TURKISH CHALLENGE

Turkey, Europe and the World
Towards the 21st Century

ONUR ÖYMEN

Published by
RUSTEM

Printed in Great Britain
by Cambridge University Press

*To my mother Nebahat Öymen and
to my father Münir Raşit Öymen,
with gratitude*

© *Öymen, 2000*

First published,Turkish edition, 1998.
Revised English edition 2000.
Translated by Özdil Nami
Edited by Helen Betts

ISBN:975-97030-0-9

Cover Designed by Keith Bomely

Contents

Tables

Preface

This book was published in Turkish one year ago. Since then important developments have taken place in Turkey, in Europe and in the world. New governments have come to power in Turkey, in Germany and in other European countries. Some Far Eastern nations have faced serious economic problems. The Russian economic crisis affected many countries including Turkey. GDP growth slowed down in general.

During the same period, NATO was engaged in a massive air operation in Kosovo to put a stop to a human tragedy that forced about 1 million people to become refugees. This was a first in the Alliance's 50-year history. The events in Kosovo demonstrated once more the importance of NATO for European security and the role of Turkey as a reliable ally in the region.

Some of the newly elected European politicians started to re-evaluate the attitude of their countries on Turkey EU relations. Significant efforts were expended to include Turkey among the formal candidates for entry to the European Union, particularly during the German Presidency and afterwards. The new German government's positive approach, supported by others, has created a fresh momentum. Now the general feeling in Turkey and in a number of EU countries is more positive than before. It seems that both sides better understand their common interests despite the existence of problems. Towards the end of 1999 an atmosphere of unity, solidarity and joint action was emerging. A rapprochement and the beginning of a long-awaited dialogue between Turkey and Greece contributed to this positive mood. Nevertheless, at the time that the English language version of this book was being

2

prepared for print, there had been no concrete changes in the official position of the EU in this regard.

In addition to a change in government, two important developments took place in Turkey. The leader of a terrorist organisation that was responsible for a campaign that took 30,000 lives over the past 15 years was arrested in a third country, flown back to Turkey and tried there. This event also revealed the international sources of support for terrorism against Turkey.

The second important development was the earthquake of August 17, 1999 when more than 15,000 people perished and 200,000 were left homeless in Turkey's Marmara region. The Turkish people rushed to the help of the victims, in close cooperation with aid organisations, civilian initiatives and the army. This was another demonstration of the human values of the Turkish people. Equally impressive was the international support that arrived in Turkey immediately after the disaster. More than 60 nations participated in the rescue operations or provided humanitarian assistance.

In reading this book one must keep in mind those events and the evolving nature of international politics. But none of these or future developments will erase from memory the facts and experiences of the past that are described in this book.

I would like to express my gratitude to Mr. Özdil Nami, who has translated the book with great care and dedication, and to Mrs. Helen Betts, who has made a valuable contribution by editing the translation and preparing it for print.

Onur Öymen
Brussels, November 1999

Foreword

December 13, 1997 will be remembered as a turning point for Turkey. On that day the European Union Summit in Luxembourg made a historic decision regarding the EU enlargement process. The countries that would join the EU in the foreseeable future were decided upon, and Turkey was not among them. This decision provoked a strong public reaction in Turkey. People of different political inclinations agreed that an injustice had been done. In fact, the Republic of Turkey, founded by Mustafa Kemal Atatürk in 1923 following one of the greatest wars of independence the 20th century has seen, had rapidly developed into a democracy and in many respects had become one of the advanced nations of the world. Such a nation should not have been prevented from taking her well-deserved place in Europe. It was a historic mistake to exclude Turkey from Europe, and this was the general feeling of the Turkish people.

The arguments used to justify the EU's decision resembled those frequently put forward during the past 20 years by certain circles whose aim was to segregate Turkey and Europe. Such unjustified arguments were employed so persistently that even some of those sympathetic to the Turkish cause in Western Europe were influenced. As the late journalist Uğur Mumcu put it, "Many people had established their opinions about Turkey without having adequate knowledge about her."

The Turkish public accepted the European Union's decision with mixed reactions. While some lost faith in Europe, others reacted by seeking alternative horizons for Turkey.

The purpose of this book is to furnish accurate information on Turkey's realities based on unbiased sources of international repute to those who wish to objectively evaluate

Turkey. A study that compares Turkey's past and present with other countries, particularly that of European nations, may help in determining the true place of Turkey in the world and highlight the political, economic and social strength that she possesses.

I would like to express my appreciation to Professor Haluk Kabaalioğlu, Bahadır Kaleağası, Professor Bilsay Kuruç, Altan Öymen and to my colleagues for the support and motivation they have given me to write this book.

I am grateful to my wife Nedret Öymen for her patience, sincere interest and assistance. I would also like to thank my children, Burak and Başak, who have supported me to the outmost of their ability.

I would be gratified if this book contributed to the identification of Turkey's place in the world, her strength and the achievements of the Turkish nation.

Introduction

There is an impressive monument at the center of Güven Park in Ankara's Yenişehir. Created by the Hungarian sculptor Thorak in 1935, the monument has a figure on one side representing human strength. Just beneath this figure the following statement of Atatürk is engraved: "Turk, be proud, work and trust yourself." This was probably one of the most important of Atatürk's messages. The Turks, who had won a great victory in their War of Independence, not only fought and defeated Greece; they also defeated the great powers of the time that had supported Greece. The Turks, founding one of the most modern states of its time on the ruins of an empire, should be proud of their success; they should work hard to reach the highest level of civilization and should have confidence in the future. This was the message.

The Turks, with the decline of the Ottoman Empire, had lost not only a sizeable amount of territory but also their self-confidence and their belief in the future. These sentiments originated in the defeats suffered by the Ottoman Empire in the 19th century and the disastrous outcome of World War I. A total of 3 million people had perished, large amounts of territory were lost and virtually no confidence remained in the future of the country. Countries that harboured political and economic ambitions against Turkey conducted a campaign of humiliation against the Turks and blamed the Turkish people for all the disasters the empire had endured.

The victory achieved at the end of the War of Independence waged between 1920 and 1922 under the leadership of Atatürk had not only saved the country from foreign occupation but also had helped the Turkish people regain their self-confidence. Turkey had become a respected country in the world. Western statesmen and press were unanimous in applauding the success of the new Turkish Republic that was founded in 1923. Eriş Ülger, in his research on an anthology of articles on Atatürk and Turkey in the German press from 1910 to 1944, uncovered many such examples.[1] This atmosphere continued even after the Atatürk era. During and after World War II, Turkey was among the countries whose friendship and support were sought by foreign nations. The move to a multi-party democracy in 1946, the heroism of Turkish soldiers in the Korean War and Turkey's membership in NATO were all met with praise in the West. The Second volume of Ülger's book contains examples of the reflections of these events in the Western press as well. Even the two interventions of the Turkish military in the political system in 1960 and 1971 were met with relatively minor criticism.

This mood continued until 1974, when, following a coup in Cyprus masterminded by the Greek junta in Athens, Turkey challenged the campaign of ethnic cleansing and terror that was being orchestrated by the leaders of the infamous EOKA terrorist organization against Turkish Cypriots. An overall campaign of criticism against Turkey began in the Western press immediately after the Turkish intervention in Cyprus. The fact that Turkey had intervened in Cyprus to save the lives of innocent civilians and that the London and Zurich agreements of 1960 not only morally but also legally justified her intervention was rarely mentioned.

However, this criticism was not to be confined to the Cyprus question alone. On August 1, 1975 35 countries including Turkey signed the Helsinki Final Act and declared, among other things, that they would respect human rights and freedoms.[2] These matters could no longer be considered the "internal affairs of a state." Thus, from the mid-1970s on, several countries began to be criticized for human rights

---

[1] Eriş Ülger, Atatürk und Die Türkei in Der Deutschen Presse, Hükeckelhoven, 1992.
[2] Fahir Armaoğlu, 20.Yüzyıl Siyasi Tarihi, Ankara, 1987, p. 654.

violations. Members of the Council of Europe were already under international obligation to respect human rights since they had signed the Human Rights Convention of 954. Turkey was one of the signatories of this convention as well. Although the scope of the Helsinki Final Act was more limited, it became the document that brought the human rights issue to a universal platform. Thereafter the Soviet Union and Eastern European countries in particular became the targets of heavy criticism on human rights issues. It was observed, however, that Western countries were trying to refrain from criticizing each other despite some shortcomings of their own. One exception to this practice was Turkey, which was often subject to harsh and in many cases unfair criticism.

The intensity of criticism against Turkey increased after the 1980 coup, but the return to parliamentary democracy following the 1983 elections created a positive atmosphere in the West. This positive trend lasted until 1987, the year that Turkey applied for full membership to the European Union. Immediately after this application a massive campaign of accusations against Turkey began. Two months after the Turkish application, the European Parliament adopted a resolution criticizing Turkey in an unprecedented manner. The arguments made in that resolution were later repeated in practically every accusation against Turkey. The anti-Turkish campaigns gradually gained momentum. Some countries trying to weaken Turkey for their own purposes exploited this criticism to damage Turkey's interests in the international arena. Some radical organizations also tried to benefit from this atmosphere, and international terrorist activities directed against Turkey increased during that period. Criticizing Turkey in the media and in the European Parliament as well as in national parliaments became fashionable. Some of Turkey's deficiencies were focused on, and many unfounded claims were brought to the attention of the international public in an exaggerated manner.

Meanwhile, the world was changing, and Europe was being rebuilt. The fall of the Berlin Wall and the reunification of

Germany signalled the end of the Cold War and the beginning of a new era. The world order established with the Yalta Declaration and the Potsdam Agreement after World War II was changing. Hundreds of thousands of people fleeing from the East to the West were evidence that the Iron Curtain dividing Europe had fallen. In the 1990s the former parameters of Europe changed. It was time to create a new order. Bridges of friendship and cooperation were established among former enemies. There was no longer any Warsaw Pact or Soviet Union. East European nations that had been de-facto under Soviet authority regained their freedom after almost half a century. Newly independent states emerged in the Balkans, the Caucasus and Central Asia. These promising developments, however, brought new risks and problems. Some regional disputes believed to be buried in history resurfaced. Extreme nationalism, religious fundamentalism and ethnic conflicts arose as new threats to peace and stability.

European institutions entered a process of reorganization in such an environment. Eastern European countries could now be members of the Council of Europe, which previously had accepted only democratic Western European states. One of the new members of the Council of Europe was the Russian Federation. Central and Eastern European countries wanted to join the EU to solve their economic and social problems, and they wanted to join NATO to safeguard their defence. These countries sought Western European Union (WEU) membership as well. In the early 1990s, the enlargement of these institutions was put on the agenda. Which countries would form the Europe of the future? This was the question that Western Europe was trying to find an answer to while working to strengthen the internal structure of the EU.

Meanwhile, as a result of the enlargement process of the late 1980s, the EU accepted its new members: Austria, Sweden and Finland. Some leading Western European countries, for historical, cultural, political, economic and strategic reasons, were willing to accept the Eastern European countries, particularly Poland, the Czech Republic and Hungary, into the

EU and NATO as full members. In order to prepare the groundwork for this process of membership, intensified aid programs were put into place. Incentives were provided to companies willing to invest in these countries. Visa requirements were eliminated, and citizens of these nations were permitted to travel freely to most of the EU states. At the same time an enormous campaign to create positive public opinion for this process was initiated. The leaders of the EU started to make statements indicating that the actual eastern borders of the EU could not be the eternal borders of the Union. Permanent committees at the presidential and ministerial level were formed among some leading EU countries and these candidates. The number of high-level visits and meetings held among these countries reached unprecedented levels.

There was a serious problem in this process. What would happen to Turkey, which had had an Association Agreement (Ankara Agreement) with the EU since 1963 and had applied for full membership in 1987? Turkey had been the closest nation to the West for the last 50 years. Among all the candidates Turkey was the only member of NATO and the only country with an economy that was strong enough to enter into a customs union with the EU. On the other hand Turkey, in many respects a powerful nation, could alter the balanced structures in Europe upon full membership in the EU. Turkey's position, potential and drawbacks were very different from those of the other candidates. More importantly, some members of the EU were not ready to see Turkey as a member of the European family, probably for psychological reasons. The idea of a multicultural Europe had not yet been fully adopted. However, Turkey had signed a customs union agreement with the EU although she knew that it would be beneficial mostly for EU countries. She expected that this agreement would serve as a catalyst on the way to full membership.

The criticism campaign against Turkey intensified in such an environment. Turkey's problems and difficulties were put under the spotlight. The aim was probably to portray Turkey as an economically underdeveloped country, a country without a real democracy, one that lacked basic freedoms and one having many problems with her neighbours. On every occasion Turkey's mistakes and deficiencies were put in the forefront, while other candidate countries' achievements in economic and political fields were highlighted. The European Parliament's critical resolutions on Turkey were largely used to support such campaigns. In fact, for many years, one could find nothing but criticism in the Parliament's resolutions on Turkey. Anyone who wanted to form an opinion on Turkey by reading only these resolutions could easily get the impression that all governments in Turkey during that period had made the wrong decision on every issue.

Some European politicians did not hesitate to make statements that not only blamed Turkey but also wounded Turkish national pride. They used some of the allegations of human rights organizations as if these allegations were based on decisions of independent courts or were indisputable realities. There were reports by the very same human rights organizations strongly condemning the human rights records of other European countries as well, but these reports were often overlooked. The Western European media rarely put this criticism in the forefront. When some Western European politicians were left in the position of addressing reports of human rights violations in their own countries, they often chose to question the reliability of the human rights organizations that had produced the reports.

Extremist organizations in Europe were among those who benefited the most from campaigns against Turkey. They used these allegations to justify their lucrative business of human trade, managing to get more than 200,000 illegal immigrants into Western Europe as if all these people were political asylum seekers.

Campaigns against Turkey were reflected across the Atlantic as well. In addition to those who address human rights issues in good faith, there are some lobbies serving the interests of the countries or groups that harbour hostile sentiments against Turkey. It is this latter group that has largely profited from such material, enabling them to foster negative public opinion about Turkey in the United States.

Turkey refrained from overreacting to such allegations. While trying to defend herself against groundless claims, she was careful not to play into the hands of those who were trying to damage her historic ties with the West. For it was well understood that one of the aims of these groups was to alienate Turkey from the West and direct her attention to alternatives other than Europe. Turkey acted with patience and prudence, never forgetting that the primary goal was her integration with the West. After the bloody wars fought against Western countries in the early 1920s, Atatürk had said that it would be a grave mistake to cut ties with the West. These words were in the minds of everyone. After gaining victory on the battlefield, Atatürk had extended a hand of friendship even to Greece, a country that had unsuccessfully attempted to invade Turkey. After the signing of the Treaty of Lausanne in 1923, Turkey established strong relations with former adversaries. It would be inconceivable to think that Turkey would change her course today just because of some baseless or exaggerated claims.

It would be wrong to assume that all politicians and journalists in Western Europe share negative sentiments against Turkey or accept all allegations against her, but their voices were dwarfed amid the intensity of the negative campaigns.

These claims had an effect in Turkey as well. Some intellectuals felt a sense of guilt, and the Turkish media strengthened its tone of self-criticism. The antithesis of this approach also emerged. The view that Europe was excluding Turkey for religious and cultural reasons began to find followers, not only among the conservative segments of the public but also among the supporters of integration with the West. The latter view was not totally groundless. It is a quite well known fact that in past centuries, there were anti-Turkish sentiments in Europe, mainly stemming from religious differences.

Prejudices against Turks go back many centuries. They were subjected to false and preposterous allegations in history as well. For example, Fatih Sultan Mehmet (Mehmet II), who is acclaimed by the contemporary historian Lord Kinross for his benevolence towards Christians, was portrayed as "the sultan who wanted to terminate Christianity" by the 16th century historian Adelphus.[3]

Martin Luther, the founder of Protestantism, saw the Turkish armies as the "armies of the devil." According to him Turks were "condemned by God, therefore, should be punished." Martin Luther collected his thoughts on this issue in two books entitled "War Against the Turks" (1528) and "Call for Prayer Against the Turks" (1541). These views influenced Western European political and religious leaders for centuries. In fact, in 1854 Cardinal Newmann put the views of the Catholic Church regarding Turks as follows:

"From Visigoths to Saracens, all races and tribes who have been in contact with Christianity have adopted the Christian faith. Turks are the only exception to this rule. Let alone adopting Christianity, they set out to wipe out Christianity, becoming the leader, spokesman as well as the symbol of anti-Christianity from the day they stepped into the scene of history in 1048. For this reason, Turks were seen as the main enemy of the Catholic Church [the Vatican] between the 11th and 18th centuries. It can even be said that the papal state spent the last millennium with nothing but war against the Turks. I am not denying the military might of the Turks; however, it is this might that makes them the relentless enemy of the faith and civilization. Therefore, we have to fight and destroy the Turks."

---

[3] Lord Kinross, The Ottoman Centuries, New York, 1977, p. 115; Bozkurt Güvenç, Türk Kimliği, Ankara 1993, p. 299.

Professor Bozkurt Güvenç, in his book entitled "Turkish Identity," reflects these views and summarizes his thoughts on this issue with a reference to Duroselle: "During the decline of Christianity and in parallel to the rise of secularism in the West, Europe could have perhaps embraced the Turks. Instead, secular and nationalistic movements adopted the traditional values and prejudices of the Church with incomprehensible and hardly defendable justifications."

Carried from generation to generation, these prejudices against Turks have reached our time. One may come across such prejudices in the textbooks of schoolchildren in many European states today. What is behind these adverse thoughts fostered against the Turks and Turkey? Could it be the traces of wars fought centuries ago? Fromkin writes that during their War of Independence, while fighting against the Greeks, the Turks were actually fighting against the whole Western world. Professor Güvenç says, "The Western world failed in its attempt to prevent the success of the Turkish nationalism movement, and that is the reason why the West still cannot forgive the Turks."

Cahen, a prominent historian, explains this negative set of values and almost reflexive attitude of criticizing the Turks at every opportunity as follows:

"Because of the fact that the Ottoman Empire was at war with the Christian World for many centuries, all matters related to Turks have been judged and condemned a priori as backward, bad, problematic and despotic."

What's even more interesting is the fact that Turkey was seen as the party responsible for all this anti-Turkish sentiment. This attitude can clearly be seen in a book of prejudices published in Germany: "Turks are the ones who are directly responsible for all of the prejudices against the Turks."[4]

---

[4] Bozkurt Güvenç, Türk Kimliği, Ankara, 1993, pp. 293-325.

One cannot explain the current approach of European political leaders towards Turkey by such prejudiced thoughts alone. Although it is a fact that enmity between religions has had catastrophic results for both sides in past centuries, people of the same religion fought against each other and endured greater catastrophes during the first and second world wars. Could sensible people today sow new seeds of conflict based on religious, cultural or ethnic differences?

Unfortunately, some European politicians have recently recreated these impressions in the minds of the Turkish public, even if this may not have been their intention. One can cite as an example the statement of Mr. Wilfried Martens, the former prime minister of Belgium, who, after a meeting of Christian Democratic leaders of Europe in Brussels on March 4, 1997, said that Turkey could never be accepted into the EU as a member because the EU is a civilization project. Although it was clarified afterwards by many participants that this was not a commonly accepted idea and that there had been a misunderstanding, the damage was done. Turks, who believed that their country was excluded from Europe due to religious differences, interpreted these words as a justification for their convictions.

The decision taken at the EU's Luxembourg Summit in December 1997 proved that the applications for membership by the Central and Eastern European states were given priority by the EU countries. Turkey was left out of this process for the time being. The summit also decided to start membership negotiations with the Greek Cypriot administration. Turkey declared that this would not only be against international law and agreements, but that it also would set back the efforts to find a peaceful settlement to the Cyprus question. Nevertheless the EU made the decision to go ahead with the Greek Cypriot application. Another interesting point of the summit decision was that Turkey was held responsible for her exclusion from the membership process. The essence of the reasons declared was that the Turkish economy was not developed enough to be included in this process, that Turkish democracy fell behind those of other applicants, that Turkey's human rights standards lagged behind those of other applicants and that Turkey had problems with her neighbours. Another concern that was not declared in the official documents but was mentioned at the closing press conference was the fear that Turkish nationals would have freedom of movement in Europe in the event of Turkish membership in the EU.

The selection of other applicants, which only seven years ago had belonged to the opposing pact, and the exclusion of Turkey from this group, putting the blame on Turkey for this exclusion, was met with strong reaction both in public opinion as well as in political circles in Turkey. Turkish President Süleyman Demirel said that the Turkish nation was hurt by this decision.

One has to remember the realities of international relations while analyzing the reasons behind the allegations against Turkey. Since states continue to be the main players in the international arena, conflicts of interest among countries shape the nature of foreign policy. While struggling to pursue their own interests, some states may often damage the interests of others. Yet, especially after World War II, countries are trying more and more to abide by international law. Possessing power is no longer sufficient to justify or legitimize the policy or the action of a state. International public opinion approval has become a necessity for the politicians of modern democracies; therefore politicians try to influence the world community at large through the mass media. They try to obtain the support of opinion-makers. At the root of all these efforts lies the will to protect national interests. If a state objects to an argument of another country, it tries to find reasons to undermine that country in the face of world public opinion. This does not necessarily mean that the argument is wrong or that it has not been explained properly; rather it may mean that to accept this argument would not be in line with the national interests of that state.

In 1994 Professor Mümtaz Soysal, the then Turkish minister of Foreign Affairs, said at a dinner hosted by German Foreign Minister Klaus Kinkel:

"We get the impression that Turkey would not be accepted as a member of the EU even if she were to fulfil all the requirements. There may be some reasons that cannot be expressed openly because it would be too shameful to publicize them."

What led Professor Soysal to express such doubts about the real intentions of European politicians? What was the truth behind these assertions against Turkey? Such assertions should be analyzed thoroughly, since they influenced European public opinion for many years; they were acknowledged by a number of Western politicians and journalists, and in the end they formed the basis of the decisions regarding Turkey taken at the Luxembourg Summit. A comprehensive study would help to understand the realities of Turkey. What is her place in the world and in Europe? What is the rate of increase and, more importantly, the composition and characteristics of her population that are cited as the main causes of concern? What is the economic strength of Turkey and its rate of growth? What is her defence power and its contribution to the security of the West? How has Turkish political life evolved towards a democracy? What was the situation in the European countries when Turkey was going through all these evolutions? What kind of developments took place in their political lives? What kinds of experiences and traditions do Turks have in the fields of human rights and tolerance vis-a-vis other cultures? What are the track records of those who criticize Turkey today on these issues? The realities of Turkey will be better understood if such questions are answered objectively.

All of the issues mentioned above will be discussed in the following chapters. Turkey will be compared to other countries on the basis of objective criteria. Some authors who made such comparisons previously have tried to show different nations, cultures and civilizations as irreconcilable entities. They developed clash-of-civilization theories instead of trying to find commonalties among nations. Therefore, it is of special importance to make these comparisons by putting the shared values of humanity to the forefront, without discriminating and without targeting any country, culture or civilization. The information, data and statistics should be used without any prejudice.

Obviously Turkey has shortcomings just like any other nation. One must accept the fact that in certain fields some nations are more developed than others. In the following chapters the reader will find some areas where Turkey is behind other nations, but also some fields where she is more advanced than many other countries of the Western world.

TURKEY AND THE WORLD

For centuries Turks have left their mark on the world. Even if the Turkish states established before it are not mentioned, the Ottoman Empire alone was born some 700 years ago. Turkey has a rich state tradition. When America was discovered, the Ottoman state was 192 years old. For centuries, Turkish statesmen attained international repute, and Turkish commanders won world-famous victories. Just as there were times when Turkey was among the three or four leading countries in the world, there were times when she was defeated and faced with great difficulties. This has been the case for many other countries as well. However, in no period did Turkey see herself as a minor country. She always made decisions regarding her future of her own free will, never bowing to external pressure. When those in government gave in to such pressure, the people buried them in the depths of history and relentlessly protected their sovereignty by establishing a new Republic. Turks have always held on to their national values, culture and traditions.

Today the New York headquarters of the United Nations, considered to be the common home of the world's nations, hosts the flags of 185 nations. Established after World War II with only 51 countries, the UN attained this increased number by accepting new members in later years. In the beginning, countries like mainland China were left out of the organization due to political considerations. Today, there are countries such as Switzerland and the Turkish Republic of Northern Cyprus, which possess all the attributes of a state but which are not or cannot be members of the UN for various reasons. Including these there are approximately 200 countries in the world, some of which have only recently gained their independence.

Many are comprised of only very small territories, and their populations number in the neighbourhood of a few hundred thousand people.

When comparing different countries, it is useful to use objective, measurable criteria such as geographic characteristics, population and economic performance. Having said this, there are factors which cannot be measured or expressed in numbers. The political structure of a country is one such factor. It is not that easy to compare countries which have liberal economic systems with those that don't. Other factors include a nation's characteristics that stem from its history, traditions, national pride and beliefs. Those in particular who criticize other countries for their shortcomings should also consider a nation's unwritten values, thoughts, beliefs, resolve, national pride, capacity for self-sacrifice and characteristics such as the ability to live with other cultures. Some writers call these "the spirit of nations" and make evaluations, putting these hard-to-measure properties and traits to the forefront of their analyses.

A comparative table prepared using OECD (Organisation for Economic Cooperation and Development), World Bank and IMF (International Monetary Fund) statistics reflects the overall situation of selected countries of the world in terms of population, area and economic strenght. (When we take a look at world geography, in particular that of Turkey, we see the following table:)

Population, Area and Economic Performance of Selected Countries (1996)

Country	Populations (million)	Area (Thousand sq. km.)	Gross National Product* (billion $)	Per Capital GNP* ($)
China	1,236	9,500	3,390	2,800
India	969	3,200	1,538	1,600
USA**	267	9,300	8,162	30,130
İndonesia	204	1,900	779	3,770
Brazil	160	8,500	1,022	6,300
Russia	147	17,000	767	5,200
Pakistan	137	796	296	2,300
Japan	126	377	2,860	21,700
Bangladesh	122	144	155	1,260
Nigeria	107	923	143	1,380
Mexico	95	1,958	777	8,100
Germany**	82	356	1,902	23,007
Vietnam	75	329	108	1,470
Philippines	73	300	194	2,600
Iran	67	1,600	343	5,200
Egypt	64	1,000	183	2,900
Turkey**	62	780	433	6,669
U.K.**	59	244	1,249	21,137
Thailand	58	514	455	7,700
France**	58	551	1,309	22,210
Italy**	57	301	1,265	21,943
Ukraine	50	603	161	3,170
South Korea	45	98	647	14,200
S.Africa	42	1,200	227	5,400
Spain**	39	505	660	16,764
Poland	38	323	246	6,400
Colombia	36	1,138	201	5,400
Argentina	35	2,700	296	8,600
Canada**	28	9,976	739	24,055
Romania	21	237	113	5,200
Taiwan	21	35	315	14,700
Netherlands**	15	37	362	23,079
Belgium**	10	30	246	24,144
Portugal**	9	92	145	14,596
Sweden	8	449	184	20,800
Bulgaria	8	110	40	4,630
Austria	8	83	157	19,700
Israel	5	20	85	16,400
Finland	5	337	97	19,000
Norway**	4	324	122	27,859
Singapore	3	6	72	21,200

*GNP figures are calculated on purchasing power parity (ppp) basis.
**1998

Leaving aside Antarctica, where no one lives permanently, the total surface area of all countries in the world is 134 million square kilometers. With 780,000 sq km. Turkey ranks 36th, corresponding to 0.65% of the total. Russia is the largest country in the world; with 17 million sq km. it is 21 times as large as Turkey. China, Canada and the United States each have more than 9 million sq km. Australia follows with 7.7 million sq km.

There are 35 countries larger than Turkey, yet most of them have populations smaller than that of Turkey. Namibia has only 1.7 million people despite 800,000 sq km. of territory. Mauritania has more than 1 million sq km. but only 2.4 million people.

In population Turkey ranks 17th in the world. There are only 11 countries having both larger populations and territory than Turkey: the United States, Brazil, China, Indonesia, India, Iran, Mexico, Egypt, Nigeria, Pakistan and Russia. On the other hand there are five countries with smaller surface areas but larger populations than Turkey: Germany, Bangladesh, the Philippines, Japan and Vietnam.

A total of 1.1% of the world's population, which came to 5.8 billion in 1997, are Turkish citizens. Together with 3 million Turkish citizens living abroad, Turkey's population is around 65 million.

When comparing the size and population of countries, we must also consider their economic strength. Among 35 countries with a size larger than Turkey there are only six with a higher per capita income, adjusted according to ppp: the United States, Argentina, Australia, Canada, Mexico and Saudi Arabia. There are two countries with smaller territory but larger populations than Turkey that also have a higher per capita GDP: Germany and Japan. If we add all countries with more than 50 million people, then we must include France, the United Kingdom, Italy and Thailand to this list.

According to this evaluation there are eight countries with larger territory or population as well as per capita GDP.

Considering all countries with more than 50 million people, Turkey ranks 13th in the world in per capita GDP.

Comparisons done without taking surface area or population into consideration may give different results, but such comparisons may be misleading. Those done without any yardstick, boundary or scale will not reflect the true position of Turkey in the world. In that event, countries such as Iceland, Seychelles, Barbados, Trinidad and Tobago and Mauritius, which do not compare to Turkey in terms of economy or any other category, with very small territories and populations and with total GNPs which are negligible on a worldwide scale, would rank higher than Turkey as regards per capita national income.

In order to make equitable and objective comparisons, economic data is adjusted according to purchasing power parity (ppp) instead of using market prices. The OECD has statistics prepared by using the ppp method, which take into consideration that a dollar buys different amounts of goods and services in different countries. According to the OECD, using 1998 figures in comparing consumer prices, the price level in Turkey is 36% that of Japan, 55% of the United States, 48% of Germany, the United Kingdom and France, 61% of Greece and 63% of Spain's price levels.

If one wants to gauge the true economic strength of a country, total GDP would be a good measure to use. Per capita national income is also an important figure reflecting the economic welfare of a nation. Using statistics published by organizations such as the UN, the OECD and the (IMF) and ranking countries according to their populations, a table has been devised as seen above.

Some of the results obtained from that table are as follows:
- When adjusted using the ppp method, the overall economic power of some Western countries with higher per capita national income is less than the economic strength of Turkey.
- Even if we do not take into consideration factors such as population and the size of the country, none of the EU

candidate countries have total GDPs that are even close to that of Turkey. Even among current EU members, there are only five with larger GDPs than Turkey, calculated using the ppp method: Germany, France, United Kingdom, Italy and Spain.

- Among the "tigers" of the Far East only Japan, South Korea, Thailand and Indonesia have larger GDPs than Turkey.

Although these issues will be analyzed in more depth in later sections, one thing is clear: Turkey not only has a larger population and territory but also a bigger economy than many EU member states.

Looking at the table above, it can be seen that there are merely a handful of countries with both a democratic system as well as a larger population or territory than Turkey. Only the United States, Germany, Australia and Japan fit into this category. Among these, Germany and Japan achieved stable democracies only after World War II. If we are to include all countries with more than 50 million people, then we would have to add the United Kingdom, France and Italy to this list. That is to say, among those countries with populations greater than 50 million or a larger territory, Turkey is one of the top eight from a democratic experience point of view. Among countries with less population there are those with strong democratic cultures. Yet historical evidence shows that compared to small countries, it is more difficult to maintain a democratic system in more populous states. The same way of thinking is valid for economic development as well. Relative to larger countries, it is much easier for a small country with rich natural resources or tourism potential to increase its per capita income.

GDP should not be the only measure used to draw comparisons among different economies. There are other yardsticks such as pace of development, public spending, internal and external debt, taxes, distribution of income, rate of inflation, savings ratio and unemployment. Where does Turkey stand when we take all these into account? What is her position in the world and in particular within the OECD, which she is a member of? The answers to these questions are examined in detail in later sections of this book. In order to make a comprehensive comparison, one must pay attention to factors besides population, geographic properties or economic situation. Demographics, level of education, life expectancy and welfare indicators as well will be analyzed later. Turkey's military strength and defence spending will also be compared with those of other countries.

Things like democratic standards, for which Turkey is widely criticized by Western governments, as well as appreciation of other religions and ethnic groups will also be taken up. Turkey's position in the human rights area will also be analyzed within this context.

SOURCES OF TURKISH STRENGTH

The most significant indicators of national strength are population, geography, economic resources and military power. One must also add the democratic standards of a country and its internal stability to this list.

It is generally accepted that there is a strong correlation between the economic-military strength of a nation and its population. The role played by a country in international politics largely depends on its economic as well as military power, but the size and the characteristics of its population are also of extreme significance, since population is a source of power in a nation.

Those who analyze the relationship between economic development and population give examples from history supporting this thesis: The population increases in the United States and Belgium in the last century accelerated the economic growth of these countries. The abundance of labor in Japan between 1894 and 1914 played a major role in the development of Japanese industry. The enlargement of arable land in Turkey between 1949 and 1962 was mainly due to an increase in population. However, the extensive use of farm equipment also played a role in the increase of agricultural products.[5] From a sociological point of view it is assumed that nations with larger and better-educated populations have more confidence in themselves. Some nations pursued an increase in their population as a national goal. Prior to World War II Japan had encouraged population growth by means of special laws; however, such incentives produced extremely

---

[5] Suat Bilge, Milletlerarası Politika, Ankara, 1966, pp. 130-141.

unfortunate results when combined with expansionist foreign policies. Therefore, while acknowledging the fact that population is one of the most important components of the power of a nation, one should not forget that rapid population growth could create serious problems.

Turkish People

Western European media and politicians often seem concerned about the size and characteristics of the Turkish population. The prospect of freedom of movement for Turks in Europe is perceived as a serious problem for European society. What is the cause of this concern? What is their discomfort regarding Turkey's population?

The rate of increase of the world's population and the economic, social and cultural problems it may entail are indeed serious issues discussed in relevant international fora. The World Population Summit organized in Cairo by the United Nations in 1995 addressed all these issues and took some important decisions.

Population growth is also widely discussed in Turkey. Both the Turkish government and Non Governmental Organizations (NGOs) are working on measures to prevent an excessive population increase.

However, it is also true that the countries which were power centers of the world, such as the British, Russian, Chinese and Ottoman empires, had, among other assets, large populations. Today, the Security Council is the most important body of the United Nations; it directs international politics to a large extent, and none of its permanent members have a population of less than 55 million. Japan and Germany, which are aspiring to become permanent members in the event of a reform within the UN, have populations of 82 million and 126 million respectively.

In international organizations such as the EU and the Council of Europe, population is considered a decisive element in many respects. In the governmental and parliamentary bodies of such organizations the weight and the representation of countries are often determined by taking into consideration the size of their populations. For example, in the European Parliament's 626 seats, Germany is represented with 99, whereas the United Kingdom, France and Italy are each represented by 87 parliamentarians. Spain and the Netherlands have 64 and 31 members respectively. Had Turkey been a member of the EU, she would have sent 87 parliamentarians to the Parliament. According to population projections, by the year 2014, provided she becomes a member of the EU, Turkey together with Germany will be the two countries with the greatest number of members in the European Parliament.

The European Parliament has been one of the centers of political activities that interests Turkey directly. Nevertheless today there are no Turkish members in this assembly to participate in discussions, respond to questions and take part in the decision-making process. A strong Turkish representation in this Parliament would affect Turkish-EU relations positively. Turkish members would be able to voice their opinion as they do today in the Parliamentary Assembly of the Council of Europe. A similar situation would exist in the EU Council of Ministers, the EU's main decision-making body. For in the EU Council, most decisions are taken according to a "weighted voting system." Countries are divided into various groups according to their population. The total number of these "weighted votes" is 87. The votes of each are as follows: Germany, France, Italy and the United Kingdom, 10; Spain, eight; Belgium, the Netherlands, Portugal and Greece, five; Austria and Sweden, four; Denmark, Ireland and Finland, three; and Luxembourg, two. Depending on the number of countries participating in the voting, 24 or 26 opposing votes are enough to prevent a decision.[6] New EU members will be allocated weighted votes according to their populations; for example, Poland will have eight. When Turkey becomes a member she will most probably be

---

[6] Paul van den Bempt, Greet Theelen, From Europe Agreements to Accession, European University Press, 1996.

considered among the largest states and therefore will be allocated 10 votes. This means that Turkey will become one of the most influential members of the European Union. Some countries that oppose Turkey's membership in the EU because of her large population might have in mind, among other things, the concern that Turkey would become too powerful and too influential within the Union.

One of the most discussed issues among the European public regarding Turkey is the question of "freedom of movement," which means the right to travel and work freely throughout the EU. A basic requirement of the Treaty of Rome, which established the EU, is granting freedom of movement to labor as well as to goods, services and capital. Yet, this does not automatically give the citizens of the EU the right to go and seek employment in whichever country or field they choose.

Even today, 40 years after the founding of the EU, there are some national rules or practices giving priority to locals when a job vacancy occurs in that country. Therefore, it would not be correct to assume that in the event Turkey becomes a member, Turkish people would have free access to the European labor market without any restrictions. It is also interesting to note that although the total population of the Central and Eastern European states is larger than that of Turkey, granting freedom of movement to the citizens of those countries did not cause any concern, whereas it is presented as a problem in the case of Turkey.

Evolution of the Turkish Population

World population is estimated to have been around 7 million in 4000 B.C. That is to say, it was less than the current population of Istanbul. Wars, epidemics and the absence of proper medical care prevented population expansion for a long period. World population around 2,000 years ago is estimated to have been approximately 300 million. It stayed below 1 billion until 1800, but doubled in just 123 years, jumping to 2 billion. By the 1950s world population had reached 2.5 billion, by 1975 it was 4 billion and continued to increase rapidly to grow to 5.3 billion by 1990. The estimates for the next century are as follows:

Projections of World Population Growth

Year	World Population
2000	6.0
2010	6.8
2020	7.5
2030	8.2
2040	8.8
2050	9.3

Source: U.S. Bureau of the Census, International Database

The average annual increase in world population is 1.4%. This is equal to that of Turkey, according to the results of the 1997 census. Developed countries have an increase rate of 0.3%, developing countries are at 1.7%, and the rate for less developed countries is 2.6%.

It has been established that 98% of all increase in population is in developing countries. At the end of the 20th century, almost 4.7 billion people lived in developing countries, whereas the total population of developed nations is 1.2 billion. By the year 2025 developing nations will have 6.8 billion people. This will obviously put significant pressure on the demographic structure of developed nations, the signs of which are already visible. This is the main trend that causes concern.

China, with a population of 1.2 billion, is the most crowded nation in the world. The population growth rate of this country is 1.1% per annum, which represents an absolute number of 13.2 million per year. There are 21 Chinese and 16 Indians per 100 of world population. In absolute numbers the increase in India is greater than that of China. India has a population of 994 million and a growth rate of 1.76%, that is to say an increase of 16 million persons annually. So each year the amount of increase in China's population in absolute terms is greater than the population of Belgium, whereas India's population grows by more than the population of the Netherlands.

There are 4.7 Americans, 2.6 Russians, 2.2 Japanese, 1.4 Germans and 1.1 Turks per 100 of world population. So one percent of the world population is comprised of Turkish citizens. In absolute numbers, the increase in Turkey's population is currently 876,000 persons per year. This may seem like a large number, but it is not even comparable to that of China or India. Among the Western nations, Turkey's increase in population in absolute numbers is not the largest, either. Each year the population of the United States goes up by 1%, i.e. by 2.69 million, which is about three times Turkey's population increase.

One can hardly talk about an increase in population in Western Europe. The population has stabilized there, and in some Western European countries it is even declining. Italy's population has hovered at around 56 million since 1977. It took Great Britain 22 years to go from 56 to 57 million. The French population increased at a relatively faster pace and reached 58.6 million in 1997 from its level of 56 million in 1989. The German population together with the former GDR has gone from 77.7 to 82 million in the last 10 years.

According to estimates from the U.S. Bureau of the Census the populations of these three countries will start to decline after the year 2000. Germany is expected to have less than 80 million by 2014 and to go down to 57 million by 2050. The same estimates predict that Italy will drop to 38, the United Kingdom to 47 and France to 48 million by 2050. However, one must be cautious in analyzing long-term projections; it is next to impossible to give accurate estimates so far into the future.

The U.S. Bureau of the Census estimates that by 2014 the
Turkish population will exceed that of Germany; thus Turkey
will become the most populated country in Europe, with the
exception of the Russian Federation.

When the European Economic Union, as it was then called,
was established, the populations of the member countries were
far less than their current levels. Compared to the numbers in
1960, the German population went up by 10 million, the
French by 13 million, the Italian by 7 million and the British
by 5 million.

As mentioned above Turkey, next to Germany, is the most
populated nation in Europe and also has the highest birth rate.
Turkey's population shows different characteristics when
compared to other Western European countries. During the
past 50 years Turkey's population increased more rapidly than
Western European nations. The forecast given by the U.S.
Bureau of the Census, considering the trend since 1950, is as
follows:

Evolution of the Turkish Population and Growth Projections until the Year 2050

Year	Turkey's Population (millions)
1950	21.1
1960	28.2
1970	35.7
1980	45.1
1990	56.1
1997	62.6
2000	66.6
2010	76.5
2020	85.6
2030	93.4
2040	96.6
2050	103.6

Source: U.S..Bureau of the Census

The 1997 census in Turkey showed that some of the previous estimates regarding the increase in population were exaggerated. While the State Planning Organization and the State Institute of Statistics calculated close to 1.8%, the census showed the rate of increase to be 1.4%. It became clear that the increase in Turkey's population would be less than previous forecasts due to birth rate control policies and rapid urban development; economic development may also decrease the birth rate, as was the case in Western Europe.

The U.S. Bureau of the Census expects an overall decline in the population of EU member states, and this is confirmed by other sources as well. In 1997 the population of the EU was 371 million; this number will go down to 364 million by 2020 and to 290 million by 2050. It is highly likely that the EU countries will face a population shortfall by the middle of the next century, as they did in the 1960s. Therefore, one should not be misled by the current high unemployment rates in EU member states while making long-term estimates.

How will the EU compensate for the population shortfall, which will get worse in the coming 50 years? Will it be by acceptance of becoming a smaller Union and a smaller market? Will it be by giving incentives to increase birth rates? Or will it be by importing population from other countries? If so, from which countries? If what they have in mind is the Eastern European states, the U.S.Bureau of the Census foresees a population decline in those countries as well. The population in the Eastern European countries will gradually go down from their 1997 level of 96 million to 89 million by the year 2050. Moreover, as happened in Spain, EU membership will lead to rapid industrialization, which will increase the local demand for labor. Therefore, the Eastern European states will have decreased populations on the one hand but an increased demand for labor on the other. This situation will of course prevent them from becoming the labor warehouses of Europe.

In some Western European states there are tens of thousands of illegal immigrants who work under harsh conditions by violating the laws and regulations of that country and who are without any rights under international law. However, from both a legal as well as a moral standpoint one cannot conceive that Europe will make up for its labor shortage through these illegal immigrants. It should not be surprising to see some Western European states turn to their traditional labor sources, especially Turkey, in the coming decades.

At this point some of the descriptions of Samuel Huntington come to mind. Huntington categorized population movements not with respect to states but with respect to civilizations. What is more, while comparing civilizations, he highlighted which civilizations controlled which populations, i.e. which nations. According to Huntington in 1900 44.3% of the world's population was under the influence of Western civilization, compared with only 4.2% under the influence of Islamic civilization. However, following the process of decolonization and independence of former colonies, the population under the "political control" of Western civilization had dropped to 13.1% by 1995. This ratio is expected to go down to 10.1 by 2025. The population under the "political control" of Islamic civilization went up to 15.9% by 1995 and is expected to reach 19.2% by 2025. The largest group is the one which is under the sphere of influence of Chinese civilization; in 1995 24% of the world's population belonged to this group. Huntington estimated that by 1993, 1.3 billion would belong to Chinese, 928 to Islamic, 916 to Indian and 805 million to Western civilizations.[7]

Latin American, African, Orthodox and Japanese civilizations follow these groups. Orthodox nations are not considered to be within Western civilization. What will be Turkey's place if one considers that her population consists of Muslims but that she started to orient herself towards Western

[7] Samuel Huntington, The Clash of Civilizations and the Remaking of World Order, p. 85.

Europe in the 19th century and that for the last 50 years has participated in the Western world? Although the answer to this question is not very clear, the overall theme of Huntington's book gives the impression that he considers Turkey as belonging to Islamic civilization. These observations are followed by "concerns" over the decline in population of those countries within Western civilization. Another area of "concern" is the fact that the populations of the Islamic nations are getting younger and more urban, which turns them from being illiterate rural populations into well-educated, urbanized, young and dynamic ones. Huntington touches on the social as well as the political implications of this development and says it will get more and more difficult to impose policies on those countries.

One should contemplate just how such approaches are in line with what is known as Western thinking after the French Revolution, based on equality, fraternity and justice.

Among the Orthodox countries Russia has a particular position, considering her population, geography and strategic location. Like Turkey, this country has also experienced rapid population growth in the last decades. Back in 1950 there were 102 million people living in what is today the Russian Federation. By 1995 this number had gone up to 148 million, which amounts to a 50% increase in 45 years. However, after 1996 the Russian population started to decline. American sources predict that the Russian population will be 145 million by the year 2000, 141 million by 2020, and by 2050 it will drop to 121 million. According to these estimates, by mid next century the population of Russia will be less than that of Iran. The political, economic, strategic and other implications of such a development require serious analysis.

Apparently, industrialization and urbanization and the social developments stemming from them have caused the population increase in Europe to slow down, then to stop and finally to regress.

In Turkey, although the birthrate is down, no decrease in population is expected for the next 50 years. When the population projections for Turkey are compared with those of the EU, Central and Eastern European countries, the United States and Russia, an interesting picture emerges.

Comparative Projections on Population Growth in Turkey, the USA, the Russian Federation, the EU and the CEES* (millions)

	1960	1980	2000	2020	2050
Turkey	28	45	66	85	103
EU	315	355	374	364	290
EU+CEES	402	456	478	468	379
Russia	119	139	145	141	121
USA	180	227	274	323	394

*CEES=Central and East European States: Bulgaria, The Czech Republic, Estonia, Lithuania, Latvia, Hungary, Poland, Romania, Slovakia, Slovenia.
Source: U.S. Bureau of the Census

As the table above indicates, the United States shows a dramatically different trend in population growth. While it had 152 million people in 1950, following a rapid increase that number had reached 249 million by 1990 and 267 million by 1997. The U.S. Bureau of the Census expects this trend to continue and reach 394 million by 2050. By then the United States population will be larger than that of an enlarged Europe and naturally will have a bigger consumer market. However, the rapid increase in population, achieved to a large extent by accepting immigration into the country, did not cause a major concern in the United States. This is because increase in population is not a problem *per se*. When the geographic position, economic situation, demographic makeup and political climate in a country are considered as a whole, prejudice regarding increase in population may change. A reasonable increase in population can be seen as a factor that contributes to the strength of that country's economy instead of being a source of concern, provided that there is enough territory, adequate infrastructure and substantial economic means to feed and educate the people and provide for their welfare.

If the forecasts are accurate, the expanded EU will have 100 million less of its present population by the first half of the next century. The population of the United States will be 204 million people less than the EU plus the Central and Eastern European countries in the year 2000. But by the middle of the next century US population will exceed the same group of countries by 15 million. Together with Canada this number will be more than 55 million. NAFTA's (North American Free Trade Area) population by then will be larger than the EU+CEEC market by 185 million people. It is not difficult to predict the economic, social and political implications of such a development.

It is worthwhile to note that Mexico's large population of 92 million, which is increasing at a rate of 1.7% per year, was not seen as a negative factor preventing her from becoming a NAFTA member. The United States and Canada, instead of seeing this country's population as a source of concern, except for illegal border crossings, considered Mexico a developing economy with natural resources and an expanding market, qualifications that make her an asset for NAFTA. Those who oppose Turkey's EU membership due to the size and growth rate of her population should draw lessons from this example. Surely, there are structural differences between the EU and NAFTA, and it is not easy to compare the two. Still NAFTA should not be considered merely a free trade zone, either.

The same population projection table gives interesting results regarding the population balance between the EU and Turkey. Back in 1980 Turkey's population was 12.6% that of the EU. This ratio will be 17.8% by 2000, 23.5% by 2020 and 35.7% by 2050. This means that by 2020 Turkey's population will be one-fourth of the EU's, and by 2050 it will reach one-third. Having new members will not change these ratios

significantly. In the event that all of the applicants are accepted
as members, Turkey's population will be 18.2% that of the EU
by 2020 and 27.3% by 2050.

If Turkey is considered as having a different group of
people vis-a-vis the EU when evaluating the change in
population balances, this difference regarding population
growth rates may be seen as a source of concern and a reason
for discomfort. However, instead of focusing on cultural
differences among the European nations, if one thinks that
each of them is as European as the others, the fact that Turkey
has a larger population than most could be perceived as being
as natural as the other population differences within the EU.
According to the most extreme estimates, by 2050 Turkey's
population will be twice as large as Germany's. But even today
Germany's population is twice as big as that of Spain, 5.5 times
the Belgian, eight times the Greek and 10 times the Swedish
population. One cannot explain with ease just exactly why the
population differences among those countries do not create a
problem but that differences with Turkey do. If the Europe of
tomorrow is to be a family formed by countries of different
sizes and different cultural backgrounds, and if it is going to be
a community of states, differences in population among these
countries should be as natural as they are now. Of course this
is true, assuming that there is no feeling of unease in having
different cultures or religions within the same family.

If Turkey is seen as a third world country with extremely
limited potential and resources, that's one thing; but if she is
seen as a rapidly industrializing country with extensive
resources, having the second largest territory in Europe after
Russia, and with a dynamic young population, that of course
will bring about another type of evaluation.

One must not forget that within the Western world Turkey
is not the only country with a significant increase in
population. Other than the United States as mentioned above,
Canada, Australia, New Zealand and Israel are among those
countries whose populations are on the rise. In Israel the

population growth rate is close to 3% due to an influx of immigrants.[8] L'Etat du Monde 1998, Paris, 1998.

Dynamism of the Turkish People

Turkey has a young and dynamic population. The number of those who are below the age of 25 exceeds 33 million. According to OECD figures those between the ages of five and 29 constituted 50.6% of total population in 1995. Turkey has the youngest population among all the European countries. Closest to Turkey in this respect is Ireland, with 41.8 %. The proportion of the 5-29 age group to total population is 31.1% in Germany, 32% in France and 34.7% in the United Kingdom and Greece.

When this comparison is done for the age group below 40, Turkey retains the same characteristics.

Population Below 40 Years of Age in Turkey and Selected European Countries (1995)

Country	Population (millions)
Turkey	43.4
France	32.1
Germany	32.0
United Kingdom	31.1
Poland	24.1
Netherlands	8.4
Belgium	5.6
Greece	5.6

Source: U.S. Bureau of the Census

[8] L'Etat du Monde 1998, Paris, 1998.

When older populations are compared, the situation is just the reverse. In most European countries the aging population is larger than that of Turkey.

Population Above 65 Years of Age in Turkey and Selected European Countries (1995)

Country	Population
Germany	9.3
United Kingdom	9.2
France	8.3
Poland	3.7
Turkey	2.4
Belgium	1.4
Netherlands	1.3
Greece	1.3

Source: U.S. Bureau of the Census

The above information also confirms that Turkey has a young and dynamic population. This is in sharp contrast to Europe's aging population, which is loosing its dynamism.

These numbers should not be seen as simple statistical figures. For example, from a social security perspective, it is clear that in Europe there are increasingly fewer young people to take on the burden of those more elderly. The proportion of the social security burden on each working person is growing. This is the basic cause of the difficulties faced by the European countries, especially Germany, in their social security systems.

Foreigners carry a part of the burden of the working population in the social security systems of Western European countries. The obligatory fees paid to the social security system by these foreigners are far more than what they receive from it. When long-term population and social security projections are studied, the economic problems created by an aging population can clearly be seen. The table below shows the change in social security burden on employers and employees over time in Turkey and various European countries.

Social Security Payments in Various Countries
(as a percentage of gross wages)

	Employees' share			Employers' share		
	1985	1990	1994	1985	1990	1994
Germany	17.0	17.8	19.4	17.0	17.8	19.4
Greece	13.2	13.7	...	21.7	23.3	...
Belgium	12.1	12.1	13.1	40.4	33.6	34.8
U.K.	9.0	7.6	8.4	10.4	10.4	10.2
Italy	8.7	8.5	10.0	45.9	45.6	46.1
Turkey	8.5	8.6	5.1	9.0	11.9	7.1
U.S.A.	7.1	7.6	7.7	9.2	7.7	7.7
Spain	6.3	6.0	6.6	30.7	30.2	31.6

Source: Coup d'Oeil sur les Economies de l' OCDE, 1996, p. 101

The table above shows that Turkey has the lowest rates for social security payments, both for employers and employees. Although various unique characteristics of the Turkish economy can be pointed out to justify this situation, it seems clear that one of the primary reasons for the difficulties that the Turkish social security system faces today lies here. These low rates increase the burden on the government. To give an example, OECD statistics indicate that the share of social security payments in GDP for the year 1989 was 24% in Germany, 26% in France, 20% in the United Kingdom, 17.3% in Spain and 20.7% in Greece.[9] Turkey's low ratio of public revenue to GDP does not allow the government to spend a

---

[9] Coup d'Oeil sur les Economies de l' OCDE, 1996, pp. 109-110.

similar percentage of its GDP on social security. As a result, revenues to meet pension and other social security payments remain low, while great difficulties are encountered in achieving an actuarial balance between revenues and the expenses of the social security system.

Today, public health expenditures in Western countries account for a significant part of their public spending. However, just as in social security, Turkey is at the lower end of the list in the ratio of public health spending to GDP.

The following table gives figures for total spending on health to GDP in some Western countries:

Health Expenditures to GDP in Some Western Countries (%)1993

	1985	1990	1993
U.S.A	10.8	12.6	13.9
Sweden	8.9	8.6	7.5
Germany	8.7	8.3	7.7
France	8.5	8.9	9.8
Belgium	7.4	7.6	8.3
Italy	7.0	8.1	8.5
Japan	6.6	6.7	7.3
U.K.	5.8	6.0	7.0
Greece	4.1	4.3	4.6
Turkey	2.2	2.9	2.7

Source: Coup d'oeil sur les Economies de l'OCDE, 1996, p. 111-112

Just as is the case with social security expenditures, the real cause of the problem here seems to be Turkey's relatively low share of public revenue in her GDP.

According to international figures on active population numbers, there were a little more than 37 million people in Turkey who were above the age of 15 back in 1993. Around

20 million of these were considered as working, i.e. active, population. The proportion of the active population in the overall figure is 54%. Compared to some selected countries we see the following picture:

Proportion of Active Population to Overall Population (1993)

Country	Population (%)
USA	66
Japan	63
United Kingdom	62
Germany	58
Turkey	54
Spain	49
Greece	49
Italy	47

Source: L'Etat du Monde 1998

A closer examination of the comparisons reveals some interesting results. For example, the percentage of active population among the males is 75 in Turkey. This percentage is 62 in Italy, 63 in Spain, 64 in Greece, 71 in Germany, 72 in the United Kingdom and 74 in the United States. Among those listed above, Japan with 78% is the only country with a higher percentage of active male population than Turkey. The reason that Turkey falls a little behind the central and northern European countries in the general average is that the true number of women who belong to the active population is not fully reflected in statistical figures. For women aged above 15 their proportion in the active population is given as 32%. When one considers that there are millions of women who work in the cities or villages but are not represented in the statistics, it becomes clear that those tables must be reviewed.

Despite this, with respect to active population Turkey is ahead of most EU countries.

Population in Eurasia: Today and Tomorrow

The population trends of Turkey's neighbours are also interesting. When the forecasts for Turkey are compared with those for her neighbours, we get the following table:

Population Forecasts for Turkey and Her Neighbours (millions)

	1980	1997	2010	2020	2050
Turkey	45.1	62.2	76.5	85.6	103.6
Iran	39.2	67.5	88.2	104.2	142.3
Iraq	13.2	21.0	31.1	39.7	65.5
Greece	9.6	10.6	10.9	10.7	8.3
Bulgaria	8.8	8.2	7.9	7.5	5.9
Syria	8.7	16.1	23.3	28.9	43.4
Azerbaijan	6.1	7.7	8.4	9.0	10.5
Georgia	5.0	5.1	4.8	4.7	4.3
Armenia	3.1	3.4	3.3	3.4	3.4
Total	**138.8**	**202.2**	**254.4**	**293.7**	**387.2**

Source: U.S. Bureau of the Census

There is a stark difference between the population figures of Turkey's northwestern and northeastern neighbours and those of her southeastern neighbours. The populations of Bulgaria and Greece have stabilized and are showing a tendency to decrease. Georgia and Armenia show similar tendencies of decline in population. On the other hand, Turkey's other neighbours have increases in population, Iran being the first among them. Come mid next century, the Iranian population will exceed that of Russia. While the

population of Turkey and her neighbours put ı
138.8 million back in 1980, this number reach
1997 and is expected to be 293.7 million in 202
million in 2050. According to these calculations, by the year
2020 the population of Turkey and her neighbours will reach
the level that the current EU members will have by then.
Coming to the year 2050 their population will exceed even
that of an enlarged EU. If the countries in this region of
extensive oil and natural gas reserves manage to solve their
structural problems and to establish cooperation among them,
they can establish a great welfare zone in this region of which
Turkey is also a part. In the Western world NAFTA will be the
only union of countries with a population larger than that of
Turkey and her neighbours.

It seems inevitable that these developments will have far-
reaching implications in the economic and social as well as
political realms. Whether she becomes an EU member or not,
Turkey, surrounded by Europe, the Middle East and Russia,
will be at the center of a market of 800 million people. When
on top of this one adds Egypt, which by that time will have
more than 100 million people, and the rest of the Middle
Eastern countries, the size of the market becomes more
striking. Here we must also consider the Central Asian states,
the Turkic republics, which possess considerable amounts of
natural resources and have extensive cultural and historical ties
with Turkey.

Though not at a very fast pace, Central Asian countries are
also experiencing population growth. While the population of
Azerbaijan, Kazakhstan, the Kyrgyz Republic, Turkmenistan
and Uzbekistan together was 43 million in 1980, this number
is expected to be 71 million by 2020 and 89 million by 2050.
Adding the population of Turkey to these figures, the
combined population of the Turkic world will be around 192
million by the middle of the next century.

Considering the well-educated populations and valuable
natural resources such as oil, natural gas and gold reserves as
well as cotton that these countries possess, Turkey and the

Turkic republics can form an extensive and productive region of cooperation. If these countries manage to recognize their common interests and implement policies for the next century that would safeguard these interests, this would benefit them, the region as well as the world, and these republics could end up possessing great economic power. One of the preconditions of this is for these countries to increase the level of education of their people. This is an important target not only for Turkey but also for her neighbours and the countries of the region.

Human Development Index

Turkey ranks low in the human development index, which takes criteria such as life expectancy and literacy rate as well as GDP per capita into account.

According to the index of 1997, Turkey ranks 74th among 175 countries. But small countries like the Bahamas and Grenada, which are ranked above Turkey, are also included in this index. Turkey ranks 11th among countries having populations exceeding 50 million. Moreover, there is only a small difference between Turkey and some countries that rank higher in the general index. The important point is this: Between 1960 and 1992, Turkey was among the top 10 countries that moved up most in the human development index. The OECD lists Turkey in the moderately developed countries category rather than the developing countries category.

The Rank of Turkey and Selected Countries in the Human Development Index

Country	Index	Rank
Canada	0.960	1
U.S.A.	0.942	4
Japan	0.940	7
Germany	0.924	19
Bahamas	0.894	28
Hungary	0.857	48
Russia	0.792	67
Turkey	0.772	74
Romania	0.748	79
Egypt	0.614	109

Source: Etudes Economiques de l'OCDE, Turquie 1997

Whatever the reason is, it is cause for concern to see Turkey ranked so low in such a listing. However, it must not be forgotten that in recent years Turkey has accomplished quite a bit in some of the criteria used to calculate this index. During the past 30 years Turkey has significantly improved her standing in life expectancy, which largely depends on the quality of health care in a country. While the life expectancy in Turkey was 52.1 years in 1967, in 1997 it reached 67.3 years. (Various sources such as the archives of The Washington Post give the average life expectancy in Turkey as 72 years.) This level was achieved only recently by some countries considered to have more developed economies. Most of the credit here should go to improvements in health services, despite financial difficulties. In fact the number of hospital beds, which was 99,000 in 1980, grew to 140,000 in 1996. The number of physicians climbed from 27,000 to 73,000 and nurses from 26,000 to 75,000. Specialists estimate that life expectancy in Turkey will be 77.5 years by the year 2010. Estimates further into the next century indicate that Turkey will have one of the highest life expectancy rates in the world.

Educational Revolution in Turkey

The level of education is accepted to be one of the prime criteria when multinational research that compares countries to each other is conducted. The human development index mentioned above is one of these.

In the Ottoman Empire the need to establish contemporary institutions of education instead of traditional ones was felt by the end of the 18th century. The first modern education institution was the School of Artillery established by Selim III in 1795. More important reforms were seen during the reign of Mahmud II. In the 1830s military secondary schools called "Rüşdiye" were opened, and the School of Medicine was established in 1832. These were the foundations of important schools such as the military academy, Harbiye, and the Faculty of Medicine, "Tıbbiye." However, education was still not widespread. In the mid 19th century, after the Crimean War, 60 "Rüşdiye" schools had 3,371 students and the religious "Medrese" schools had 16,752. In order to achieve widespread education, cooperation with France was initiated. Napoleon III's minister for education Duroy arrived in Istanbul and prepared a modernization program for the Ottoman education system. Galatasaray Lycee opened in 1868 with the cooperation of France. The modern schools of the time accepted not only Muslim students but also students from other religions. Again in conjunction with Duroy's project Istanbul University, or "Darülfünun," was established.

Despite all these efforts education could still not be made as widespread as was desired. By the end of the 19th century the literacy rate in Turkey was below 10%. In that period Western Europe had not fully solved its education problems either. In the early 19th century the Germanic states were the most advanced in education, but even in those countries the literacy rate was only 50%. The Newcastle Commission, established in England to analyze the education system in the cities after the Industrial Revolution, reported that most people in England were illiterate. In response to this report, a new education law was passed in 1870 aiming to broaden primary education. These efforts proved to be inadequate. In 1876 another law was promulgated which involved penalties for not attending school. The situation in the rest of Europe was not much different.

From the beginning of the last century the Ottomans grasped the importance of education and despite the fact that they could not make education widespread, they did not discriminate among those children who received an education. They allowed minority and missionary schools to be established. For example in 1871 in Istanbul alone there were 48 Armenian schools, and the number of these schools in the rest of Anatolia was 469. Greeks also had many schools. During that period there weren't that many Jewish schools, but their number increased rapidly, and by the end of the 19th century their number had reached 50. In 1863 American missionaries established Robert College. By 1870 the number of American missionary schools alone was 205. French schools being the foremost among them, the number of European missionary schools was in the hundreds.[10]

Did the people in all European countries have the same equal access to education in those times? In Russia during the reign of Alexander III, who came to the throne in 1881, the children of workers and villagers were not accepted into secondary schools. His predecessor, Alexander II, allowed only those who could be "trusted" into universities. Alexander III introduced strict restrictions on the education of Jewish children, only a small amount of whom were allowed to go to secondary school. It seems the educational level of those

[10] Robert Mantran, Histoire de l'Empire Ottomane, Paris, 1989, pp. 480-481.

countries that wanted to portray Turkey as a backward country was not perfect either.

In some Western countries relatively high standards in education had been reached, but this was not enough to make these societies live in prosperity, security and peace. In particular, the wars that took place in the first half of the 20th century among countries with well-educated people show that increased schooling is not enough to create a high level of civilization in a society. As Churchill said, the leaders of those countries with the best-educated people have turned Europe into hell. While Atatürk relied on an uneducated, mostly illiterate people and on their common sense and high values when establishing a new republic, leaders in Europe were forcing their well-educated people to be governed by outdated regimes.

In 1923, when Atatürk established the Republic the educational standards of the country very poor; in all of Turkey there were only 4,894 primary schools, 72 secondary schools and 23 high schools. In 1927 the literacy rate was 10.7%. For women this figure was only 4.8%. Then, an unparalleled education campaign was initiated. Adopting the Latin alphabet instead of the Arabic facilitated the spread of education. The literacy rate went up to 20.4% by 1935, a 100% increase compared to 1927. This percentage became 30.2% in 1945 and 34.6% in 1950. When considering the level of education achieved by Turkey today, one must think also about the starting point and how fast she reached today's level.

School Enrollment in Turkey Between 1923 and 1997

Year	Primary School	Student	Technical School	Student	High School	Students	Higher Educ.	Students
1923	4,894	341,941	64	6,547	23	1,241	9	2,914
1930	6,598	489,299	59	9,296	57	5,699	17	4,186
1940	10,596	955,957	103	20,264	82	24,862	20	12,844
1950	17,428	1,616,626	326	53,289	88	32,269	34	24,815
1960	24,398	2,866,501	530	107,547	194	75,632	55	65,297
1970	38,513	4,939,516	913	235,086	518	244,569	152	159,231
1980	45,660	5,694,860	1,864	520,332	1,167	534,605	321	237,369
1992	50,701	6,878,923	2,973	977,010	1,888	894,047	424	759,047
1997	44,862	8,944,425	3,305	1,135,000	2,555	1,313,892	536	1,323,345

Source: Ministry of Education, Republic of Turkey

In the early years of the Republic there was a significant increase in the number of schools, and ministers of education made revolutionary changes in Turkey's cultural and educational system. The table above shows the results of these efforts.

For all educational levels, the increase in schooling is greater than theincrease in population; this proves that the general level of education and culture did in fact improve.

The educational reforms of the Republic were not confined to school-age children and youngsters. For adults too there were community schools and workshops. Village Institutes were established to educate and train the children of the villagers. The goal as to leave no village without a school. For that purpose the Village Institutes Law was passed on April 17, 1940. Those graduating from elementary school would be further educated in the Village Institutes boarding schools for five years. These students would then become teachers themselves and would also be knowledgeable enough to help villagers become more productive. Within 15 years there were to be no villages without a school or a teacher. Four existing schools for training teachers for villages would be turned into Village Institutes, and 17 new ones would be established.

By the end of the fifth year 3,000 teachers for villages would be trained. This was the target. The founder of the

Village Institutes was the head of the Elementary Schooling Department, a prominent educator, İsmail Hakkı Tonguç. President İsmet İnönü saw this initiative not only as an important development for education but also as an important vehicle to help Turkey regain her strength. In 1939, İnönü said, "We firmly believe that when we manage to improve the education and prosperity of our villagers, the might of our nation will be so great that it is difficult to envision today."

The Village Institutes created excitement not only among education circles and the public in Turkey but also around the world. A former general director of UNESCO, Julian Huxley, said, "In Turkey an interesting education system called Village Institutes has been put in practice, and this can be used as an example for all developing countries."

The Village Institutes were closed in 1954. Up until that time, around 20,000 teachers for villages had been trained. İnönü reflected his thoughts on this matter in 1946 as follows: "Without taking into consideration any of the duties I have undertaken as a politician or a soldier, I can easily say that when I die I will leave two things to the Turkish nation: the Village Institutes and the multi-party system."[11]

With these and similar measures, education in Turkey became widely available, and the literacy rate increased dramatically. By 1990 82% of the people had become literate. As a matter of fact, the older segment of the population pulls down this rate. The literacy rate of the age group above 65 is only 36%. This figure is above 90% for those younger than 30. A significant increase is seen in schooling levels as well. While the elementary schooling rate in the 1960-1961 period was 70%, by the 1993-1994 period this had reached 83.1%. Within the same time frames the proportion of those who attended secondary school went up from 20.5% to 61.9% and high school from 18% to 45.1%. The percentage of those

[11] Erdal İnönü, Anılar ve Düşünceler, Istanbul 1995, vol. I, pp. 87-94.

attending to universities or institutes of higher learning climbed from 3.3% to 16.9%.[12]

In the 25-64 age group in Germany the proportion of those who graduated from high school is 62% and in France, 54%. There are countries more comparable with Turkey as well. Spain and Portugal's figures are less than the average of Europe and closer to those of Turkey.[13] We should remember that Spain and Portugal have been EU members for a long time now and have benefited from education funds of the Union. Whatever the case and the position of other countries may be, it is a reality that Turkey still has not achieved the desired levels in education.

Nevertheless, one should not underestimate the significance of what has been accomplished so far. The number of those receiving higher education in Turkey has tripled in the last 20 years. Back in 1975 only 6.7% of Turkish youth was able to receive a higher education. That number reached 8.9% in 1985 and 19.6% in 1996. There are improvements in other countries as well, but it is difficult to find more rapid development than in Turkey. As an example, in the same 20-year period the increase in Spain was twofold, and in Italy it was half of that.[14]

The United States is one of the most advanced countries in public education and schooling. In some fields the gap between the United States and Europe is no smaller than that between Western Europe and Turkey. Moreover, the current advanced level of education in the United States has been achieved only with the developments of the past decades.

Another criticism leveled against Turkey is the fact that Turkey falls behind Western countries in educating the female population of the country. Yet the difference between Turkey and Western Europe in this respect is not as great as one might suspect. According to research conducted in 1983 regarding

---

[12] Emre Kongar, 21. Yüzyılda Türkiye, Istanbul, 1998, p. 533.
[13] Regards sur l'Education, les Indicateurs de l'OCDE, Paris, 1997.
[14] Education at a Glance, OECD Indicators, Paris, 1998.

elementary schooling, 47% of the students in cities are females and in villages, 45.1%. In 1980 26% of university students were female. This number was 30% in Switzerland, 33% in Japan and 51% in the United States.[15] In the 22 medical faculties in Turkey the percentage of female faculty members is 28.2%.The female faculty members account for 26.8% of the overall system.[16]

Turkey is making huge investments to improve standards in the field of education. In 1994 3.3% of the GDP was spent on education. While 20 years ago the amount spent for defence was twice as much as that spent on education, their percentages now are closer to each other. Still, the proportion of money spent on education is smaller than that of many other countries. Spain spends 4.7%, Germany 4.8%, Italy 5.2% and the United States 5.5% of GDP on education. Putting aside the Western countries, Iran spends 5.9% and Egypt 5.0%.

Having said this, if national budget figure is used instead of GDP as a yardstick, then it will be seen that Turkey is ahead of many countries in spending on education. Turkey spends 14.7% of her budget on education. This figure is 9.4% in Germany, 10.8% in France and 8.8% in Italy. The two indicators produce different results due to the fact that the ratio of public spending in the overall GDP is relatively small in Turkey. We will come back to this issue in the chapter on economics.

Of all the expenditures regarding education, the amount spent on investment is also quite high in Turkey. In 1991 14% of all education expenditures went towards investment. Today among the OECD countries, Japan with 16% is the only country that invests in education relatively more heavily than Turkey.

[15] UNESCO, Statistical Yearbook, Paris, 1996.
[16] Eser Danyal Köker, Education, Politics and Women in Turkey, Istanbul.

Here we must also consider the fact that in Turkey practically all of the public spending on education is met from the general budget. Other than Ireland and New Zealand, there is no Western nation that funds the expenditure on elementary and secondary education from the general budget alone. Canada covers (spends) 3% of the (national budget for the) expenses of elementary and secondary schools from the national budget. In the United States this rate is 8%. The rest is met with regional and local resources.

The situation with the universities is a little different. Until recently, seven Western countries including Turkey funded practically all public spending on universities from their general budget. Others use local resources in varying proportions.

The number of Turkish students abroad is also increasing. Turkey is among the top three Western countries with students overseas. The others are Germany and Greece.

In 1995 there were 33,305 Turkish students receiving higher education in the West. Germany hosted 22,747 of them and 6,716 were in the United States.[17]

The efforts to improve educational standards in Turkey have begun to bear fruit. But Turkey has decided to take even bigger steps in reforming this sector. On August 16, 1997 the Turkish Parliament took a decision to increase compulsory education to eight years. Some of the goals set by this reformist law are as follows:

- In the year 2,000 1.1 million students in the 12-14 age group will have three more years of elementary education;
- The average number of students per classroom will go down to 30. (Today this number exceeds 50 in some schools.);
- To achieve these goals 140,000 more classrooms will be built, and 190,000 more teachers will be employed;

---

[17] Regards sur l'Education, OCDE, Paris, 1997.

- The number of regional elementary schools will be increased from 171 to 571; and
- To this end Turkey will spend $10 billion in three years.

Hence, Turkey is entering the 21st century with an unprecedented rate of improvement in her education system. The standards reached today will eventually be replaced by even better figures comparable to those of the most advanced countries of the West.

So far, Turkey has met the increased demand for education and has improved the system's quality relying only on her own resources. On the other hand, members of the EU receive considerable funds from the EU budget for such purposes. Lately, those countries that have been selected as candidates for EU membership have started to receive sizeable financial aid to bring their education systems up to EU standards. To this end Poland, for example, received ECU 180 million up until 1996.

As these figures show, despite a lack of funds relative to the West and a population increase of more than 800,000 people per year, Turkey has accomplished significant advancements in the field of education. Turkey today has more than 3 million university graduates and more than 60 universities. Private universities are being opened up and, thanks to donations from charitable organizations, the infrastructure for better-quality higher education is being put in place.

With a better-educated population Turkey will increase her power and influence in the region as well as in the world, and all indicators show that Turkey will catch up with Western educational standards in the near future.

There is a good reason why so much emphasis is put on education. If the lack of education of the Turkish people is the main concern of those criticizing the size of Turkey's population, the figures above show that the gap between Europe and Turkey will be diminished in the near future. One should also remember that the priority of those who invited Turkish workers into their countries 35 years ago in order to employ them in heavy industry and mines was not whether these workers had a higher education. At that time the demand was for manpower. However, those workers trained themselves as best as they could and strove to better educate their children. To a large extent they have been successful in this effort.

Referring to Turkish workers abroad, some try to argue that Turks are more prone to commit criminal acts. Some crimes committed by Turks at home or abroad are over-publicized so as to "prove" this argument and give the impression that crime rates among Turks are higher than the rest of the population. The fact that the Turkish media gives more coverage to ordinary crimes compared to the Western press leaves the impression that Turkey has an overall crime rate which is much higher than that of other countries. Furthermore, critics use this argument to imply that a country with such a high crime rate and with so many criminals does not have a place in the community of civilized countries. Could these impressions and publications reflect the truth?

Research conducted by the United Nations for the period 1970-1994 analyzing the crime rates in different countries came up with some interesting results. In 1990 there were 44,826 prisoners in Turkey. This number was 77,778 in the United Kingdom, 95,096 in Ukraine, 51,147 in Poland and 120,220 in South Korea.

We get a more accurate picture of the crime rate in a country when we compare the number of people imprisoned with that country's population. The table below gives the total number of imprisoned persons for the year 1990 as well as per 100,000 of the population for selected countries:

Prison Population in Selected Countries (1990)

Country	Population	In Prison	Per 100,000
Denmark	5,140,000	15,421	300
Austria	7,717,000	20,944	271
Sweden	8,558,000	15,833	185
Belgium	9,962,000	17,693	177
Netherland	14,951,000	25,320	169
U.K.	56,428,000	77,770	137
Poland	38,108,000	51,147	134
Slovakia	5,262,000	6,866	130
Portugal	9,870,000	11,122	112
Czech Rep.	10,309,000	11,418	110
Turkey	56,123,000	44,826	79

Source: UN Statistics on Crime Rates, 1990

According to the official UN statistics Turkey, despite the increase in population, has experienced no increase in the number of those imprisoned. One can even observe a decrease compared to the figures of 1965, 1970 and 1975. Turkish criminality statistics show that in 1965 the ratio of crimes per 1 million people was 2,638. This figure went down to 1,006 in 1997.[18]

The table above shows crime tendencies in various countries. It can clearly be seen that the tendency towards crime in Turkey is lower than in those countries whose people are considered to be more educated than Turks. The crime rate in Turkey is half of what it is in Sweden and a quarter of Denmark's. There are more up-to-date figures for those imprisoned in EU countries. In 1995 there were 66,164

---

[18] 75.Yılında Sayılarla Türkiye Cumhuriyeti. T.C. Başbakanlık Devlet İstatistik Enstitüsü, p. 38.

prisoners in Germany, 53,178 in France, 51,265 in the United Kingdom and 49,642 in Italy.[19]

According to the State Institute of Statistics, the number of those imprisoned in Turkey in 1997 was 62,946.[20]

The crimes committed by Turks living abroad are given extensive coverage in the Western media. Turks are shown as crime-prone elements in society who damage Europe's social fabric and public order. From time to time figures supporting this argument also are found in the media. Those who base their impressions regarding Turks on such information start to see the Turkish people as a source of problems for their community, as individuals who lack the ability to adapt to contemporary society. This sentiment gradually spreads to the public at large, influences politicians and creates the impression that granting freedom of movement to the Turkish people could result in the destruction of social order in Europe. Yet the above statistics prove that these concerns are not justified. If the crime rates among Turks living abroad are higher than those in Turkey, then one should seek the reason for this, not in the national traits of these people but in the environment in which they have to live and in the difficulties they face in adapting to the prevailing social conditions in foreign countries. What's important is to be able to see the Turks as an integral part of the society they live in as well as to acknowledge the positive contributions they make, instead of trying to single out the problems they may have.

Turks Living Abroad

After World War II one of the problems faced by Europe was a lack of population. As there weren't enough people locally, it was necessary to import labour in order to rebuild

---

[19] Eurostat, Yearbook, 1997, Luxembourg, p. 175.
[20] 75. Yılında Sayılarla Türkiye Cumhuriyeti, T.C. Başbakanlık Devlet İstatistik Enstitüsü, p. 38.

the European economies. Turkey was among the most important suppliers of this Labor. In 1955 Germany signed her first Labor agreement with Italy. In 1960 similar agreements were concluded with Greece and Spain, then with Turkey in 1961, with Morocco in 1964, with Tunisia in 1965 and with Yugoslavia in 1968.

Celebrations organized at train stations to greet the "guest workers" are still vivid in people's minds. Specialists on the topic give figures on exactly how much of a contribution these workers have made to the German as well as other European economies. According to official German statistics, relative to their population foreign workers, in particular the Turks, add as much value to the German economy as the Germans themselves. Although we will come back to this topic later in the chapter, it is important to note the fact here that Turkish workers in Europe, who are viewed as a source of concern, even considered a reason to block Turkey's membership in the EU, are those who have shouldered the heaviest and most difficult jobs in Europe and contributed enormously to the economy. Back in the 1960s one could not even imagine that efforts to meet the demand for labour in Europe, would result in the 1990s in initiatives aimed at closing the doors of Europe to Turkey.

According to Turkey's Social Security Authority there are 3.4 million Turkish citizens living abroad. Most of these are in Western Europe. There are 40,000 in the former Soviet republics, some 21,000 in Australia and 800 in Libya.

The Turkish Studies Center in Essen says that in Western Europe alone, there are 2.9 million Turks. The total number of Turks living abroad is larger than the population of Ireland, half of Denmark and Finland and six times that of Luxembourg. The total number foreigners living in EU countries is close to 17.6 million. Thirty-two percent of these are EU citizens living in a country other than their own, and 68% are from other nations. A total of 16.5% of all foreigners are Turkish citizens. If we consider only those from non-EU countries, then the ratio of Turkish citizens goes up to 24.5%.

Seventy percent of these Turks live in Germany. After Germany comes France with 12%, the Netherlands with 7% and Austria with 5%.

Germany is the first country that comes to mind when one talks about foreign workers in Europe. Although this preconception is true in absolute numbers, when one considers the amount of foreigners relative to the rest of the population, there are other EU countries with higher ratios than Germany. A total of 32.6% of Luxembourg's population, for example, is comprised of foreigners. Belgium and Austria have higher figures than Germany. The proportions for these are 9.1% and 9% respectively. Foreigners comprise 8.6% of the population in Germany.

The priority of the Turks who came to Germany was to work for a while in order to save enough money to establish their own businesses back in Turkey. Contrary to the common view, for most Turks Germany or Western Europe in general was not the utopia in which they wanted to spend the rest of their lives. While on the one hand increasing in number and becoming the most numerous foreign group in Germany, returning to Turkey has always been in the back of these people's minds.

By 1996 the number of Turks in Germany exceeded 2 million. According to the Turkish Studies Center in Essen, the population distribution of Turks in Europe is as follows:

Foreigners and Turks in Western Europe(1995)

Country	Foreigners	Turks
Germany	6,990,000	2,049,100
France	3,596,000	254,000
UK	2,096,000	29,000
Belgium	922,300	85,981
Netherlands	757,100	154,310
Austria	720,900	142,231
Italy	683,600	3,700
Sweden	537,400	20,252
Spain	460,800	322
Denmark	196,700	35,739
Portugal	157,100	100
Greece	152,800	3,100
Luxembourg	132,500	-
Ireland	96,400	-
Finland	62,000	1,200

Source: The Economic Power of the Turks Living in the European Union, Turkish Studies Center, Essen, May 1998

There are many thought-provoking aspects to this table. It is clear that in absolute figures Germany has the largest number of foreigners. France has half as many, and the 2 million foreigners in the United Kingdom are no small number, either. However, for some reason the amount of discussion over Turks in Germany is not matched by any other country or for any other foreign group. One does not, for example, come across that many articles in the press on the number of the Basque or Catalan workers from Spain. No one conducts research to determine how many of the workers from Greece are of Hellenic, Macedonian or Turkish origin. Similarly there isn't much discussion taking place over the ethnic, regional or religious origins of the Indians in the United Kingdom. Yet the German press frequently estimates how many of the Turkish citizens in Germany are of Kurdish origin. Using these numbers they then go on to argue that Turkish and Kurdish groups have brought their conflict in Turkey to Germany.

However, there aren't that many people who investigate whether there is in fact an ethnic-based conflict in Turkey or not. Is there any conflict based purely on difference of ethnicity among the Turkish citizens in Germany? An objective observer would have to answer "no."

In that case, why the discomfort? Have the Turks started to become a burden on the German economy? Yet as mentioned above, official German figures tell us that the value added by Turkish workers is quite high. Moreover they are paying a considerable amount of taxes. Their contributions to the social security fund are much larger than the benefits they receive.

The social structure of the Turks who arrived in Germany in the 1960s has also changed. All of them came as workers, but some of them established their own businesses and are now employers themselves. A significant number of their children became university graduates, and they too began to have their own businesses. The welfare and educational level of the Turkish people has significantly improved.

In the beginning Turks were not allowed to own businesses. When this restriction was removed in 1975, the number of Turkish enterprises grew dramatically and reached 42,000 in 1996. The Turkish Studies Center estimates this number will grow to 49,500 by the year 2000 and 90,000 by 2030. These companies were employing about 186,000 people in 1998.

These figures refer only to the Turks in Germany. The numbers for the whole of the EU are even more impressive. In 1997 the number of Turkish enterprises in the EU was 62,100, with a total turnover of DM 50.4 billion. The total investment made in EU countries by Turks is DM 11.8 billion. This number is larger than the total amount of foreign investment in Turkey in the 1980-1995 period. A total of 256,900 people work in Turkish-owned firms in the EU. In 1997 every Turk living in the EU contributed, on average, ECU 17,188 per year to the GDP of the country he or she was residing in. This is almost equal to the amount contributed by EU citizens themselves which is ECU 17,310. In other words, Turks on average are creating as much value as the citizens of the EU. The total contribution of Turks to the GDP of the EU is ECU 49.7 billion, which is more than half the EU's budget.[21]

Turks living abroad have made great leaps in education as well. The first generation who went to Germany without receiving adequate education in Turkey faced many difficulties. In particular, the educational level of women remained low. According to research conducted by Professor Nermin Abadan on the subject, compared to their sisters who had moved to Germany, women who stayed in Turkey received better education. But those days are a thing of the past. The second and third generation of Turks accomplished revolutionary improvements in their level of education. According to 1995 figures 21,000 young Turks are studying at German universities, and 407,889 Turkish children are attending various German schools. A growing number of these are going to schools that either pave the way for university education or are technical schools.

These achievements accomplished despite difficulties are encouraging. That so many Turkish children are receiving education in Germany is also proving to be helpful in solving the adaptation problem faced in the early years of moving to a new country. Shouldn't everyone involved be pleased by this development and see this as an avenue to move the Turkish and German nations closer together? Should the illegal acts of some pro-violence groups who went to Germany as well as to other European countries just to provoke incidents be a factor that could prevent these fundamental, positive developments from being recognized as such? Wouldn't it be unfair to those who have given their life's work to those countries and who saw themselves as part of those countries if, just by looking at the actions of some fanatics, they are given the impression that

---

[21] Avrupa Birliği Ülkelerinde Yaşayan Türklerin Ekonomik Gücü, Türkiye Araştırmalar Merkezi, Essen, Mayıs 1998.

Turks are not wanted in Europe? Isn't it possible to punish those who commit crimes instead of hurting the law-abiding majority? Just as one cannot make a judgment on all Europeans merely by looking at the actions of some racist extremists, the acts of some violent groups from Turkey cannot be attributed to the entire Turkish community, either.

In a country with so many foreigners problems are inevitable. However, as can be seen above, positive developments are much more numerous and far more important. In other European countries too there have been improvements akin to those in Germany. Emphasizing these positive developments would surely prove to be more effective while trying to solve the problems facing all concerned.

One should not have the impression that all Turks are eager to spend all their lives in Germany or in any other European country. The number of people returning to Turkey from Germany is quite large. According to the Turkish Studies Center, 1.7 million Turks went home from Germany between the years 1974 and 1995, and since 1960 more than 2 million have done so. The latest figures show that approximately 45,000 people per year go back to Turkey from Germany. Yet the Turkish population in Germany rose even after 1973, when Germany stopped taking in more foreign workers. This is due in part to births in Germany and in part to those arriving from Turkey to reunite with their families.

Foreign workers have from time to time been a source of concern to Germans. When Spain was to become an EU member, they were worried that hundreds of thousands of Spaniards would occupy the rest of the EU. The results, however, were quite different. When EU membership resulted in increased investment and demand for labour in Spain, Spanish workers started to return home.

Turkish workers used to arrive in Germany without their wives. This changed in later years, and now 45% of the Turkish population in Germany is comprised of women.

The Turks living abroad contribute to Turkey's economic and cultural strength in those countries. This becomes even more evident when, in addition to those living in Europe, we consider the Turks living in the United States and Australia. Turkey's power abroad cannot be measured solely by looking at the income levels of her citizens living in foreign countries. In fact, Turkey's greatest gain from these people is the know-how they acquire by living overseas. Using German figures as a reference, we can estimate that today around 700,000 Turkish students are being educated in the most advanced countries of the world. Thirty thousand of these are university students. The foreign language, professional and academic training these students receive increases Turkey's overall wealth and strength.

The investments made in Turkcy by the Turks who live abroad are not generally considered to be foreign investment; they are instead counted as local investment. According to European Turkish Businessmen's Association (ATIAD) statistics, the total amount invested in Turkey only by the Turkish businessman in Germany had reached DM 750 million by 1994. The success of the Worldwide Turkish Businessmen's Conference, which held its first meeting in 1996 and the second in 1998, demonstrated the influence of the Turkish businessmen around the world as well as their potential to invest in Turkey.

ATIAD makes projections for the future as well. As compared to the figures of the Turkish Studies Center, ATIAD has more optimistic estimations. Their forecasts show that by 2010 there will be 100,000 Turkish entrepreneurs in Germany alone. They bring to mind the fact that the Hinduja Group of Companies, established by Indian businessmen living in the United Kingdom, have a worldwide turnover of $11 billion, and that 70% of all foreign investment in China is made by Chinese businessman living abroad. Turkish entrepreneurs are also engaged in similar efforts.[22]

---

[22] Almanya'daki Türk Girişimcilerinin Görünmeyen Gücü, ATİAD, Düsseldorf, 1997

When determining Turkey's place in the world, it would be a mistake to ignore the fact that there exists a large and powerful Turkish community abroad, which Turkey can and does profit from enormously.

Turkey's Natural Resources

As mentioned earlier, geographic properties play an important role in determining national strength. Throughout history nations with great power have emerged from among those possessing large territory. Although having large territory has never been sufficient to be a great power, it has always been a prerequisite to play an important role in world politics. This, however, has been one of the basic causes of many battles in history. When the world ran out of vast and empty territories, states started to attack each other. Such bitter experiences led the nations of the world to accept the principle of territorial integrity and inviolability of borders as a cornerstone of international relations. One of the most important principles of the UN Charter and the Helsinki Declaration is respect for the territorial integrity of independent states.

It has not been easy to reach this stage. Yet, there are still those who talk of spheres of influence of states or groups of states. Samuel Huntington, who argues that civilizations are on a collision course, investigates what parts of the world were under the control of which civilizations and when. According to his research, the territory under the control of Western civilization was around 51.2 million sq km. back in 1900. After World War I this area went up to 65.3 million sq km. However, following World War II and especially after its colonies gained their independence, this amount was halved. In 1993 the area under the political sphere of the West was around 32.5 million sq km.

The most striking change took place in Africa. In 1900 most of this continent was under colonial rule; therefore, the area under the control of African civilization was a mere

419,000 sq km. By 1993 it became 14.3 million sq km. Territory under the political influence of Islamic civilization went up from 8.9 million sq km. in 1900 to 28 million sq km. in 1993.

In 1900 the area under the control of Western civilization was 38.7% of the world, whereas the area under Islam was 6.8%. That is to say, territory under Western civilization was six times than that under Islam. Towards the end of the century, however, these ratios changed, and new balances formed. By 1993 area under the control of the West was down to 24.2%, and that under Islam was up to 21.1%. Orthodox civilization, which is not considered part of Western civilization, used to control 16.6% back in 1900; now it is down to 13.7%.[23]

Is such an analysis whereby world geography is divided among different civilizations compatible with a modern outlook towards the world? The UN Charter, which came into being after World War II, has come to be accepted as the constitution of the new world order. With this document and the Universal Declaration on Human Rights, the principle of the equality of people and of states was accepted irrespective of gender, religion, language or race. Today international relations are regulated based on this philosophy. This is why it seems odd to divide the world up along the lines of different civilizations.

Unfortunately, the proponents of such civilization ideologies are not alone in their approach of dividing the world into various spheres of influence. In the final analysis, world-famous American strategist Zbigniew Brzezinski's views run along the same lines. He accepts that nation states form the nucleus of the world order, but he argues that some of these countries have sovereignty areas around the world. He thinks that geographic properties constitute the starting point

---

[23] Samuel Huntington, Clash of Civilisations, p. 84.

for the development of national policies and that the size and status of territory are the main criteria of national power.

There is no doubt that geography is among the most crucial factors of national power. But to interpret this as a search to extend a country's sovereignty beyond internationally accepted borders is contrary to the concept of contemporary statehood established after the French Revolution. National power should be seen as something that enables a nation to live freely within its territory, independent of other states, allowing the country to effectively protect its interests within its borders. Turkey's geography should be viewed with this general understanding as well.

How was the world of today shaped after the long and bitter experiences of the past? Keeping in mind the understanding we mentioned above and looking at the world geography by taking the nation-state as the basis of analysis, we come up with the following table:

Area of Some Countries

Country	Area (thousands of sq km.)
Russia	17,075
Canada	9,976
China	9,596
USA	9,363
India	3,267
Kazakhstan	2,717
Turkey	780
France	547
Germany	357

Source: Images Economiques du Monde

Russia is the largest country in the world, with 17 million sq km. Following Russia are China, Canada, Australia, the

United States and Brazil. There are 29 countries with more than 1 million sq km. Among these is Turkey's neighbour Iran. Kazakhstan is twice as large as Iran.

These areas should be considered together with their geographic properties and not just by their size. For example, due to their harsh climate large portions of Russia and Canada are not suitable for settlement. Almost the entire Canadian population lives in an area ranging no more than 200 kilometers from the United States border.

Other than climatic conditions, the landscape of the territory also imposes its own restrictions. Australia is as big as the United States but only 6% of its territory is arable. This figure is 8% for Russia. Turkey is the second largest country in Europe, next to Russia. Turkey's land is almost as large as France and the United Kingdom put together. Turkey's territory is bigger than the sum of Poland, Hungary, the Czech Republic and Romania, all candidates for EU membership. Climatic conditions are hospitable all around Turkey. It is no coincidence that quite a number of early civilizations were established in the land that today is Turkey.

Turkey has 8,272 kilometers of coastline. This is important both from a strategic as well as an economic point of view. Thirty percent of its land is arable, and 26% is covered with forests. According to 1989 figures an area of 22,200 sq km. is irrigated. As the Southeastern Anatolia Project (GAP) becomes functional stage by stage, this area will become even larger.

Turkey's arable land is as large as that of France and Hungary combined, countries that are traditionally viewed as the most advanced European countries in farming. Contrary to the common view forested areas in Turkey are twice as great as Germany's and larger than all French and Italian forests put together. Naturally the fertility of the land and the type of forests must be taken into consideration as well.

Turkey is not among the richest countries of Europe with respect to water resources but still has sizeable water potential, which also forms the backbone of energy supplies in the country. Thanks to her suitable climate, fertile land and irrigation systems Turkey is the fifth largest producer of cotton in the world.

Turkey also possesses rich mines. With 3 million tons per year, she is the 25th largest producer of coal in the world. In Europe, she is ranked seventh along with Romania. Among the EU candidates only Poland and the Czech Republic have higher production rates than Turkey.

In brown coal production Turkey ranks higher. Here, the output levels of Turkey, Greece, Poland and the Czech Republic are close to each other. The rest of Europe falls behind in this category.

Turkey is the 15th largest producer of iron ore, which is an important material from an economic as well as a strategic perspective. In Europe only Sweden produces more than Turkey, and that is only by a minimal amount; the yield of the remaining EU countries is smaller.

In the production of boride, another strategic material, Turkey ranks 14th in the world. Only Hungary and Greece produce more of this material in Europe.

Turkey is 16th in the world in copper production. In Europe, only Poland, Sweden and Yugoslavia have higher rates of production.[24]

We could give more examples; however, the point is that Turkey is among the countries with the highest production rates of strategically important materials. Relying on one's own resources while developing economically is an important factor contributing to the strength of Turkey.

---

[24] UN Monthly Bulletin of Statistics, New York, Vol. U, No.12, December 1997.

Strong Army, Permanent Peace

Defence power is regarded as an important factor in positioning a country. Fifty years after the end of World War II and at a time when bipolar world order has lost its meaning, there may be those who think that possessing a strong defence has lost its significance. The fact is, however, there has been a surge in regional conflicts since the end of the balance of horror that existed between East and West for the last 40 years. For more than 20 years acts of terrorism, costing the lives of many people, have been on the rise. Fundamentalist movements in some countries have had serious consequences on their structure and stability, and efforts to export fundamentalist ideologies are perceived as serious ongoing threats. In the 50 years that followed World War II, when the world was thought to be going through a relatively peaceful and stable period, 17 million people were killed in local and regional wars, conflicts or uprisings. More than a million of these were in the Balkans, the Middle East and the Caucasus, all areas bordering Turkey. In Greece alone, 160,000 died during the civil war that took place between 1945 and 1949, while wars in the Middle East claimed 972,000 lives and fighting in the Caucasus in 1992 left 60,000 dead.[25] The death toll in Bosnia back in 1991 is estimated to be close to 200,000.

Located in an area surrounded by local fighting and intense terrorist activity, Turkey has no alternative but to have a strong army. Her geography as well as the historical background of the region imposes this condition on her.

Due to this, Turkey has engaged in important reforms to modernize her army since the early 19th century. Mustafa

---

[25] IISS, Military Balance, London 1997-1998.

Kemal had won the War of Independence with an army that lost most of its fighting power during World War I. He went on to update the military and lay down the foundations of the armed forces, which now has exemplary strength, morale and discipline. When he first initiated the Independence War, all that Mustafa Kemal had was militia scattered around the country and a small number of troops that had survived from the Ottoman period. When the Turkish Parliament was established in 1920 there were only 70 soldiers in Ankara.[26] Later, a regular army was established with a decree from Parliament. The main war was fought with this army, and the militias were dispersed.

Despite the acute financial difficulties of the time, whatever the resources at hand, they were all made available to strengthen the army. At the outbreak of World War II, the Turkish Army was still not among the strongest in Europe, yet it was powerful enough to be a deterrent against the larger military powers of the time. Turkey remained non-aligned until the end of the war. None of the warring parties made an attempt on Turkey; maybe they were simply unable to do so. This was due in part to a successful foreign policy and in part to the resolve of the Turkish nation to defend herself.

Before starting to make comparisons, one point must be stressed. When contrasting defence capabilities, writers like Samuel Huntington take civilization background instead of individual countries as a basis for comparison. According to Huntington 43.7% of the world's total military power was controlled by Western civilization in 1900. Islamic civilization used to control 16.7%; Orthodox civilization, 16.6%; and Chinese civilization, 10%. After World War I the military power controlled by the West went up to 48.5%, while the Islamic world's dropped to 3.6%. This picture changed dramatically in 1970. While the power of the West declined to 25.8%, that of Orthodox civilization, its foremost country being the former Soviet Union, climbed to 25.1%, with the

---

[26] Kongar, op. cit., p. 90.

Chinese world's control growing to 24.7% and the power of Islamic civilization reaching 10.4%.

With the collapse of the Soviet Union the balances changed once again. The West's share decreased further and came down to 21.1%. We see a dramatic decline in the Orthodox category as well, to 14.3%. The Islamic proportion, however, went up to 20%, establishing a numerical balance with the West. Chinese civilization shows an even higher increase, with 25.7%. These are followed by armed forces under the control of Latin American, Indian, African, and Japanese civilizations.[27]

How fruitful is it to compare defence forces along the lines of differences in civilization? Will Turkey be viewed in the Western category, the security of which she has been contributing to substentially for the last 50 years, or in the Islamic category, since her population is almost entirely Muslim? To what extent could the Soviet Union be viewed in the Orthodox category? Won't these comparisons, based on civilizations instead of individual countries, pave the way for even more dangerous conflicts and enmities?

Is replacing the ideological Iron Curtain, which took 40 years to tear down, with new iron curtains based on differences in religion, culture and civilization the right thing to do?

Those who dissect defence capabilities along civilization lines are not the only source of concern. There are strategists who divide the world up into spheres of influence among the greater powers as well. American strategist Zbigniew Brzezinski says Eurasia has been the power center of the world for the past 500 years and argues that whoever controls this region can control the world.

Brzezinski says that 75% of the world population, 60% of its GNP and 75% of all known energy resources are located in the region called Eurasia. For him Eurasia is a chessboard

---

[27] Huntington, op. cit., p. 88.

upon which world domination games are played. For the first time in history a non-Eurasian country, i.e. the United States, has been influential in this field. According to Brzezinski there are five countries that are geostrategic players: France, Germany, Russia, China and India. Right next to these and playing critical roles are Ukraine, Azerbaijan, South Korea, Turkey and Iran. He then goes on to analyze the potential of these countries to dominate their regions as well as the relations between them.

Brzezinski writes that Turkey is a source of stability in the Black Sea region as well as the country that controls the gateway from the Black Sea to the Mediterranean. He stresses the fact that Turkey is an antidote for Islamic fundamentalism and a strong pillar of NATO's southeastern flank. He says that for 300 years the world was under Western domination. There were only four entities that could not be subjugated: China, Russia, the Ottoman Empire and Ethiopia. At this point he approaches Huntington's views and talks about the predominance of the European civilization in the world.

It is difficult to reconcile such theories of supremacy and domination with a contemporary democratic world outlook, especially after the catastrophes of the first half of the 20th century, which claimed the lives of millions.

Countries must carefully evaluate the geopolitics of their regions based on their national interests. Therefore, we must keep in mind the fact that 75% of the world's energy resources are in Turkey's vicinity, making her geographic location of paramount strategic significance.

The only way for Turkey to live in peace and security in such a sensitive region is by having a strong military. This fact has been known since the Ottoman period, but Turkey was able to actualize it only after World War II, when she became a member of NATO. Next to Russia, Turkey now has the largest conventional forces in all of Europe.

Compared to the early 20th century, there are large differences between the powers and areas of responsibility of different nations' armed forces. At the beginning of the century, Britain was the world's largest military power. In 1914 it had 28 million sq km. and 400 million non-British people under its sovereignty.[28]

After World War I, the United States emerged as an important military power, and especially after World War II it became the most powerful in the world. The Soviet Union's claim to being the second superpower disappeared with the end of the Cold War. The international balance based on nuclear arms has, to a certain degree, lost its significance, and the political balances established in Europe have changed the value of military strength in its global sense.

The strength and structure of the armed forces of Europe today are very different than those of World War II Europe. The development of high-tech weapons has made it possible to have more effective defences with fewer people. However, in the final analysis one of the determining factors of military strength is still the number of well-trained personnel. Even 15 years after the end of World War II most European countries had defence structures based on large armies.

In the last 40 years there have been significant changes in the number of troops of different countries around the world. It is a well-known fact that France used to have 1 million troops in the early 1960s, when she still had overseas territories and had to have men stationed in places such as Algeria.

When East-West relations were still strained, almost all European countries had large armies. Immediately after the end of the Cold War the United States, Russia and Western European countries as well as Eastern European nations made large cuts in their military personnel. Between 1980 and 1996 there was also a significant decline in the Chinese armed forces.

---

[28] Zbigniew Brzezinski, The Grand Chessboard, New York, 1997, pp. 19-21.

Japan is the only country that has not decreased its number
of troops significantly since 1960, because they have
maintained only a small military since the end of World War
II. The size of the Japanese Self-defence Force is half Turkey's
army and less than one-tenth that of China, which is the
greatest military power of that region.

The cutback in Western countries' armed forces is not
confined to the number of troops. From 1985-1995 there
were serious declines in arms purchases as well. To give an
example, at the beginning of that period the U.S. Navy used to
purchase an average of 29 ships per year, but at the end of that
same period this number had gone down to only six; new
aircraft purchases went down from 943 to 127 per year; and
tanks dropped from 720 to zero.[29]

The effective force of the Turkish Army is determined
based on considerations imposed by the region as well as
Turkey's defence requirements. According to the London-
based International Institute of Strategic Studies (IISS) Turkey
has more than 600,000 troops, and her army has been
equipped with the latest equipment, particularly in the past 15
years.

Turkey's long-term modernization process is planned to be
actualized in all sections of the armed forces in the coming 20
years. The Turkish Navy has the responsibility of defending an
8,272-kilometer-long coastline. It too has been furnished with
modern ships, as Turkey is one of the few countries capable of
building its own frigates, submarines and fast patrol boats
carrying guided missiles. The Air Force is also in a similar
situation. Turkey has manufactured 160 F-16s, and with 80
more planes currently under production, will have completed
a second lot by the end of 1999.[30]

---

[29] Huntington, op. cit. p. 89.
[30] Defence Policy of Turkey and Turkish Armed Forces, The White Paper,
Ankara, 1996.

Turkey has the largest and one of the best-equipped gendarmeries in all of Europe, operating under the Ministry of Internal Affairs. The power of the Turkish Armed Forces emanates not only from its number of personnel but also from its arms and equipment.

As mentioned above, the Turkish Armed Forces is the largest of its kind in Europe, with the exception of Russia. It ranks seventh in size after China, the United States, Russia, India, South Korea and North Korea.

It would be useful to look at this matter from the point of view of Europe's future. With the 1992 Maastricht Treaty, the EU targeted the acquisition of a defence dimension, in addition to its political and economic dimensions. Therefore, one cannot consider Europe's future without taking into account its defence.

The enlargement process of the EU should be carried out also keeping this consideration in mind. Looking at it this way, it is worth remembering that the total number of troops of Poland, the Czech Republic and Hungary, countries declared as candidates for EU membership, is half as large as Turkey's.

In international statistics, defence expenditures are accepted as an important criterion. The table below gives these expenditures for various countries for 1985 and 1996. These figures are not official numbers but are from the IISS, widely regarded as a reliable source.

The share of defence spending to GDP in Western countries fell after the table below had been prepared. For example, the United Kingdom's proportion went down to 2.7% and is expected to go further down, reaching 2.4% by 2001. When comparing the defence expenditures of the United States and Europe, the amount spent on research and development should also be taken into consideration. In this regard, the United States is far more advanced than Europe. While the United States spent $36 billion on R&D for 1998, the total amount spent by the European members of NATO was $10 billion. These R&D activities enable countries to decrease their total spending on defence while making their armed forces more efficient and better equipped.[31]

Defence Expenditures (billion $)

Country	Expenditures on Defence		Share in GDP(%)	
	1985	1996	1985	1997
USA	352.5	265.8	6.5	3.4
Germany	48.1	38.4	3.2	1.6
UK	43.5	32.7	5.2	2.8
France	44.6	46.2	4.0	3.0
Italy	23.4	23.2	2.3	1.9
Spain	10.2	8.4	2.4	1.4
Greece	3.1	5.4	7.0	4.6
Poland	7.8	3.0	8.1	2.3
Hungary	3.2	0.7	7.2	1.4
Czech R.	-	0.9	-	2.2
Russia	329.4	69.5	16.1	5.8
China	27.1	34.6	7.9	5.7
India	8.5	10.1	3.0	3.3
Japan	29.3	43.6	1.0	1.0
Turkey	3.1	6.8	4.5	4.2

Source: IISS Military Balance 1998-1999

This table shows that since World War II there has been a decline in defence expenditures both in absolute numbers and in proportion to GNP in Western countries as well as in Russia. This fall continued into the late 1990s. For example, the United States expenditure on defence went down to $222 billion in 1998, resulting in a decline of $130 billion for the entire period. The US government has shifted these funds to other areas such as social programs, scientific research and the space program. Germany's savings in defence expenditures are around $10 billion, and those of the United Kingdom amount

---

[31] IISS Military Balance 1998-1999, p. 33.

to $11 billion. Eastern European countries also had large savings, with Poland's being close to $5 billion in that period.

Turkey, however, is among those countries that have increased their military spending. In order to modernize her armed forces, Turkey has spent on average 4.8% of her GNP, or 21.7% of her budget, for the last 40 years. The annual increase in Turkey's defence expenditures totaled 5.4% between 1950 and 1994.[32]

Relative to 1985, Turkey spent $3.7 billion more for defence purposes in 1996, thus reducing the gap that existed between her and the most advanced countries of the world.

There are others, such as France and India, which have also increased their military budgets. Greece, China and Japan show higher proportional increases in their military spending. The sum of the 1996 military budgets of Poland, the Czech Republic and Hungary, three EU candidates as well as new members of NATO, is only two-thirds of the Turkish defence budget. This is yet further evidence of Turkey's significance to Europe's security.

There is a strong relationship between a country's strategic position and the amount it is willing to invest in its national defence. It is Turkey's location that forces her to spend so much on defence relative to GNP. The reverse is true for Western countries. The reduced risk of armed conflict in their regions has enabled them to significantly reduce their military spending. Yet the story is different for Turkey. Back in the 1980s two of her neighbours were engaged in a war that cost the lives of almost a million people; as a result they spent most of their national income on weapons. The following table gives a general idea of the situation:

[32] Selami Sezgin, Country Survey, XI, Defence Spending in Turkey, Defence and Peace Economics, Vol. 8, p. 384.

The Armed Forces and Military Spending of
Iran, Iraq and Syria

Country	Defence Spending		Defence Spending /GNP		Number of Troops
	1985 ($ bn.)	1996 ($ bn.)	1985 (%)	1996 (%)	1996 (000)
Iran	19.4	3.3	36.0	5.0	513
Iraq	17.5	1.2	25.9	8.3	382
Syria	4.7	1.5	16.4	4.8	421

Source: IISS Military Balance 1997-1998

The ratio of these countries' peacetime military spending to their GNP is greater than that of any NATO country. They devoted tremendous resources to their armed forces during times of war. Although they suffered staggering losses during the war, the military capabilities of these countries have developed significantly. They have more troops than any NATO country except the United States and Turkey. Syria, for example, has more soldiers than France. Even after the war, Iraq has more soldiers than Germany.

These are not Turkey's only neighbours. When all of them are considered, it becomes obvious why Turkey needs a large army that requires a higher proportion of her GNP compared to that of her Western allies.

When considering the amount of money spent on defence, money spent from sources other than the budget must also be taken into account. If only the numbers reflected in the budget are looked at, then it is obvious that Turkey's defence expenditure is one-thirty-eighth of American, one-fifth of British and German, and one-sixth of French spending. In Europe, Turkey is the one that spends the least amount per capita on defence. Yet, she is able to maintain and equip a larger army than those of other Western European states.

Though some of these countries pay additional costs due to their nuclear arsenal, their earnings from arms exports compensate to a certain extent for these expenditures.

To give an example, in 1990 France exported FF 38.8 billion worth of arms. Changes in the political environment in the world and the decline in armed conflicts have decreased the demand for arms since then. This has taken its toll on the French as well as other defence industries. French earnings from arms exports went down to FF 16.8 billion in 1994. Still, this number is higher than the total exports of many other countries.[33]

Thanks to her strong deterrence capability Turkey has been the only country that has not become involved in any major war in its region since 1922. This enabled her to develop her economy under conditions of peace. Turkey's ability to live in peace and stability cannot be attributed to her military strenght alone.

A foreign policy based on Atatürk's motto "Peace at home, peace in the world," correct assessments of the balances in international relations and being a member of NATO for 45 years have all helped Turkey achieve this result. But despite all these, had Turkey lacked a large and disciplined army, it would have been extremely difficult to live in peace and stability in such a strategically sensitive region. Therefore, the financial costs incurred for defence must be seen as necessary sacrifices on Turkey's part. It must be remembered that the cost of war is always larger than costs incurred to preserve peace.

Turkey has consistently used her military power as an instrument to aid her peaceful foreign policy. Protecting Turkey's independence, sovereignty, territorial integrity and national interests is the basis upon which Turkish defence doctrine rests. For this reason Turkey follows a strategy with

---

[33] Ramses, Institut Français des Relations Internationales, Paris, 1997, p. 97.

defence at its core. Therefore, the Turkish Armed Forces are a force for peace.

Turkey has used her military strength to defend other countries as well. Since the Korean War the Turkish Armed Forces have participated in many peacekeeping operations around the world. For a period of time, the commanding officer of the UN peacekeeping troops in Somalia was a Turkish Army general. Since 1992 Turkish units have been serving with UN forces in Bosnia. Turkey has contributed a frigate, one F-16 squadron and 1,300 troops to the SFOR operation in Bosnia led by NATO. Next to the United States, Turkey ranks second in casualties suffered under the UN flag since World War II.

The high level of technology possessed by Turkey and the progress accomplished in the country's defence industry have made the Turkish Armed Forces a force to be reckoned with, not only in its own region but in the world as well. Today Turkey is capable of producing F16 C-D airplanes and their engines. Turkey also produces CN-235 cargo planes under license from Spain, and Agusta training aircraft under license from Italy. Various heavy and light weapons as well as electronic equipment are produced in Turkey, some of which are exported. As can be seen, similar to the size and strength of her armed forces, Turkey's defence industry is also more advanced than that of many other European countries. The high level of morale and discipline stemming from the cultural background of the Turkish people should also be taken into account when one tries to judge the strength of the Turkish Armed Forces.

Thanks to her deterrent power, Turkey has played a crucial role in the defence of the West for 50 years and will continue to do so in the foreseeable future. A strong defence capability can only be maintained if supported by a strong economy. For this reason Turkey's economic development is necessary not only to improve the welfare of her people but also to maintain her effective defence capability.

TURKISH ECONOMY
PAST, PRESENT AND FUTURE

As in other sections, the historical development of the Turkish economy should first be looked at. What kinds of stages did it go through? How did its relations with other countries evolve? Under what circumstances did other nations' economies develop? In the field of economics, too, there may be lessons to be learned from history.

The Ottoman Period:
A Difficult Start

The Ottoman Empire had a role in international trade just as it did in international politics. Some of the problems faced today have their sources in history, notably from the 19th century. It is a fact that Turkey was late in joining the Industrial Revolution. The absence of a strong economy and an inability to develop adequate financial resources during the last two centuries are among the factors that led to the collapse of the Ottoman Empire. The capitulation system, which had a stranglehold on the Turkish economy for centuries, prevented the implementation of economic reforms. Under this system, major economic concessions were granted to Westerners by the Ottoman Empire in the 16th century as a goodwill gesture, but they were later misused by Western countries against the economic and political interests of the Ottomans, particularly in the 18th and 19th centuries. There were also external factors that kept the Turkish economy from developing parallel to Western economies.

From the time of its foundation, the Ottoman state had
been located on the trade routes between Europe and China.
Even before the Ottoman period, the Turkish states in
Anatolia used to trade with the Far East using the "Silk Road,"
which remained the major route until the discovery of the
Cape of Good Hope, thus facilitating maritime commerce with
the Far East. The Black Sea and the Mediterranean, both of
which have been among the most important sea trade routes
throughout history, were also largely used by the Ottomans.

In the early years of the Ottoman Empire the economy was
based on agriculture. All of the land belonged to the sultan,
remaining that way until 1857, when a law regulating property
ownership and allowing citizens to hold title to their land was
implemented for the first time. Yet the state continued to own
a great majority of the land for many years that followed.[34]

In time, handicrafts developed. Textile production began in
the 14th and 15th centuries. Shipyards were built. There were
also workshops producing people's daily necessities as well as
manufacturing goods such as guns. The silk fabric produced in
Bursa attained international repute. Mints and workshops that
worked gold, silver and copper were established. The first
Ottoman golden coin was minted in the first half of the 15th
century, and the first significant regulation concerning these
matters came with a decree from Sultan Beyazıt II in 1502.

During that period the requirements of the army had
priority in industrial production. There were shipyards
producing battleships, and small manufacturing facilities
putting out cannons, guns and gunpowder, whereas clothing
for soldiers was supplied by the local textile factories. In those
days, the Ottoman economy was not far behind other
economies. Yet production was not sufficient to meet demand.
This necessitated imports from places like England, Spain and
various other European countries. Fatih Sultan Mehmet, who
had conquered Istanbul and taken it from the Byzantines,

---

[34] Kongar, op. cit., p. 62.

introduced customs duties to regulate the empire's international trade. In the 15th century the tax rate on non-Muslims was 4%, whereas Muslim traders had to pay only 1%. During his reign Fatih Sultan Mehmet granted capitulations to the Venetians. The sultans that followed also gave similar concessions to other countries.

The empire continued to expand with the annexation of various countries to Ottoman territory in the 16th century. The population went up by 41% between 1520 and 1580. This was reflected in the economy and to a large extent the country became self-sufficient. Using Professor Braudel's definition, the Ottoman Empire formed a "world of economy."

In this period, the state effectively played its role in directing the economy. There were many laws regulating production, commerce, prices and capital. The Ottomans were tolerant towards the use of interest, which is forbidden by Islam. In the 16th century interest rates were between 10-15%. During that century the Muslims played as active a role in commerce as did the empire's minorities, although the Greek, Armenian and Jewish minority groups became more dominant in later periods. Farming was still the main economic activity however, in 1528 87% of all arable land belonged to the state, since Ottoman law did not allow private land ownership.

During this century many foreigners began to trade with the Ottomans, but the discovery of new trade routes had its effect on the commercial life of the empire. The close friendship of Sultan Süleyman the Magnificent with French King François I resulted in granting of commercial privileges to France. In 1569 a capitulation agreement was signed between the two countries. In later years similar agreements were concluded with England, Holland and other countries. We know that the sultans of the time were warned by their advisers of the potential impact that developments taking place around the world would have on Ottoman interests. In a report dated 1580, Murad III was informed that European settlements in America, India and the Gulf would harm the commerce of the Islamic world. The study suggested digging a canal in the Suez region, which would enable the conquest of the coastline as far as India.

A specialist named Ömer Talip had also prepared a similar report in 1625 which stressed that Europeans had discovered the entire world, sending their ships everywhere and putting all harbours along the way under their sovereignty. This brings to mind the fact that Chinese and Indian goods used to be transported by Muslim traders to Suez from their points of origin, yet now these were being shipped directly to Europe and distributed around the world via Portuguese, Dutch and English ships, sending only poor-quality merchandise to Istanbul and charging five times its fair price. The report shows this as the reason why the amount of gold and silver in the Ottoman Empire was decreasing. It then goes on to recommend the capture of the coast of Yemen and warns that if this was not done, Europe would gain control of the land of Islam.[35]

The report shows that even in those days the Ottomans were aware of the political as well as strategic dimensions of economy and commerce. However, the upper hand gained by Europe at sea and in world trade limited the Ottomans' ability to compete. They were not able to duplicate their success on the battlefield in the area of trade. One of the Ottomans' major sources of income was the spoils of war, along with taxes levied on conquered peoples. Still the analysts were warning the sultans that things were changing and that they needed to adapt.

Despite these warnings the Ottomans continued to grant capitulations to foreign countries, which influenced Ottoman economy and commerce for centuries and had great repercussions on the political and economic developments in the centuries to follow. In 1673 the capitulation agreement

---

[35] Bernard Lewis, The Emergence of Modern Turkey, London, 1961, p. 28.

with France was extended, and import taxes were decreased from 5% to 3%. In the years that followed the Poles, Austrians and Russians all benefited from capitulations. Greek, Armenian and Jewish traders first became the agents of these foreigners, then moved on to take control of the commercial as well as financial life of the empire. Meanwhile, due to a lack of newly conquered lands, the income of the state began to decline.

These were the main traits characterizing the Ottoman economy until the 19th century. With the start of the period of decline, a strong and modern army was needed to reverse the trend. More than any other reason, this is why the reforms were first initiated in the army. The reformist policies of Selim III and Mahmud II at the beginning of the 19th century required large sums of money. This, together with other economic problems, caused the devaluation of Ottoman currency. During the reign of Mahmud II gold coins were devalued 35 times and silver 37 times. In 1814 one pound sterling was worth 23 kuruş. In 1839 one pound sterling could buy 104 kuruş. For the Turkish people their history of living with inflation started during that period. An Ottoman bank was established by decree of the sultan in 1840, and paper money began to be printed the year after. A 12% annual interest rate was paid on this paper, more like government bonds in nature, which became a serious economic burden on the economy during the Crimean War. In 1858 negotiations to borrow funds from international sources began. These economic difficulties brought the country to the financial collapse of 1875.[36]

After the Crimean War, an improvement in the Ottomans' foreign trade occurred. There was a significant increase in cotton, tobacco and silk exports to France and England. In 1840 the total exports of the empire had been around 4.7 million pounds sterling, but this number reached 20 million

---

[36] Ibid., p. 109.

within 40 years. During the same period, imports also went up
from 5.2 million to 24 million pounds sterling. During the
previous 50 years foreign trade had grown by only 80%.
Tobacco, cotton, wheat, raisins, figs and silk accounted for
60% of total exports. European traders, in search of
alternative markets due to the Civil War in the United States,
looked to the Ottoman Empire. Towards the end of the 1870s
England was the empire's most important trading partner, with
45% of all imports coming from there. France and Austria's
shares were around 12%. The balance of trade was
consistently in favour of the Europeans, pushing the Ottomans
to borrow even larger sums from the West. The capitulations,
which forced the Ottomans to pursue an extremely liberal
economic policy, allowed the West free access to Turkish
markets. While an agreement with England, signed a year
before the political reforms (Tanzimat) of Sultan Abdülmecit
in 1839, established an import duty of 5% on all industrial
imports from England, the duty on trade taking place among
the different regions of the empire was 8%. The traditional
foreign trade policy of the Ottomans can be summarized as
incentives to imports and restrictions on exports.[37] In 1913
foreign trade's share of national income was around 30%. This
figure is high even for the most advanced contemporary
economies. The trade deficit was around 8% of GNP, forcing
foreign debt to snowball. The goal of those policies might have
been to achieve stability in the local market, but they ended up
destroying the economic and financial balances of the country,
devastating local industry along the way. The world-famous
silk production in Bursa went from 20,000 pieces per year in
1843 to 3,000 pieces 20 years later due to unfair competition
from the West. There were similar stories in other regions as
well and the already weak Ottoman industry collapsed mainly
due to the privileges given to Western countries through

---

[37] Yakup Kepenek, Nurhan Yentürk, Türkiye Ekonomisi, Istanbul, 1996, pp.
14-19.

capitulations. Despite all this, a few factories were built to meet the demands of the army in particular.

The great potential of the Ottoman Empire was better understood in the second half of the 19th century, resulting in increased foreign investment flowing into the country. Meanwhile, foreign banks started to open up branches one after another. The first of these was the Ottoman Bank, established in 1863 as a Franco-British partnership. Foreigners concentrated their investment in railroads, the first of which connected Izmir and Aydın, built in 1863 with British capital. From 1882 to 1908 2,350 km. of railroad were built between Damascus and Hejaz; however, only 1,850 km. of track was laid in Anatolia during the same period. The empire was spending its already scarce resources in its outlying regions instead of on its own center. City electricity and tramways were introduced in Damascus even before Istanbul. This indicates the difference in mentality between the Ottoman Empire and colonial empires. The Ottomans did not aim to devour the regions tied to the empire; to the contrary they devoted a large proportion of national income to develop these regions. The protectionist measures adopted by the West in response to the 1873 economic crisis led them to seek new sources of raw materials as well as new markets where they could freely sell their products. Capitulations made the Ottoman Empire one of the most attractive markets.

The exorbitant size of the foreign trade deficit made the Ottoman Empire insolvent. In November 1881 the government issued a decree and consolidated its debt. The income from a salt monopoly and revenues from taxes on alcohol, tobacco, fish and silk were put aside to pay off the country's debt. An institution called the Debt Administration, or Düyunu Umumiye, was established to oversee the operation. The chair of this institution alternated between the British and the French, and its board had a German, an Austrian, an Italian and an Ottoman representative. The bankers of Galata, who had developed a poor reputation by loaning the government money in times of hardship under unfavourable terms, also were represented. The Düyunu Umumiye was totally independent of the Ministry of Finance; therefore from that time on one cannot speak of an independent financial policy for the Ottoman Empire. By the end of Sultan Abdülhamid's reign, this institution had 720 branches around the country and 5,500 employees. It controlled 30% of all the state's revenues. This exploitation of the national economy by foreigners instigated anti-Western sentiments among the people.

While public finance was in ruins, foreign investment flowed into the economy. The Ottoman market, which was unable to protect itself from the unfair competition of foreigners, seemed to be an attractive place to be. The French were the foremost among these. Their investment climbed from FF 85 million in 1881 to FF 292 million in 1895 and FF 511 million in 1909. A total of 40% of all investment made prior to 1914 took place between 1888 and 1896. Only a small amount of this went into manufacturing; the majority went to building railroads. This was because the railroads enabled their owners to extend their economic as well as political influence in the region. A German company bought the concession to the Anatolian railroads in 1888. While there had only been 1,800 km. of railroads back in 1878, this figure had jumped to 5,800 km. by 1908. Fully 73% of all foreign investment was made to build harbours and railroads, geared towards preparing the infrastructure to facilitate the trade of foreign companies. The state was unable to control strategic investments such as ports and railroads. It was only after the victory stemming from the War of Independence and the signing of the Lausanne Treaty that these facilities reverted to the Turkish nation.

Aware for a long time that the capitulations were preventing the development of the economy and infringing upon national sovereignty, the Ottomans worked to remove them.

At the Paris Congress held after the Crimean War, Ali Pasha did all he could to abolish these but failed. In 1900 Abdülhamid wanted to increase import taxes by 3%, but this met with such a strong reaction from the West that he had to abandon his plans. Increasing import taxes became possible only in 1907 and that only after granting some other concessions. The state came under foreign economic influence so much so that an agreement signed with Japan to mutually open up embassies could not be implemented because the Ottomans did not give capitulations to the Japanese.

The commercial privileges granted to foreigners and minorities strained the financial resources of the state as well, forcing it to collect a sizeable portion of its revenues from the agricultural sector. From 1909 to 1910 40% of all public income was derived from taxes on agriculture and stockbreeding. Despite these difficulties some industrial development can be observed. In 1908 there were 250,000 workers in the empire, most of whom were in the textile sector. Foreigners, however, controlled most of the trade; there were 97 shops in Izmir and 34 shops in Aydın owned by foreigners in 1893.

From 1913 to 1915 an industrial survey was conducted in the Ottoman Empire. The results were interesting: 50% of all industrial concerns belonged to the Greeks, 20% to the Armenians and 5% to the Jews. The Turks' share was only 15%, with the remaining 10% belonging to other foreigners.[38] A similar situation existed in mining as well. In 1911, with the exception of coal mines, the Turkish people owned only 20% of all mining concessions; foreigners owned 75% and minorities 5%.

German acquisition of the rights to the Baghdad Railroad drew reactions from other Western countries, and in the end the French managed to secure a 30% share of this as well. Together with this, the right to manage all the forests and mines along the route of the railroad were also granted to the

[38] Mantran, op. cit., pp. 539-542, 553.

owners of the foreign companies. This went on until the start
of World War I. Before that, however, the Ottomans passed a
law subsidizing local industry in 1909. With the start of World
War I the Ottomans unilaterally abolished all capitulations and
put a 15% duty on all imports.[39] During the war more than
100 local companies were established in the banking,
transport, mining and construction sectors; however, the war
damaged the country in all respects.

This has been a brief history of the economy of the
Ottoman Empire. The concessions granted to foreigners as a
sign of friendship during periods of great strength destroyed
the empire afterwards. In periods of decline, when the empire
was at its weakest politically and had lost a large portion of its
territory, it did not have the power to revoke the capitulations.
When it intended to do so, intense pressure was exerted to
prevent such a development. Foreign investment was often
used as an instrument of exploitation for the country and had
little to do with its development.

What was the world economy like when the Ottomans
were going through such times? In the mid-18th century China
supplied one-third of the world's production. India's share was
one-fourth, and the West's was less than one-fifth. In the
1830s the Industrial Revolution began to have an effect, and
the West overtook China. In the years that followed, the
West's industrialization resulted in the decline of other
countries, which began to undergo the same experiences that
the Ottoman Empire had. This process continued well into the
20th century. In 1913 the level of production in non-Western
countries was two-thirds its level in the 1800s. In 1928 the
West's share was 84.2%, yet it dropped to 57.8% in 1980.
This trend can be observed not only in industrial production
but also in other sectors of the economy. The share of the
West in world production decreased to 49% in 1980 from

---

[39] Kepenek, op. cit., p. 20.

64% in 1950, and there are estimates that it will go down to 30% by 2013.[40]

As he does in other fields, Huntington approaches the field of economics from a view based on differences among civilizations and calculates the share of each in world production. According to Huntington while the West's share was 64.1% in 1950, that of the Islamic world was 2.4%; the proportion of Orthodox civilization, which he doesn't consider as belonging to Western civilization, was 16%. The Chinese world's percentage was 3.3%, just above that of the Japanese portion, at 3.1%. During the 40 years that followed, these balances changed significantly. By 1992 the West's share was down to 48.9% while the Islamic portion was up to 11%; the Japanese civilization's reached 8% and China's, 10%. The Orthodox world's share of world production decreased to 6.2%. These figures are interesting as far as giving a general view of the situation, yet here again such analysis viewing the world from a competition-among-civilizations perspective is hardly compatible with contemporary approaches. Moreover, it is not always easy to categorize countries into different civilization groups. How would one define Turkey, whose people are Muslim but which at the same time is a Western country? Therefore, it is not a valid method to make such categorizations. As states are the basis of analysis in international relations, comparisons should be made among states instead of civilizations. To what extent were such mentalities responsible for the hardships and economic problems faced by the Ottomans? It is worth investigating. But the experiences of the Ottomans and the consequences they faced at the end of their era were clear: The country was under enormous economic and financial strain due to the capitulations. The Ottomans were unable to keep up with the Industrial Revolution, could not control trade routes, had no specialized economists and lacked infrastructure as well as the

---

[40] Huntington, op. cit., p. 87.

resources to maintain a strong army. What's more, years of war had destroyed whatever little capital the country possessed and had cost the lives of many.

This was the economy Atatürk assumed when he first set out on his journey to establish a new republic on the ashes of an empire.

The Economic Situation in Turkey and the West in the 1923-1960 Period

The Turkish Economy After the War of Independence

Turkey's War of Independence put a further strain on the already scarce resources of the country. During the war, production levels were down while the prices of gold and foreign exchange were up by 700%. Taking 1914 as the base year with an index of 100, the cost of living index was 1,406 in 1920 and 999 in 1922.

During the war, the Soviet Union sent 1 million gold coins and the Muslims of India 300,000 of them as aid. Taxes were increased as well.

A large part of the difficult negotiations that took place in Lausanne in 1923 centered on the capitulations. The representatives of the Western governments soon realized that İsmet Pasha, who headed the Turkish delegation, had no intention of compromising on the issue; therefore they agreed to abolish all the capitulations. The task, however, was not all that easy to achieve. During the Lausanne Conference the following conversation took place between the representative of Britain, Lord Curzon, and İsmet İnönü, who wrote about it in his memoirs:

"I was with Lord Curzon at a meeting. It was late in the evening. We were together with the United States representative, Mr. Chaild. Lord Curzon turned to me and said:

" 'We will reach a conclusion during this conference, but we will not be happy about it. You are not compromising on anything. You are rejecting whatever we say without even considering whether it is reasonable or justified. We have decided to put whatever you reject in our pockets. Your country has been devastated. Aren't you going to rebuild it? You will need money to do that. Where will you find it? The only people in the world who have it today are me and this man next to me. Don't forget, whatever you reject goes into my pocket. Where will you find the money? From the French?'

"I said, 'Yes.'

"Curzon continued: 'No one has money. Only we can give it to you. If we are not happy with you, who will you get it from? How are you going to rebuild a destroyed country? When you come on your knees asking us for money, we will one by one show you the things which we are putting in our pockets right now.'

"I never forgot Lord Curzon's words. It has been 45 years since the Lausanne Conference, and during all this time I was always mindful of the likelihood of such an eventuality.

"When Lord Curzon finished what he was saying, I told him: 'Let's settle what's facing us now. If I come asking for money, you can show me your pocket then.

"The fact is, until World War II we did not receive any financial assistance from anyone, and Turkey saw herself through World War II by relying only on her own resources."[41]

In the postwar era Turkey suffered economically but did not grovel before anyone. She faced all the hardships alone and developed on her own, through the selfless efforts of her people.

In Lausanne, aside from the abolishment of the capitulations, additional rights which would pave the way for the development of the economy were also won. One of these was the right to coastal commerce. From then on only Turkish ships could carry people and cargo in Turkish waters.

There was also an agreement on repayment of the Ottoman debt, which amounted to TL 129.4 million. Turkey's share was estimated to be TL 85.6 million. Turkey was to start repaying

---

[41] İsmet İnönü, Hatıralar, 2. Kitap, Ankara, 1985, pp. 89-90

this debt in 1929, in yearly installments of TL 5.8 million. In later years this debt was rescheduled through the mediation of the League of Nations. In 1933 Turkey's total debt was calculated as 8 million gold coins. Turkey spared a sizable portion of her income to pay off the Ottomans' debts. While these payments were 7.6% of the 1924 budget, they rose to 17.8% in 1930.[42] Turkey had paid off all these debts by 1954. However, some restrictions were also agreed to in Lausanne, such as maintaining the 1916 import duties for the coming five years. So the Turkish Republic not only assumed the debt of the Ottomans but also conceded to prolonging the concessions granted to the West despite the fact that she had just emerged from a war and desperately needed all available funds. This clearly demonstrates how keen the Western powers were to preserve their privileges in Turkey. We must take into account all these difficulties and drawbacks when trying to evaluate the economic development initiatives in the early years of the Republic.

From the very first days the government adopted Swiss civil law and ensured the private property rights of its citizens. With the laws passed in 1927 and 1929 land reform was enacted, and land was distributed to villagers. According to a calculation done in 1927 only one-seventh of arable land was in fact planted. Opening up new land for farming was put on the agenda, but the population was still not sufficiently large to reach that goal. Ziraat Bankası (Agriculture Bank), which had been established during the Ottoman period, was reorganized, and an effective system of credit was put in place to help the farmers.

Again in 1927, a law to subsidize industry was passed. But as the Treaty of Lausanne did not permit import taxes to be increased for five years after its signing, it had not been possible to protect local industry until 1929.[43] During that period 43% of all industry was based on agriculture and 23%

---

[42] Kongar, op. cit., p. 349.
[43] Kepenek, op. cit., p. 38.

on textiles. Industrial production could not meet demand. Sugar production could only supply 14.5% of consumption. It was the same with clothing; in 1928 41% of all imports were in the textile and clothing category.

The economic priority of the new government was development of the country's infrastructure; here again construction of railways topped the list. Within 15 years the length of track in the country grew from 2,352 km. to 6,800 km..

In 1930, one year after the freeze on import taxes came to an end, the Turkish trade balance moved into a surplus position.

Bitter experiences in the Ottoman era had made the young Republic extremely cautious about its economic policies. The goal was to preserve economic as well as political independence, and a balanced budget policy was followed to achieve that goal. In the 1923-1930 period, with the exception of one year, the budget was always in surplus, keeping inflation under control. In 1931 and 1932 there was in fact deflation, and prices were down below their 1923 levels. The money supply was kept under strict control and decreased a little in the early days of the Republic. Annual depreciation was around 4%. While trying to retire the debt accumulated from Ottoman times, the government did its best to avoid financing it through additional borrowing.

At the Izmir Economic Congress of 1923 the economic policies of the government were announced: There would be a switch to the liberal economic system, and development of the private sector would be given priority. However, the private sector lacked the funds to undertake the necessary investment. Therefore, the state also assumed the role of entrepreneur. The first development plan was adopted in 1933, aimed at coordinating the economic activities of the government.

The involvement of the government in the economy was seen as an act of necessity imposed by the economic conditions of the country and was not based on an ideological predisposition. At a speech he gave at the opening ceremonies of the Izmir International Fair for Trade and Industry in 1935, then Economy Minister Celal Bayar explained Atatürk's views on this matter as follows: "The policy of state control of the economy as it was applied in Turkey was not copied from the ideas of 19th century socialist thinkers. Our system takes into consideration private enterprise and individual talent, but it also considers the needs of the people and recognizes the amount of work that needs to be done. The state directs the national economy with this understanding."

A few large factories were put under construction. New railroads and ports were built. The wounds of war were healed, the structure of the new state was put in place and the public was educated, and all this was done with almost no external financial aid or borrowing. The only exception was the construction of some factories with the technical and financial aid of the Soviet Union due to the friendly relations that existed at time. Meanwhile, between 1938 and 1944 20 foreign companies were nationalized. During the early years of the republic significant increases in GDP were achieved. In 1924 this increase was 14.8%; and was even higher in 1926 at 18.2%. There was a crop failure due to severe weather conditions, and the yield was down by 30.9%. Naturally this shrank the overall economy; yet, it recovered within a year. The GDP expanded by 11% in 1928 and by 21.6 in 1929. These are just a few examples reflecting the successful, rapid, economic development of the young Turkish Republic. In the 1924-1939 period, with the exception of three years, the economy managed to grow significantly. Agriculture constituted the major component of the economy; between 1925 and 1953 the share of agriculture in GNP almost never fell below 40%. In 1923, the first year of the Republic, the share of industry in the Turkish economy was only 10.6%, but this went up to 15.5% in 1936.[44]

---

[44] Kongar, op. cit., pp. 353, 404.

A report published by the World Bank in 1951 says that Turkey developed significantly during the period when the state was given a prominent role in the economy and adds, "Considering the legacy of the Ottoman period, it was doubtful that the private sector could have attained the same level of success."[45]

While Turkey was trying to lay the foundations of a new republic, the world went into the Great Depression of the late 1920s. Precautions were taken to protect the local economy from its adverse effects; however, it was impossible not to be influenced by a global economic crisis. Despite this, Turkey managed to attain a high level of economic growth in the early days of the Republic. During the 1924-1940 period the Turkish economy grew by an average of 6.5% per year.

Economic Cycles of Western Countries in the First Half of the 20th Century

Western economies underwent significant structural changes both during and after the war. Prior to 1914 the government share in economies had been extremely low, especially in the United States, where the share of public spending in the GNP was between 5-10% and the proportion of public revenue in the GNP was 9%. In Germany it was twice as much, at 18%; in the United Kingdom it was 13%; and in France this percentage was larger than the rest. However, Japan and Russia were the two countries in which the state had almost total control over the economy and in which the government was active in nearly all economic sectors.[46]

During the 19th century the economies of the West were by and large stable. Large price increases were quite rare.

---

[45] Lewis, op. cit., pp. 281-282.
[46] Paul Johnson, A History of the Modern World, London, 1983, p. 14.

Inflation started to rise in 1908 and with the war reached extraordinarily high levels. If the index for 1913 is accepted as 100, the wholesale price index in the United States immediately after the end of the war in 1919 was 212, 242 in the United Kingdom, 357 in France and 364 in Italy. A year later in 1920 prices in some countries showed an even more rapid increase. The wholesale price index was two-and-a-half times as much as its pre-war level; in the United Kingdom it was three times, in France five times, and in Italy six times as much. In Germany, the biggest looser of the war, which had to assume a huge debt with the Treaty of Versailles, inflation was higher than all in the other countries: it was almost 20 times more than the pre-war average. The 1913 index figure of 100 had gone up to 1,965 by 1920. For the first time since the 16th century the West encountered "hyperinflation."

By the end of World War I almost all the Western countries owed large sums of money to each other. The largest creditor was the United States: including interest it had $11.8 billion in receivables. The amount owed to the United States by Britain was $4.6 billion. The total amount owed to Britain by France, Italy, and Russia combined was $6.5 billion. In order to pay off this debt, it was decided that Germany should pay substantial war reparations in the amount of 132 billion gold marks, 52% of which would go to France. Germany also had to supply 2 million tons of coal per month to the victors as part of the reparations.

Germany was unable to carry this financial burden, and in 1922 she was declared a country that could not pay off her debts. In response to this French and Belgian troops crossed the German border and occupied the Ruhr region, confiscating its economic wealth, factories and other facilities. This resulted in an economic catastrophe for Germany, and following the occupation of the Ruhr basin, the price index shot up to 16 million from its level of 100 in 1913.

The German mark also depreciated sharply from DM 1 = $2.13 in 1913 to DM 1 = $.07 in 1918. The value of 1 cent was DM 100 in 1922, but in 1923, after the occupation of the

Ruhr basin, the economic collapse reached its peak: $7.00 bought DM 4 billion, and banks demanded 35% daily interest on loans.[47] Small savers lost all their personal wealth. Schact, who was appointed head of the Bundesbank, stabilized the value of the deutsche mark, but the economic crisis combined with other political factors made an impression on the German people that would pave the way for the devastation to come.

Germany was not the only country hit hard by World War I. Although not to the same extent, the French economy was also adversly affected. In 1926 the value of the French franc depreciated to one-tenth its pre-war value. To prevent a disaster akin to that of Germany, precautionary measures were taken in taxes and other areas. Stability was achieved and exports increased; however, after 1930 high unemployment, low production levels and increased poverty hit France. The effects of these were felt until the end of World War II. In 1948 the wholesale price index was 105 times its 1902 level, and gold prices were up 174 points. By the end of the 1930s the industrial production level was even lower than that of 1929.

The conditions in the United States were different. It was not influenced by the war in the same way the Western European countries had been. The term of President Calvin Coolidge, in office during the 1923-1928 period, is defined as one of increased economic development, industrialization and prosperity. By 1929 the United States economy had become the largest in the world, putting out 34.4% of the world's production. The British share was 10.4%, Germany's was 10.3%, Russia's 9.9%, France's 5% and Japan's 4%, while Italy's portion was only 2.2%. While traditional sectors like textiles and coal mining were in decline in the United States, new industries were making giant leaps. Car manufacturing jumped from 569,000 units produced in 1914 to 5.6 million in 1929. There were 9 million cars in 1920; this number had

---

[47] Johnson, Ibid., pp. 36, 134.

reached 30 million by 1930. The combined number of cars produced by the four largest industrial nations of Europe in 1924 was only 11% of the cars produced by the United States.

There was a big boom in the stock market as well. Income earned in industrial production had been invested in stocks for speculative gain, but, in October 1929 the American stock market on Wall Street crashed, and prices collapsed. This crisis affected the entire industrialized world, especially the United States. The four years following the crash, known as the Great Depression, were years of social unrest and hardship in the United States, with the number of unemployed soaring to 15 million. Franklin Roosevelt, who became president in 1932, involved the government more heavily in economic affairs and introduced the New Deal, which gave state enterprises a leading economic role in helping the country climb out of the depression.

Great sums of public money were transferred to the banking sector to prevent financial institutions from becoming insolvent. The Tennessee Valley Authority was established in 1933 as a governmental institution with responsibility for directing investment and other economic affairs covering a large region of the country. Again in 1933 the National Economic Development Law was passed, establishing the Public Works Administration. In the agricultural sector, too, legislation was implemented enabling the government to play a key role in undertaking regulatory measures. Although some of these laws were declared unconstitutional by the U.S. Supreme Court, their influence was felt on the economy, which entered a period of recovery. The New Deal was only partially successful; although the rate of unemployment went down during the 1933-1937 period, it went up again in the following years.[48]

The Great Depression hit the United Kingdom as it did other Western countries. The number of unemployed rose to 2.7 million in 1931. Strikes followed one another, and the

---

[48] H.L. Peacock, Europe and Beyond, London, 1984, pp. 163, 200.

government passed legislation outlawing politically motivated strikes as well as general strikes.

The years of World War II caused great devastation in Western Europe, and one can speak of a complete economic collapse. The IISS estimates the cost of the war to be $4 trillion using 1995 prices. [49] Countries felt the effects of this devastation for a long time.

In the years following the war they tried to overcome this catastrophe and rebuild their industries. The Marshall Plan gave them extensive financial aid; yet, not until the mid-1960s did the Western European economies achieve stability in the true sense of the word.

The Marshall Plan provided significant financial facilities. Through this program the United States offered aid in the amount of $13 billion between 1948 and 1951. In 1949 the amount of Marshall Plan assistance received by the Netherlands was equivalent to 16-23% of its GDP. This proportion was 10-11.5% for France, 9% for Italy and 5% for Britain and Germany.

By the end of the war Great Britain's foreign debt totaled more than 3 billion pounds sterling; it had lost one-third of its commercial fleet, and exports were at 60% of their pre-war level. The government nationalized many industries. In 1946 the Bank of England was nationalized. Mines were turned over to the National Coal Administration, and electricity and natural gas were also put under the control of governmental commissions. The British Transport Commission was formed in 1947 to control the railroads and waterways. Despite all this, the private sector's share in the economy did not drop below 80%; yet the use of ration cards continued until 1954 for some basic commodities.

There were 2 million unemployed in the United Kingdom in 1947. During those years even bread was sold through ration cards. In the first half of 1951 Britain's trade deficit was

---

[49] IISS, Military Balance 1998-1999.

151 million pounds sterling, resulting in the government decreasing imports by 6%. By 1955 the standard of living began to rise and with the increased international trade that came with the end of the Korean War, British exports started to pick up. However, this positive trend did not last long. In 1957 rising inflation started to threaten the economy. Trade and current account deficits ate up the gold and foreign exchange reserves of the country. The government prepared a long-term economic plan in 1962. In the same year the National Economic Development Commission was established with the participation of experts in economics, representatives from the private sector and trade union leaders, who were tasked with advising the government on the economic policies to be followed. By 1961 the GDP growth had slowed down significantly, and in some regions the unemployment rate reached 7%.

France also experienced economic turbulence in the years following the war. When de Gaulle came to power, gold reserves were almost down to zero. The current account was in deficit. In order to prevent inflation the government imposed wage and price controls.

With measures taken by de Gaulle and Monet as well as assistance from the European Economic Community, the French economy took off. Gold and foreign exchange reserves began to rise, but the government did not loosen its grip on the economy. The Socialist-Communist coalition government of 1973 made improvements in the social arena, but in the meantime it also nationalized some of the country's most important financial institutions as well as a number of the larger industrial facilities.

In the 1970-1980 period, as in some other European countries, France too experienced recession, inflation, unemployment and social unrest. By 1980 inflation had gone up to 13.3%, and the unemployed numbered 1.5 million.

Thirty-six banks and numerous industrial concerns were nationalized in 1981.[50]

The list can be enlarged upon; however, it is obvious that in the 20 years following World War II, Western countries experienced great difficulties and turbulence, even having to resort to ration cards to curb the public demand for goods. There had been periods when they gave the public sector the lead in their economies and undertook extensive nationalization programs. They frequently experienced trade as well as current account deficits. There were also spells of wage and price controls. Entry into the EEC, now the European Union, has been the cornerstone of their economic development. Freedom of movement of goods, capital and labor gave them the opportunity to develop together. However, it must not be forgotten that they had economic difficulties after becoming EU members as well. Moreover, the fact cannot be ignored that these countries industrialized long before Turkey, not to mention that they had profited from the resources of their colonies for long periods of time, accumulating great wealth in the process. They developed their commerce by benefiting from the markets of these countries. While reconstructing their economies on the ruins of World War II, they relied on their past amassment and made extensive use of their trained technicians, specialists and scientists.

State-Supported Development in Turkey

The economic development of the Turkish Republic and the results obtained in its early days should be analyzed within the context of the prevailing economic conditions in the world at that time. For Turkey, the above-summarized turbulent years for the West, especially the years that followed 1930,

---

[50] Peacock, op. cit., p. 291.

were years of stability, with budget and trade surpluses. Major steps were taken to bring the infrastructure of the economy, especially the railway network, up to contemporary levels as well as develop the agricultural and industrial sectors.

The 1923 decision to give the private sector the lead in the economy could not be implemented due to the economic conditions being experienced worldwide as well as a lack of capitalization of the private sector. The country followed state-led economic policies out of necessity during the 1930s. A great portion of total foreign capital left the country following nationalization of the railroads along with some other major infrastructure facilities. Between 1930 and 1938 the annual increase in the money supply was around 0.5%. With the exception of 1933, 1939 and 1944 the budget was in a surplus position, and Turkey did not need to borrow any significant amounts of money until the end of World War II. A $10 million loan from a United States institution was used to establish the Central Bank of Turkey, while a $10.5 million loan obtained from the Soviet Union was used in the financing of the first Five-Year Industrial Development Program. The Karabük Iron and Steel Factory was established with a 16 million pounds sterling loan received from Britain.

During the same period the land available for farming tripled. In mining too, especially after the establishment of the Technical Research Institute for Minerals, significant developments occurred. There were sizable increases in the production rates of coal and copper mines after their purchase from the French and German firms that had previously owned them. While in 1933 1.8 million tons of coal were produced, this reached 3.7 million tons in 1947. The increase in brown coal was even larger, going up from 29,000 tons to 624,000 tons. Iron ore production begun in 1938 doubled in 1945, totaling 124,000 tons. Oil was first discovered in 1940 at a town called Raman. By the end of 1930 textile production was able to meet 80% of local demand.

The trade balance had a surplus every year but one between 1933 and 1945. Exports had reached 173.4% of imports by

1945, yet the volume of foreign trade did not change; in fact it even went down. The trade surplus caused gold reserves to go up, increasing from 14.5 tons to 210.8 tons between 1932 and 1945. Together with foreign exchange reserves, the total reserves of the country were $260 million.[51]

The rapid GDP growth experienced in the period between the establishment of the Republic and World War II slowed down during the war, and even regressed in some years. Immediately after the war, however, in 1946, there was a large increase of 31.9%.[52]

During the war, a commission formed by the government prepared postwar development strategies. The Economic Development Plan adopted in 1947 once again gave the private sector the leading role; motorways were given priority over railways; and the share of foreign investment in the development of the economy was determined to be 49%.

The United States sent specialists in 1947 to help Turkey within the framework of the Marshall Plan under the Truman Doctrine. These specialists suggested that basic reforms be implemented and the private sector be given priority. The instilling of these principles may have influenced the 1947 decision to do just that.They also had another suggestion: Turkey should not establish iron and steel, petrochemical, in particular chemical fertilizer, or cellulose paper industries. Turkish industry should concentrate on processing agricultural products, light metal, construction materials, forestry products and handicrafts. The World Bank, the IMF and the OEEC (later OECD), which were given the task of executing the Marshall Plan, all suggested the same economic policies to Turkey. That is to say, Turkey should develop herself but should not have heavy industry.

Although Turkey did not join the war, the money spent in order to be prepared for such an eventuality strained the

---

[51] Kepenek, op. cit., pp. 65-70.
[52] Selami Sezgin, op. cit., p. 383.

economy. This demanded heavy sacrifices by the people. Some basic goods could not be found, and extraordinary taxes like the "Wealth Tax" were imposed. On the other hand, remaining neutral during the war saved Turkey from economic devastation.

After the war, reconstruction efforts began. Here, United States aid became an important factor supporting these efforts. However, in order to benefit from this aid certain rules had to be adopted. Privatization of state-owned companies was put on the agenda but could not be implemented. To the contrary the State Economic Enterprises (KITs) gained more importance after 1953. Major industrial investments were made through these enterprises, and their capital was supplemented. Meanwhile, partnerships were formed between the state enterprises and private firms, the number of which had gone up to 72 by 1962.

During the early years of the Republic, except when it was absolutely necessary, the policy of refraining from external borrowing was adhered to, although it was partially abandoned during the war. Foreign debt went up a little, but thanks to high levels of gold and foreign currency reserves Turkey's net foreign debt remained close to zero. In the years that followed, in line with the requirements of rapid economic development, sizable amounts of external loans were secured. The United States was the primary source of these funds. In addition to the funds received from the Marshall Plan, funds from the Agency for International Development (AID) were also received. In addition the United States installed a system called PL 480, which collected the lira equivalent of aid received in the form of excess United States agricultural production in a special fund and spent it in line with a bilateral agreement. Until 1950 most US aid was in the form of loans. In the 1950-1960 period it primarily took the form of grants. Between 1946 and 1962 the amount borrowed from the United States was $585 million. Grants totaled $995 million, with $497 million coming from other sources.

In the 15 years that followed the end of World War II when Turkey accelerated its rate of development, the total amount of aid and loans received was $2 billion. Although changes in the value of the U.S. dollar must be taken into account, when compared with the amount of aid supplied today to a medium-sized country, the dwarfish size of the aid received by Turkey becomes apparent. Having said this, with these limited amounts of assistance Turkey still managed to emerge from being an underdeveloped country and took important steps towards industrialization while modernizing her agricultural sector. By building dams, roads, ports and power plants, the infrastructure for future leaps of the economy was prepared. Though in limited quantity foreign capital started to flow back in, 40% of it originating in the United States. In contrast to the foreign investment of the 19th century, 95% of the investment arriving was channeled into the industrial sector. Most of the foreign companies investing in Turkey were forming partnerships with local private companies, whose share of the capital was, on average, three times as much as the foreign capital. It was possible then to talk of a new Turkey and a new Turkish economy.

In the agricultural sector, too, important developments were taking place. The amount of cultivated land went up from 12,664 decares in 1945 to 23,215 in 1962. The wheat harvest had increased from its postwar yield of 4 million tons to 7.8 million tons by 1962. During the same period the number of tractors increased from 1,156 to 43,747. The amount of loans given to the agricultural sector, especially at the start of the 1950s, shows an annual jump of 65%.

In the same time frame local production was encouraged, and a policy of import substitution was pursued to produce locally what used to be imported. The private and public sectors developed simultaneously. But it must be remembered that the capital accumulation of the private sector was still not sufficient. For this reason the state took the initiative on most industrial investments. The state's share in industrial investment was around 57% in the 1950s, 60% in 1955 and 78% in 1962.

This rapid industrialization brought with it an increased demand for energy. Between 1950 and 1960 the power generating capacity jumped by 350% to 3,560 kwh, achieved by building numerous dams and hydroelectric generators. The share of hydroelectric power went up from 3.8% in 1950 to 31.2% in 1962.

Significant improvements occurred in mining, as well. In 1960, coal production rose to 3.6 million tons from its 1950 level of 2.8 million tons. Brown coal (lignite) production also increased twofold, hitting 3 million tons.

During that period, roadways were given priority over construction of railroads, for which only 224 km. of track were laid. On the other hand, roads grew to 10,750 km. by 1965 as compared to only 1,700 km. in 1950.[53]

Directly after the war, in 1946, the Turkish lira was devalued. One U.S. dollar, which until that time could buy TL 1.30, now bought TL 2.80. Foreign trade expanded. Especially after arrangements were completed to remove obstacles on imports, the period of trade surpluses came to an end. In later years, the ratio of exports to imports kept falling steadily. Due to the trade surplus, this ratio was 1.93 in 1946, dropping to 0.61 by 1962. However, the increased share of machinery and raw materials in imports shows that Turkey was going through a period of industrialization. The result of the trade deficit was a growing foreign debt and an increased burden on the budget to repay this debt together with its interest.

From the mid-1950s, institutions giving foreign aid to Turkey, and the IMF in particular, insisted that Turkey should devalue the lira further. As a result, in 1958 it was depreciated to the point of $1=TL 9.

In the same period a stability program was put in place, and the money supply and public borrowing were tied to certain rules. At that time, the foreign debt was $422 million.

---

[53] Kepenek, op. cit., pp. 84-97, 107.

After 1950, until early the 1960s, the GDP shows a steady increase. It went up by 12.8% in 1951. In the two years that followed this growth was more than 11%. Turkey entered into a rapid development process, and the GDP per capita showed continuous growth.

The Turkish Economy Between 1960-1980 and the Five-Year Plans

In order to complete its infrastructure and become a competitive country Turkey relied, to a large extent, on her own resources until the end of the 1970s. During this period, Turkey protected her local industries against unrestricted foreign competition, refrained from excessive borrowing and tried to keep inflation under control. Starting from the 1960s five-year plans were prepared to give direction to the economy.

When the first Five-Year Plan was prepared, 15-year long-term goals were also set. In order to progress in all fields, these goals called for educating a sufficient number of qualified scientists and technical personnel, 7% annual GDP growth, solving the unemployment problem and achieving all these in accordance with the principles of social justice. All the necessary calculations were also made to estimate the required amount of investment needed to achieve these goals.

The plan called for an investment amount equivalent to 18.3% of the GDP, with 14.8% from internal and 3.5% from external sources. The funds from internal sources were obtained as planned, but external sources amounted to only 1.8%. The same situation was faced during implementation of the second Five-Year Plan. The targeted growth rate was once again 7% annually. Yet, external funds proved to be inadequate. A total of 1.9% of the GDP was expected to be obtained from external sources; however 0.6% was the actualized number. During the second Five-Year Plan's term locally funded investment also fell below expectations. In the third Five-Year Plan, however, the opposite occurred. The targeted growth during this period was 8%. The share anticipated from external sources was 0.8%, but the actual amount was 4.2%. Sixteen percent of the GDP, instead of the planned 21%, was able to be obtained from local funds, and the share of foreign funds in investment increased.

In Turkey, the development plans were binding on the government but acted only as guides to the private sector. Investments made by the private sector during the first 15 years of the planned period were in line with the targeted amounts, and in fact they even exceeded the levels forecast in the first and third Five-Year Plans. In short, the planned development achieved its goals to a large extent. Turkey completed the infrastructure necessary to attain more rapid economic development and strengthened the base of local industry.

At the start of the planned period in 1963, Turkey signed an Association Agreement with the European Economic Community, and with the Additional Protocol signed in 1970 agreed to enter into a customs union by 1995. That is to say, entry into the customs union was decided upon at that time, together with the year in which it was going to be implemented.

Despite the success of the planned period, continuous increases in oil prices after 1974 and high levels of inflation together with unemployment in Western countries with which Turkey had close economic ties upset the Turkish economy. Between 1962 and 1978 the share of public spending on investments was on average 34%. In the 1973-1977 period this was 38.8%.

During the first Five-Year Plan period, i.e. between 1963-1967, the total amount of foreign capital entering Turkey was $115 million. In the next year five-year period this grew to $183 million and reached $362 million during the third five years. The share of foreign capital in Turkey's development was very small, being even less than the amortization and interest payments of the Turkish foreign debt made during the same period.

During the first Five-Year Plan $671 million was paid in amortization and interest; during the second, $850 million; and during the third, $1.5 billion.

Turkey had repaid $3 billion in foreign debt during a 15-year period of time. The foreign capital that flowed into the country during the same period was only $560 million. Turkey succeeded in retiring one-sixth of her foreign debt. Foreign debt amounted to 7.8% of GDP in 1977. In later years this increased, going up to 12.1% in 1979 and 37.4% in 1993. In that same year domestic debt was 16.8% of GDP. As we will see in later sections this figure is below the average for Western countries. Total external debt climbed to $82 billion in 1997. As indicated above, internal debt had gone up to $30 billion in the same year, giving us a total debt stock of $112 billion, approximately 56% of that year's GDP.

The short-term debt, which was at negligible levels in 1972, started to increase rapidly during the third Five-Year Plan, reaching $6.6 billion in 1977. This was a very important development, which later became one of the prime reasons behind the country's economic difficulties. Short-term debt was around 3% of total debt in 1973, becoming 56.3% in 1977. [54]

During the same period the average duration of medium- to long-term debt dropped from 22.1 years to 12.7 years. The interest burden grew to 7.6% from its level of 4.4%. The percentage of grants from creditor countries, which had been 75% during the early 1960s, shrank to 18% during the second half of the 1970s.[55] After 1977, all these adverse developments made it more difficult to repay the foreign debt. At the same time this picture reflects the bottleneck Turkey got into in her economic and financial relations. It is difficult to explain this

---

[54] Kongar, op.cit., p. 374.
[55] Kepenek, op. cit. pp. 161, 164, 232.

development merely by the rapid increase in oil prices. There are those who question whether or not political influences had any effect on the extremely difficult conditions that Turkey rapidly found herself in regarding her foreign debt. Some find it thought-provoking in particular that these adverse developments occurred right after the intervention in Cyprus. However, these suspicions, unless backed by solid evidence, should be viewed with caution. Having said this, it is impossible not to see that when compared with the amount of aid supplied to Russia as well as Central and Eastern European countries in the early 1990s and to Far Eastern countries in later years, there has been a reluctance to transfer funds to Turkey. This issue will be revisited later when discussing the relations between Turkey and the EU. Yet, the following words in the strategy section of the fourth Five-Year Plan explaining the difficulties faced during that period must be brought to mind: "For five years extraordinary oil price increases and the resulting rapid and continuous increases in the prices of the intermediate and investment goods squeezed economies like Turkey, which imports oil as well as these intermediate and investment goods. The exhaustion of the privileges granted to Turkey in our partnership relations with the EEC together with the continuation of various other stumbling blocks in this relationship have been a significant factor making our economic development more difficult and expanding our balance of payments deficit." That is to say, it is pointed out that the economic difficulties faced by Turkey during the 1970s did not stem solely from domestic causes but to a significant extent from external sources. Despite these difficulties the fourth Five-Year Plan called for an 8% GDP growth rate.

The oil price increases of the 1970s caught the economy under such conditions. Whatever the reasons, towards the end of the 1970s Turkey faced difficulties in paying her debt, and a new schedule was devised to retire these obligations. Despite this, Turkey showed success in stabilizing her economy and continued her rapid pace of development.

Another sign of success achieved in industrialization during the planned development period and the following year is the composition of foreign trade. At the start of the first Five-Year Plan in 1963, 77% of Turkey's exports were agricultural products; only 19.8% were industrial, and 3% comprised minerals. By 1980, the agricultural product share went down to 57%, while that of industrial products increased to 36%. In the following years this transition became even more apparent, and industrial products in exports grew to 80%. This picture is one of the indicators reflecting the rapid industrialization process experienced by Turkey in the last 30 years. It also shows the competitive power of Turkish industrial goods in world markets.

Up until the worldwide economic shock created by oil price increases, Turkey had followed a relatively closed economic policy. During that period the share of foreign trade in the GDP was much lower than its current levels. For example, in 1974 it was 10.3%, less than half what it is now. Not including transfers made by Turks working abroad, foreign exchange earnings from construction, transportation and tourism were almost negligible. The Turkish lira was protected by strict regulations. Economic balances could only be maintained with such harsh measures and restrictions. Even the stage by stage lowering of import taxes as required by the Association Agreement signed with the EEC in 1963 and the Additional Protocol of 1971 could be implemented only with great difficulty and delay. The private sector was not yet ready to open up to unfettered competition with the world. In such an environment it was difficult to make the political decision to join the EU. Towards the end of the 1970s this issue was debated extensively. In the early 1980s the decision to apply for full membership was taken, but due to the coup of September 12, 1980 relations with the EU were frozen for a long time, and the official application was only able to be made in 1987.

Turkey tried to do the best she could under the difficult conditions of the pre-1980 period, when she had great difficulty obtaining foreign loans and faced shortages even in basic goods. She undertook great infrastructure investments. Save for one or two years, she managed a higher growth rate than the EU average. It would prove to be more useful if one were to evaluate that period and the decisions regarding economic policies within the context of the time. Another point that should not be missed is the fact that the infrastructure constructed during and before that period served as the base for the industrial development that took place in later years.

The Turkish Economy After 1980

On January 24, 1980 Turkey took a historical decision to liberalize her economy and restructure the whole system. This can be seen as a turning point. However, liberalizing the economy was not the end of the planned economic development. The fifth Five-Year Plan was a tool to realize the January 24, 1980 liberalization decisions. This plan too points to growing foreign debt as the underlying factor behind most of the economic problems faced by Turkey. A 6.3% growth rate was targeted by the fifth Five-Year Plan. The rapid process of industrialization would be continued with a planned growth rate of 7.5%. The sixth Five-year Plan covered the 1990-1994 period, with a projected annual growth rate of 7% and a slowing down of the population growth rate. The seventh Five-Year Plan targeted the 1996-2000 period. This reformist plan put forward 20 major projects. It forecast an annual growth rate between 5.5% and 7.1%. It envisioned decreasing the share of the agricultural sector in the GDP to 11% and increasing industrial production's proportion to 43% by the end of the period. The plan was still binding on the public sector but acted only as a guideline for the private sector. Although the share of state-owned companies in the economy was on the decline, the state took into consideration the targets set by the plan while undertaking infrastructure investment through public funds.

Though various aspects of the post-1980 period have been the subject of many discussions, even those criticizing Turkey in other areas could not argue that the economy had not been fully liberalized. Today, even when compared with the world's largest economies and most industrialized nations, Turkey stands out in this respect. Refraining from protectionism is widely accepted as a leading measure of adherence to the principles of a liberal economy, and according to this criteria Turkey is the eighth most liberal economy in the world. That is to say, Turkey is among the few countries which gives foreign investors extensive facilities and does not discriminate between domestic and foreign investors. Likewise, Turkey is among those countries which give the least amount of subsidies to state-owned companies, ranking ninth in this area. Turkey ranks 11th on a list of countries that interfere the least with their economies. In creating equal opportunity for everyone irrespective of race, religion or nationality, Turkey again ranks 11th.[56]

When after 1980 Turkey started to implement a liberal economic system in its true sense, she made changes to some of the policies that had been followed in the past. Import restrictions were removed in 1984, and in 1989 the Turkish lira became a fully convertible currency. Prices and interest rates were totally set free, and support decreased for state-owned companies, which had played a crucial role in leading the economy during the early days of economic development. These companies were transformed into institutions that could compete in market conditions. Privatization was initiated. The resources of the economy were mobilized to achieve rapid economic development. Increasing exports was set as the prime goal. Tourism investments were given priority. Legal restrictions protecting the value of the Turkish lira were removed. Hence, Turkey became one of the most liberal economies in Europe as well as the world. This is a point that should not be ignored while making comparisons between Turkey and other countries with rapid development rates, such as those in the Far East. To give an example, the reforms demanded by the IMF from the Korean government during the 1998 crisis had already been undertaken by Turkey a long time ago.

---

[56] World Competitiveness Yearbook, 1997.

Meanwhile, it is well worth noting that in South Korea, until the 1998 financial crisis, foreign investors could not own a majority stake in companies; foreign banks could not enter into the South Korean financial market; foreign industrial goods such as Japanese cars could not be imported freely; and the South Korean Central Bank was not as independent as its counterparts in the West.[57]

The liberalization movement that first manifested itself with the January 24 decisions subsequently continued at a more rapid pace. The actual transition that Turkey went through can be seen if one compares 1975 and 1996. During this period Turkey's population went up from 40 million to 61.8 million. Population density went up from 51.2 to 79.2 per sq km. The population growth rate declined from 2.09% to 1.4%. Infant mortality went down from 120 per thousand to 53 per thousand; the rate is still high, but the progress made is clear. Doctors per thousand increased from 0.542 to 1.02, i.e. doubled. Life expectancy went up from 60.3 to 67.3 years.

Rapid Development, Rapid Industrialization

For a long time now Turkey has been in a process of rapid growth. Its current national income cannot even be compared with its past levels. In rate of growth, Turkey leaves behind most other countries. According to the OECD's GDP calculations using ppp, the Turkish economy is among the six largest in Western Europe. Per capita GDP calculations are surely important tools showing the average individual wealth and living standards of a nation. Yet these numbers do not fully reflect the economic power of a country. Therefore, if one is to compare the total economic power of a nation, then total GDP must be used as a yardstick.

---

[57] Martin Feldstein, Refocusing the IMF, Foreign Affairs, vol. 77, No. 2, p. 26.

Indicators comparing 1974 to 1996 give the following results: Turkey's GDP with current prices went up from $35.8 billion to $187.4 billion. According to more recent data Turkey's GDP reached $232 billion in 1997. Using current prices, Turkey's GDP is larger than six EU countries, and using ppp calculations it is larger than 10.

In the 1974-1996 period the structure of the Turkish economy also changed. The share of agriculture declined from 35.8% to 16.9% of the GDP. Industry's portion went up from 14.7% to 30.7%. The share of services was also on the rise, from 49.5% to 52.2%. Using ppp, Turkey's per capita GDP went up from $1,634 to $6,381. OECD statistics indicate that Turkey's total GDP increased by 40% between 1987 and 1996. [58]

Within the OECD, a group comprising most industrialized nations in the world, Turkey is among those with the highest GDP growth rates. Between 1965 and 1980 Turkey's average annual growth rate was 6.3%.

In the 1980-1993 period, Turkey's average annual growth rate was 5.2%, higher than the OECD average. If a longer time frame is looked at, we can see that from 1950-1994 Turkey's average annual GDP growth rate was 5.4%, calculated with 1987 prices.[59]

Given below is a table prepared by the OECD comparing Turkey with EU countries, using ppp.

[58] La Turquie, 10 Ans Après sa Demande d'Adhèsion à l'Union Européenne, Centre des Relations Européennes, CRE, Bruxelles 1997, p. 32.
[59] Selami Sezgin, op. cit., pp. 383-384.

GNP of Turkey and European Union Countries
on the Basis of Purchasing Power Parity (1995)

Country	GDP (Billion $)	GDP per capital ($)
Germany	1,673	20,497
France	1,159	19,393
Italy	1,114	19,465
UK	1,041	17,776
Spain	557	14,226
Turkey*	408	6,381
Netherlands	305	19,782
Belgium	210	20,792
Austria	167	20,773
Sweden	165	18,673
Greece	127	12,174
Portugal	123	12,457
Denmark	112	21,529
Finland	91	17,787
Ireland	62	17,228
Luxembourg	13	31,303

Source: Etudes Economiques de l'OCDE, Turquie

The above table shows the following realities: When we look at total GDP, Turkey's is one-fourth that of Germany and half that of the United Kingdom. Yet, it is six times larger than Ireland's GDP, three times larger than Denmark's and more than twice as large as those of Sweden and Austria. The total of Austria, Denmark and Finland's GDP is equal to Turkey's economic power. Here, however, we must pay attention to one crucial factor: Turkey has to develop at a faster pace if she is to catch up with more advanced nations. When we take absolute numbers, a 1 percent growth in the German economy, for example, translates into a $16 billion increase in national income. One percent growth in Turkey, however, yields only $4 billion. To close the gap Turkey must develop at more than 4% per year while Germany develops at 1%. To reach Spain's level is relatively easier, since the value of a 1 percent increase in the Spanish economy is around $5.5 billion, a little above that of Turkey. Yet it seems inevitable that in order to catch up with the most advanced nations Turkey must develop at a very fast pace. Similarly, Turkey's rapid development will widen the gap between her and countries with smaller national incomes, in Turkey's favour.

When the calculations are made using market prices instead of ppp the numbers in the above table change. In this case, some countries ranking lower overtake Turkey. But, as indicated above, a dollar buys different amounts of goods and services in different countries, comparisons based on the ppp method may be thought as more reflective of the true situation. As the table shows, in relative terms Turkey has become one of the largest and most powerful economies in Europe. Provided that her growth rate does not decline and her birth rate is kept under control, Turkey will have a stronger economy by early next century. Moreover, it can even be said, as mentioned earlier in the foreign trade section that despite economic hurdles and restrictions imposed by the EU Turkey has achieved this success with extremely limited assistance from that organization or from other sources. It is worth bringing to mind once again that Turkey's GDP is larger than that of all candidates for EU membership, irrespective of the method of measurement.

This level of achievement brings Turkey to an important position, not only as regards Europe but also as regards the industrialized nations of the world. Rates of development are important as far as the base indicators are concerned.

Sustaining a high growth rate is not an easy task, even for the strongest economies in the world. Japan, which has had high levels of economic growth for many years, had to revise its target growth rate for 1998 down to 1.9% following the economic crisis of that year. Foreign observers find even that number over-optimistic and think the Japanese economy will actually shrink by 1.6-1.8% in 1998. A similar decline can be observed for China. During the 1992-1994 period the average growth rate of the Chinese economy was 13-14%, but in 1998 it fell to 7.2%. In China, a one percent decline in growth rate increases the number of unemployed by 5 million.[60]

Every year except five between 1980 and 1997, Turkey's growth rate has been higher than the OECD average. Within 12 years of this period Turkey was ranked among the top three countries in the OECD. In six of the last 18 years Turkey achieved a higher growth rate than all the European members of the OECD. In some years the Turkish GDP has grown as much as 9.4%, and in one year it fell by 5.4%. However, when looked at over a long period of time, it can be seen that her rate of growth has been well ahead of many other nations.

In GDP terms and using ppp and not taking into account the unregistered economy, Turkey ranks 17th in the world, with a total income of $408 billion. There are five countries in Europe with larger GDPs: Germany, France, the United Kingdom, Italy and Spain. We must add Russia to this list as well. In North and South America there are four countries with larger GDPs than Turkey: the United States, Canada, Mexico and Brazil. Only six countries in Asia have a larger GDP than Turkey: Japan, China, India, Indonesia, South Korea and Thailand. In addition to these countries Australia also has a greater national income than Turkey. Among her neighbours none has a higher GDP, and only Greece has a higher per capita income.

The table below shows GDP growth in Turkey and in EU candidate Central and Eastern European countries; the last two columns show the GDP index with 1989 as the base year.

---

[60] The Economist, 24 October 1998.

GNP Growth Rate of Turkey and
Central and Eastern European Countries

Country	GDP Growth			Index (1989=100)	
	1995	1996	1997	1996	1997
Turkey	8.1	7.6	*8.3	137	144
Poland	7.0	6.0	5.5	104	110
Slovenia	3.9	3.5	4.0	96	100
Slovakia	7.4	6.8	5.0	90	95
Czech R.	4.8	4.1	4.0	89	92
Hungary	1.5	0.5	2.5	86	88
Romania	6.9	4.3	-2.5	88	86
Estonia	2.9	3.3	4.0	69	71
Bulgaria	2.6	-10	-4.0	68	66
Lithuania	-1.6	2.3	4.0	52	54
Latvia	3.1	3.0	4.0	42	43

Source: La Turquie 10 Ans après sa Demande d' Adhèsion à l' Union Européenne

That some Central and Eastern European countries have shown rapid development in recent years is without doubt a good sign. However, we must not forget that these countries experienced large drops in their national income right after the end of the Cold War, when they started implementing liberal economic policies. This is why the numbers in the last column are important in reflecting a more accurate picture. As this index shows Slovenia has succeeded in getting its economy back to its 1989 level. Poland has managed to exceed that level by a margin. Others still have not managed to attain the 1989 levels. In per capita GDP growth Turkey managed a better rate than not only all Eastern and Central European countries except Poland, but also all EU countries, with the exception of Denmark and the United Kingdom.

Turkey has been successful not only in general indicators like GDP but in production, employment, investment and international trade as well. When one evaluates Turkey's position in various fields and her production and export levels compared to other countries, this success becomes even more striking.

According to comparable figures available, Turkey ranks 11th in the world in increase of agricultural production.[61]

According to UN statistics with a 1990 index of 100, Turkey had reached 150.9 in industrial production by September 1997. Except for a few small countries, Turkey's performance has been slightly surpassed only by South Korea, Malaysia, Chile and Poland.

The Strengthening Private Sector

Especially after the 1980s the private sector began to increase its share in the Turkish economy and gain dominance. In 1995 the private sector's share was 85.8%, and 445 of the largest 500 Turkish firms belonged to the private sector. In Central and Eastern European countries, which are often compared with Turkey, these levels were unable to be achieved despite all efforts. The Czech Republic has the closest percentage at 70%, followed by Estonia with 65%.

When total number of firms is looked at, one comes across an even more interesting set of figures. Ninety-nine percent of all large and small firms in Turkey belong to the private sector. Yet because some state-owned companies are quite large, the share of the public sector goes up to 15%. The state has more or less totally withdrawn from manufacturing. Of 10,541 firms in this sector only 405, i.e. 3.8%, are owned by the state. Investment made by State Economic Enterprises (KITs) in manufacturing has decreased, whereas investment by the private sector has gone up. While KIT investment totalled around $640 million in 1992, this number had fallen to $374 million by 1996. During the same period investment on the

---

[61] World Competitiveness Yearbook, 1996.

part of the private sector went up from $6.2 billion to $9 billion. Therefore, when compared to private sector investment in manufacturing, the public sector's share has dropped from 10.3 to 4.1%. In the production index, too, this change can be followed. With an index of 100 for 1992, the public sector's production went down to 98.4, whereas that of the private sector went up to 124.6. Yet, in other countries the situation is much different. In the Czech Republic, for example, 24% of all companies in manufacturing belong to the state. This figure is 33% in Hungary and 59% in Poland.[62] With respect to the Copenhagen criteria for EU membership one should pay close attention to these numbers.

Some private companies in Turkey have managed to become among the largest in the world. To give an example, with its $12.2 billion turnover the Koç Group ranks 362nd on the Fortune 500 list. Koç's 1996 turnover was equivalent to 3.6% of Turkey's GDP. In the same year this company's exports were $857 million.[63] Sabancı Holding's numbers are close to these.

The private sector, which used to try to bring foreign capital into Turkey, now sells technology and know-how to other countries as well as opening up factories there. Today Turkish firms own numerous facilities in Germany, Azerbaijan, Belgium, Algeria, Georgia, the United Kingdom, Switzerland, Lebanon, Egypt, Romania, Turkmenistan and Uzbekistan and have invested $24 billion in 32 countries.[64]

From time to time Turkey is criticized for over-subsidizing her firms in the private or public sectors. This criticism also appears in the press. However, international statistics do not support these claims.

Turkey is among those countries, not only in Europe but also in the rest of the world, which extends the least amount

---

[62] La Turquie: 10 Ans après sa Demande d'Adhèsion à l'Union Européenne, op. cit., p. 100.
[63] Doing Business in Turkey, IBS Yayıncılık, Istanbul, 1997, pp. IV.1-14.
[64] Executive's Handbook, Intermedia, Turkey, 1998, Almanac, p. 43.

of subsidies to firms. There are only seven countries that lend less support than Turkey. Among these none are European, and only the United States and some Far Eastern countries fall into this category.

The table below shows the proportion of support given by some countries to their private or public sector companies as a percentage of their GDP in 1994.

Public Support to Companies as a Percentage of GNP in Selected Countries

Country	Support Ratio (%)
USA	0.58
Turkey	0.63
Japan	0.73
Poland	0.79
UK	1.21
Germany	1.42
France	1.62
Spain	2.02
Italy	2.23
Belgium	2.71
Netherlands	2.93
Hungary	3.06
Finland	3.38
Sweden	5.62
South Korea	8.88

Source: La Turquie: 10 Ans Après sa Demande d'Adhésion à l'Union Européenne

The table above also highlights the fact that behind the competitive advantage of the firms in many Western countries that are accepted as being more economically advanced than Turkey lies the support of the state. Contrary to conventional wisdom, international competitive power stems not only from these firms' operations or their success under market conditions. The share of the support they receive from their governments plays a significant role in this phenomenon. It seems that behind the overwhelming success and competitive edge of South Korean firms in recent years lies also the support of the South Korean government, which at times has reached 9% of GDP, or $50 billion in absolute numbers. This table makes the competitive power attained by Turkish firms and the increase in exports they have achieved, despite a lack of government support, all the more significant.

In undertaking her economic development in recent years Turkey was not hidden behind protectionist barriers and in most of the cases has been less protectionist than not only Eastern European countries but also Germany, the United Kingdom, France, Italy and Spain. Turkey achieved the results she did in foreign trade through her own competitive power, instead of prohibiting foreign imports. With the customs union agreement all barriers against EU countries were effectively removed. Hence, in this respect Turkey has overtaken the non-EU countries, since today there is no other non-EU country in the world that has entered into a customs union with the EU.

The Public Sector in a Changing Environment

In previous years the Turkish State Enterprises- KITs, together with protectionism, were among the main tools helping the government regulate the economy. Starting from the early days of the Republic the KITs have played an important and leading role in Turkey's economic development.

Turkey adopted a policy of privatization of state-owned companies 10 years ago. The legal basis for this move has been prepared, and despite some difficulties, $3.5 billion worth of privatization has been accomplished.[65] Most of the state-owned companies that are to be privatized have been put under the administration of a governmental agency called the

---

[65] Ibid., p. 49.

Privatization Administration. In April and May of 1998 $1.6 billion was received from the privatization of cellular telephone lines and the sale of the state's shares in Türkiye İş Bankası.

In recent years other countries too have managed successful privatization operations. Leading among these is the privatization program undertaken by the German government in the former GDR. The institution responsible for this privatization process was called the Treuhand, and in a short period of time it privatized thousands of facilities. Equipped with extensive powers the Treuhand turned some of these facilities over to the private sector for symbolic amounts. Yet this was subject to strict requirements, such as introducing new technologies, making new investment, continuing with production and keeping lay-offs to a limited number of workers as well as being tied to certain principles. Compliance with these rules was under strict supervision, and facilities were taken back from those who did not abide by them. As a result most of the East German facilities that were thought to be of no use and inefficient were incorporated into the economy and became the thrust of the region's welfare.

In Turkey, parallel to the privatization process, the KITs' share in the GDP shrank, dropping from 7% in 1990 to 5.7% in 1996. The state shifted its investment to the fields of energy, transportation and communications. In 1996 total fixed investment by the private sector in Turkey amounted to $27.3 billion, while that of the public sector was $6.5 billion.

Despite privatization and its decreased share in the economy the public sector's contribution to production and employment should not be underestimated. The KITs, which were established in the 1930s and supported by the state at a time when private enterprises were limited in number, rendered a great service to the Turkish economy.

Especially after World War II the KITs formed the backbone of the economy. New technologies were introduced to Turkey through these KITs in many different fields.

Managers who became quite successful in the private sector had gotten their experience in these organizations. The KITs made important contributions to exports as well, helping Turkey earn billions of dollars. These state enterprises also helped create jobs for hundreds of thousands of people. Naturally, in time the state had to withdraw from various sectors. Today there are only a few who would argue for total state control over production and the economy in general.

Those who had argued for an active government role in the economy to achieve rapid economic development and strength when the private sector was very weak were correct in their arguments. However, today those who agitate for the government to withdraw from non-essential sectors and concentrate its resources on things like education, health, infrastructure and defence are in the majority.

As a result, the KITs share in the economy is clearly less than what it used to be. All this reflects general trends. But there may be a more crucial point: Since the time new rules were adopted for KITs and the present day, the KITs have ceased to be a financial burden on the government to a large extent. The public borrowing required in 1992 was mainly due to the losses incurred by the KITs. During that year these organizations' total losses amounted to $6.4 billion; yet, in following years major changes took place. With some exceptions, removing controls over prices charged by the KITs for their products and services together with better management resulted in beneficial results for the economy.

In 1996 the total amount of KIT losses were down to $900 million.

Thirty percent of the public borrowing requirement used to stem from the KITs; however, this is now down to 8%. In 1990 the borrowing needs of the KITs were equivalent to 4.2% of GDP; this figure has dropped to 0.2%. There used to be complaints regarding over-staffing at the KITs; they employed 643,000 in 1990, but this number was reduced to 483,000 in 1996, a decrease of 160,000.

As can be seen above, despite all the changes the KITs' weight and power in the Turkish economy is not to be underestimated. Fully 55 of the 500 largest Turkish companies are from the public sector. Yet, 40.1% of the value added by these 500 companies comes from these KITs. Thirty of the KITs on this list were profitable, with profits amounting to $1.5 billion. However, it is a fact that the number of firms on this top 500 list that belong to the private sector and make a profit was much higher.[66]

When making comparisons regarding Turkey's public sector, we must also bear in mind the situation in other countries. The thing that draws one's attention is the fact that despite great privatization moves in fields such as communications, the public sector continues to play an important role in key strategic sectors. For example, according to OECD figures, with the exception of Japan, there is no OECD country that has left electricity production solely to the private sector. In countries like France, Italy, Austria, Canada and Greece all electricity production is done by public sector companies. The United Kingdom, Denmark and Portugal managed to shift to a mixed system of private as well as public production only after 1990. Turkey has used the mixed system since 1975.

A similar situation exists in electricity distribution. In countries such as France, Italy, Canada, Greece, Norway and Australia the state has a monopoly in this area. Even in those countries with a mixed system in power generation, distribution rights have been reserved only for the public sector. Denmark, Norway, Sweden, Portugal and Turkey fall into this category.

In telecommunications some OECD countries have recently opened up to free competition. Other OECD countries either have semi-open markets, or state monopolies. However, in

---

[66] Doing Business with Turkey, op. cit., pp. IV, 1-7.

recent years new trends are developing, and privatization of telecoms is being put on the agenda of many countries.

In transportation, too, the weight of the public sector can be felt in most Western countries. In addition to railroad systems, which with few exceptions are almost all state-owned, the public sector has a major role in air transportation as well.

For example, countries such as Germany, Italy, Greece, Spain and Turkey used to have state monopolies over air transport, but they then shifted to a mixed system. Today airline companies belong solely to the private sector only in countries like the US, the United Kingdom, Canada and Japan.

State banks have assumed significant roles in the banking sector in many countries, and public sector entities still maintain their influence in some nations. In France, for example, Renault is a major public sector company operating in the automotive industry. Public sector companies have been grouped under state-owned holding companies in countries such as Italy and Spain. In Denmark and the Netherlands there are state-owned companies established with the sole purpose of giving direction and support to the private sector so as to be able to engage in joint ventures with the private companies of other nations.

In order to present a better picture of the public sector's place in the economy, it may be useful to give the proportion of people working in this sector to the total active population.

The table below gives the numbers for those working not only in state-owned enterprises but also in the public sector in the most general sense of the word:

Public Sector Share of Employment in
Selected Countries (including the military) (%)

Country	1980	1990	1992	1993
Turkey	8.3	8.7	9.3	9.5
USA	16.0	15.2	15.6	15.6
Germany	14.5	15.1	15.6	15.6
France	20.3	22.6	23.4	24.3
Italy	15.3	16.7	16.8	17.9
Sweden	30.7	32.2	32.7	33.2
OECD	16.4	17.4	17.8	17.9

Source: Coup d'Oeil sur les Economies de l'OCDE

At some points in time perhaps Turkey did employ too many people in the public sector, but overall it can be seen that the share of the public sector in employment in Turkey has been less than the OECD average. In some Western countries the employment levels in the public sector reached twice the level in Turkey. However, in looking at these numbers, the efficiency as well as the value added by those working in the public sector must be taken into consideration.

The results obtained from these figures are as follows: There is no significant difference between Western European countries and Turkey regarding the financial burden or the size of the work force in their public sectors. This is despite the fact that in places that are strategically located, such as Turkey, the public sector carries greater significance in terms of economy and national security. Certainly, under current conditions prevailing in the world and Turkey, it is only logical to privatize some state-owned companies. Yet, it must not be forgotten that the public sector in general and KITs in particular have been and still are a significant part of Turkey's national strength. It is important for those KITs that are not going to be privatized to continue their services to the fullest extent possible, in line with conditions existing in the market economy.

Investments and a Giant Project: GAP
(Southeastern Anatolia Project)

Today's high production capacity seen both in the public as well as private sectors is largely due to heavy investment. When compared to other countries, Turkey seems to be in good shape from the standpoint of an increase in domestic investment. Between 1991 and 1995 Turkey was second only to the Czech Republic in the increase of gross domestic investment rate among other European countries, who all lagged behind Turkey, with Austria next in line at half the level.

While capacity was expanding both in the private and public sectors, the quality of goods produced also improved, a fact acknowledged by objective parties. The European Foundation for Quality Management award was granted to Turkish companies in the "large firms" category in 1995 and in the "medium-sized firms" group in 1996. Turkey's infrastructure investments started to bear fruit, and some of them became world famous, the most important being the Southeastern Anatolia Project (GAP). Not only Southeastern Anatolia but all of Turkey has already started to benefit from this initiative.

The project entails the building of 21 dams and 17 hydroelectric power plants, the irrigation of 1.6 million hectares of land and the production of 26 billion kwh of electricity, with a plant capacity of 7,500 MW. The land to be irrigated will be larger than the half of all the land irrigated in 1993 in Turkey, more than 2.5 times the size of Belgium. When the project is completed the share of the six provinces in the region will go up from 8% to 20% in agriculture, from 1.9% to 8% in industrial production and from 5% to 10% in services. This is the expectation for the year 2002.[67]

---

[67] Semih Vaner, Deniz Akagöl, Bahadır Kaleağası, La Turquie en Mouvement, 1995, p. 77.

Turkey undertook this project with her own budget, using almost no external loans. This is one of the underlying reasons behind the budgetary problems that Turkey has had to face in recent years. GAP will contribute the economic development of the country as well as help reduce regional economic differences within Turkey, and in the coming years even more achievements in the area are anticipated.

After significant achievements in developing her infrastructure and production capacity, as said above, Turkey has been removed from the developing countries category and put into the middle-income level group by the World Bank and the OECD.[68]

Direct Foreign Investment

The Turkish private and public sectors have made most of the investment in Turkey, and foreign investment is well below that of most other countries. The following table shows the cumulative amounts of such investments in OECD countries.

---

[68] Ibid., p. 56.

Direct Foreign Investment in Selected Countries ($ million)

Country	1971-1980	1981-1990	1991-1996
USA	56,276	368,309	279,846
UK	40,503	130,477	113,782
France	16,908	43,194	109,148
Belgium-Lux	9,215	28,182	60,357
Spain	7,060	46,000	55,955
Netherlands	10,822	27,850	42,233
Mexico	-	24,178	37,077
Canada	5,534	11,448	36,787
Italy	5,698	24,888	19,944
Germany	13,969	18,028	19,021
Denmark	1,561	3,388	14,673
Hungary	-	512	12,519
Portugal	535	6,258	8,473
Austria	1,455	3,274	7,950
Japan	1,424	3,281	5,333
Greece*	-	6,145	5,290
Turkey	228	2,340	4,880

*Except 1996
Source: OECD International Direct Investment Statistics Yearbook 1997

The table above puts forward some interesting facts. Compared to the decade before it, the 1981-1990 period saw a significant increase in foreign investment. The United States attracted the largest amount of capital, and among the EU countries the United Kingdom ranked first. Structural differences between the British, French and German economies are small, and particularly after the United Kingdom became an EU member, these differences diminished even further. It would be interesting to learn why the United Kingdom has attracted so much foreign investment despite this lack of structural differences. Another interesting point is the small amount of foreign investment that Japan has had. Despite its being one of the largest and most rapidly developing countries in the world, the fact that it ranks among the lowest in drawing foreign investment may be explained by the polices she follows. It is clear that Japan does not encourage foreign companies to play significant roles in its economy. Another point is the remarkable increase in the amount of foreign investment received by Spain after becoming an EU member. The foreign investment arriving in Spain from 1981 to 1990 was twice as much as that going to Italy during the same period, and more than seven times that of Greece. This sheds light on the reasons behind the recent economic development seen in Spain. In later years foreign investment continued to flow in larger amounts, with China and other Far Eastern countries being among the primary recipients.

By 1996 the global amount of direct foreign investment had reached $349 billion. The cumulative figure reached by the end of the same year was around $3.2 trillion. $129 billion, i.e. 37% of all direct foreign investment in 1996, went to developing countries. $86.7 billion of this amount was shared among seven countries only; China received $42.3 billion, Brazil $9.5 billion, Singapore $9.5 billion, Indonesia $8 billion, Mexico $7 billion, Malaysia $5.3 billion and Poland $5.1 billion. The cumulative foreign investment in China reached $270 billion.[69] The Economist, 24 October 1998. Foreign investment plays an important part in the increased foreign trade and GNP of these receiving countries. 25% of the gross domestic investment in China is of foreign origin. There are 17 million people employed in the 120,000 foreign firms operating in China. A total of 47% of all Chinese exports are conducted by these firms, whereas this figure was just 5.6% only a decade ago. Large foreign investment has also had an impact on China's foreign trade. For example, during the 1991-1998 period China's trade with the United States multiplied by 15 times and climbed to $75 billion. Similar numbers can be given for other countries as well. Investments in Central and Eastern European countries will be analyzed in the section on EU enlargement. In these countries foreign

---

[69] The Economist, 24 October 1998.

investment has an important place. The situation in Turkey, however, is quite different. The share of foreign investment in economy, production and exports is more limited than in those countries. Turkey managed its economic development, production and export expansion by relying on her own resources, labour, capital and companies.

Despite this, however, relatively speaking there has been an increase in foreign firms investing in Turkey. In 1989 there were 1,525 of them, reaching 3,582 in 1995.

One can argue that the high inflation rates experienced by Turkey are keeping foreign investment from being made. There might be some truth to this. Yet, one must then explain why Russia, which has had much higher inflation than Turkey, received so much foreign investment: $2 billion in the 1995-1996 period alone, reaching a cumulative total of $7.5 billion.[70]

Looking at the sources of foreign investment may also give interesting results. One would expect all investor countries to enter into a market having attractive conditions. If that is not the case, and if a few nations are taking the lead over others in entering particular countries, then one may conclude that political considerations are determinant in such nations

Obviously state subsidies are not the only factor influencing foreign investment. The bottom line is the internal dynamics, scales and preferences of each country. Therefore one must not neglect factors directing such investment. However, one thing is certain: If states would like to channel the foreign investment of their companies towards particular countries for their own political aims, they have the means to do it. This issue will be revisited in the EU section.

Some international rating agencies also play a crucial role in directing foreign investment to various countries. The ratings given by these act as guidelines to investors, informing them about the general economic conditions of the countries and

---

[70] Le Courrier des Pays de l'Est, Août, 1997, vol. 421, p. 18.

their ability to pay back their debts. Depending on these, investors make their choices. Likewise, international banks and financial institutions also take these ratings into consideration when extending credit to these countries or determining the conditions as well as the duration of this credit. Ratings given to Turkey are usually fairly low. In 1991 Turkey received a BBB rating from Standard & Poor's, which means "able to pay back its debt." From then on her rating went down and remained low. In 1997 D&P gave Turkey a BB rating, meaning "declining ability to pay back debt." In previous years as well similar ratings were given. Yet, despite these poor ratings Turkey kept paying back her debts on time and still continued her rapid economic growth. The fact must be emphasized that Turkey met her financial obligations even in 1994 when she had a serious economic crisis. This must be seen as a sign of power and discipline. We do not know whether rating agencies take this into account. The ratings given by these institutions to some other countries reveal an interesting picture.

Other than Bulgaria all Central and Eastern European countries in recent years received better ratings than Turkey. However, among them are those which defaulted on their debt or rescheduled it. None of them attained the same kind of economic development as Turkey. None have foreign currency reserves as high as Turkey's. Without doubt these rating agencies use justifiable methods while giving their ratings. But one wonders how they ended up giving good ratings to some Far Eastern countries just six months before the economic collapse that was experienced in that region. When we take an average of ratings by S&P and Moody's, we see that in July 1997 Indonesia's rating was four grades better than Turkey's, and South Korea's was 10 times better. We have no reason to question the objectivity of these agencies, but the ratings and realities are all there. Who will compensate those banks and investors that entered those collapsed markets as a result of relying on ratings given by these institutions? Who will compensate countries like Turkey that undeservedly received low ratings and lost credibility in international financial circles? These questions have no answers.

Evolution of the Turkish Stock Exchange

While some foreign investors prefer industrial investment, some prefer putting their money into the Turkish stock exchange (Istanbul Stock Exchange or IMKB), which has become one of the fastest growing and most profitable stock exchanges in the world.

As regards the greatest number of companies listed on a stock exchange, Turkey ranked seventh in Europe in 1995. None of the Eastern European exchanges have more companies listed. In this respect, Turkey also leaves behind eight EU countries. The IMKB is among the most rapidly developing exchanges in the world. It grew by 210% in 1993, and its daily turnover went from $34 million in 1992 to $200 million in 1997. Its annual turnover, which was $8.5 billion in 1992, had gone up to $51 billion by the end of November 1997.[71] Now the goal is to increase the capitalization of the exchange. The table below gives the daily volume for the IMKB as well as for some other European stock exchanges.

---

[71] Executive's Handbook, op. cit., p. 35.

Daily Turnover in Some European
Stock Exchanges 1997 (million $)

EXCHANGE	VOLUME
Paris	1,608
Italy	757
Madrid	526
Istanbul	209
Brussels	134
Barcelona	88
Lisbon	75
Ireland	58
Vienna	51
Warsaw	33
Athens	9
Luxembourg	4

Source: TUSIAD Opportunities and Challenges
in the Eurasian Area, November 1997

Returns in stock exchanges are as important as their volume. The following table gives dollar-based returns for some of the world's stock exchanges.

Stock Exchange Revenue in Selected Countries
(12/31/96-10/22/97)

STOCK EXCHANGE	INCOME (%,$ based)
Russia	190.6
Turkey	111.9
Greece	63.3
Hungary	63.3
Mexico	61.1
Portugal	43.1
India	31.0
China	29.9
Poland	4.4
Taiwan	0.5
Hong Kong	-13.7
South Korea	-14.9
Czech Republic	-16.2
Indonesia	-49.0
Malaysia	-56.1
Thailand	-69.3

Source: TUSIAD, Opportunities and Challenges in the Eurasian Area, November 1997

The figures above fluctuate from time to time. The financial crisis in the Far East during the first half of 1998 affected almost all of the stock exchanges around the world. The Russian and Far Eastern exchanges experienced steep declines. The IMKB also felt its effects but subsequently recovered.

In Turkey there have been significant improvements not only in the stock exchange but also in capital accumulation, which has been above the OECD average. Between 1970 and 1979 Turkey's yearly average was 4.5%, whereas the OECD average amounted to just 3.8%. In the 1980-1996 period, with the exception of a few years, Turkey's average was again higher than that of the OECD. In some years Turkey ranked first.

Banking in Turkey

Just as in any other country, banks and other financial institutions have played an important role in the economic development efforts of Turkey, where contemporary banking began with the foundation of the Republic. During the Ottoman era, prior to 1847, the bankers of Galata ruled the empire's financial sector. The 1847-1908 period saw the growing dominance of foreign banks. The Osmanlı Bankası (Ottoman Bank) was established in 1856 as a British-French partnership and acted as a central bank until 1923. Ziraat Bankası (Agriculture Bank) was the first Turkish bank, founded towards the end of the last century. During the first seven years of the Republic, Turkey did not have a separate central bank. Türkiye İş Bankası was the first bank established after the declaration of the Republic. Among its responsibilities were encouragement of industrial investment and capital accumulation.

Turkey's banking sector started to grow after World War II, then entered into a period of rapid development following the move into a liberal economy in 1980.

By the end of 1997 there were 71 banks in Turkey, 19 of which were foreign, with 6,500 branches. According to OECD reports, Turkish banks are among those with the highest profitability rates in the world. In June 1997 the total assets of Turkish banks were valued at $87.2 billion, and their loans totalled $38 billion, with deposits of $55.4 billion. There were 24,951 ATMs and 2,216,010 credit card holders in Turkey in 1995. In recent years Turkish banks have started to improve their consumer credit lines, and 4,635,439 people benefited from such credit in 1995. Compared to the previous year this reflects a 34% increase.[72]

---

[72] Ibid., p. 38.

Having said this, when compared to the balance sheets of banks in other developed countries, those of Turkish banks remain quite weak. The following table gives the 1995 figures for the balance sheets, taxes and net profits of banks in various countries.

Bank Turnover, Profit and Taxes in Selected Countries (1995)

Country	Balance Sheet ($ Billion)	Profit After Tax ($ Billion)	Profit/ Balance Sheet(%)	Tax/Net Income (%)	Profit/Net İncome AfterTax(%)
USA	7,555	83.0	1.15	30.7	55.5
Germany	4,152	11.0	0.26	32.6	28.8
France	3,728	1.9	0.05	13.5	7.2
Italy	1,478	0.4	0.03	29.2	2.4
UK*	1,204	9.3	0.77	27.0	52.5
Spain	1,052	4.8	0.46	7.3	34.5
Switzerland	925	5.9	0.64	14.9	48.2
Netherlands	919	4.7	0.52	24.7	57.4
Belgium	840	1.8	0.21	21.3	36.9
Austria	517	1.6	0.31	9.4	35.6
S.Korea	317	1.4	0.38	4.0	28.7
Sweden	217	2.3	1.07	21.6	90.3
Denmark	165	1.9	1.16	11.3	53.6
Greece	130	1.0	0.87	23.6	59.3
Turkey*	62	2.6	4.17	7.4	74.4
Poland	53	1.1	2.20	35.8	55.3
Czech Rep.	64	0.1	0.13	11.7	7.6

Source: OECD Bank Profitability, 1997. (Foreign Exchange rates are calculated on the basis of the data provided by OECD Economic Outlook, June 1997.)

The table above gives the following results: There are significant differences between the total volume, taxes paid and profitability figures of Western banks. The balance sheets of German banks are triple those of Italian banks, Spain's are five times higher than Sweden's and Denmark's balance sheets are triple those of Turkey. On the other hand Turkey ranks second after Sweden in after-tax income. In absolute numbers, Turkey ranks seventh in profitability. Despite being among those with the lowest balance sheet numbers, Turkey seems to be ahead of others in profitability on balance sheets. Poland, which comes a distant second, has profitability rates that are half those of Turkey. The situation is very different when taxes on net income are examined. Turkish banks are among those paying the least amount of taxes. This is probably one of the reasons why their profits are so high. Taxes paid by Turkish banks out of their net income is equal to the amount paid by Swiss banks. Only the South Koreans pay less. Yet while commenting on this table, eroding bank equities due to inflation must also be taken into account. Rapid devaluation of the Turkish lira makes it difficult to compare the figures of Turkish banks with those of other countries. The table above has been prepared by taking the average values for the balance sheets. Countries inform the OECD of their statistics using their own currencies. Therefore, the conversions in the table were done using the average daily exchange rate for the year 1995. For Turkey and the United Kingdom the numbers only reflect the positions of their commercial banks. For other countries all of their banking sectors have been included; therefore, discrepancies that arise due to this factor must be allowed for. Moreover, there may be differences from one year to another. For example, we see marginal profits by Italian banks for the year 1995; yet in previous years they have achieved higher figures.

The stability and credibility of banks and other financial institutions are of extreme significance. It should not be forgotten that it was the problems with the banking sector that caused the 1998 economic crisis, leading Far Eastern economies into financial difficulties. The most striking examples of these were in South Korea, Japan and China. In Japan alone the amount of bad debts has been declared as

$600 billion.[73] In China the total amount of bad debts were estimated to be around $270-360 billion.[74] Nevertheless the above figures give a general view of the relative position of the banking sectors in various countries. It seems that the total assets of Turkish banks remain limited for a country the size of Turkey. It is a well-known fact that many people in Turkey prefer to hold their savings themselves in gold instead of in bank deposits. Therefore, the total deposits in banks do not accurately reflect the true total savings of the country. The recently established gold exchange is expected to change these habits.

The total assets of banks should not be seen as the sole measure of a country's financial strength. Financial assets traded on the stock exchange as well as other financial instruments should also be taken into account. It must be remembered, however, that similar instruments exist in other countries as well. The fact that total assets of Turkish banks are low relative to their counterparts in the West indicates one of the reasons behind the difficulties with Turkey's economic development efforts.

In foreign currency reserves, Turkey ranks 26th in the world, and in gold reserves she is 25th. In May 1998 the foreign currency reserves of the Central Bank had reached $25.8 billion. None of the Eastern European countries possessed more. In foreign currency reserves Turkey ranks 26th and in gold reserves, 25th in the world.

The Construction Sector

The Turkish construction sector has been one of the most rapidly developing sectors, one which also managed to internationalize just as fast. Turkish contractors won their first

---

[73] IHT 23.11.1998.
[74] The Economist 24 October 1998.

foreign contracts in Libya in the early 1970s. Later, they were awarded larger projects in Western Europe, Russia, the Central Asian republics and in the Middle East. The total value of these projects exceeds $33 billion, and $15 billion of these are still under construction. Turkish contractors work in 25 different countries, and the value of the projects they have undertaken in Western Europe alone is more than $8 billion. In Russia there are more than 30,000 Turkish labourers working with Turkish construction companies. Turkish firms have recently started to establish retail chains, enabling them to be influential in the commercial sector as well. In the Turkic republics of Central Asia and in the Caucasus Turkish firms have undertaken large projects and have proved their competitive capabilities as well.

Tourism in Turkey

Tourism is another important source of foreign exchange for Turkey. Turkey has been one of the most rapidly developing tourism destinations in the world. In 1996 8.6 million and in 1997 9.7 million tourists visited Turkey. In the first eight months of 1998 there was a 2.2% increase in the number of tourists coming to this country. The increase in the number of arrivals from Eastern European countries is particularly significant. While ranking 28th in tourist arrivals in the world back in 1985, in 1996 Turkey moved to 19th place.

The rate of increase between 1995 and 1996 was 12.5%. With the exception of Russia, Egypt, China and Macao no other destination showed a larger increase. Income from tourism went up to $6 billion in 1996, and the increase in 1997 alone was 21%. In tourism-related investments as well Turkey is among the leaders in the world. In 1985 there were 75,000 beds in touristic establishments; in 1996 it reached 276,000. This means that within a decade capacity had increased by 267%, a rate unmatched by any other country in the world. The rate of increase in Hungary, which is second to Turkey, was half as large.

In evaluating the tourism sector those who travel abroad from Turkey as well as those coming into the country must be considered. That is to say, although Germany, for example, is one of the most popular destinations in the world, due to the high number of Germans travelling abroad its tourism account shows a deficit of $34 billion. The expenditures of Turks travelling abroad were $912 million in 1996. Therefore, the net tourism account gives a surplus of more than $5 billion. In "tourism surplus" Turkey ranks fourth in Europe, with only Spain, Italy and France coming in higher.

In conjunction with tourism, the transportation sector also developed. Turkish Airlines flew 3.8 million people in 1988, and in 1996 this number went up to 9.3 million.

There have been developments in the maritime sector as well. The Turkish commercial fleet had 3.1 million gross tons of capacity in 1988. This increased to 6.5 million gross tons in 1996.

Development Indicators in Turkey and the World

Next to general economic indicators other important figures regarding production capacity must also be taken into consideration when comparing Turkey's economic development with that of other countries.

Foremost among these comes power generation, which constitutes the backbone of all industrial production. The reason behind power shortages experienced from time to time in Turkey is the fact that industrial production has expanded more rapidly than electrical generating capacity. In fact, when considered on its own, Turkey's power generating capacity has increased significantly.

Since the early 1970s Turkey has made huge investments to increase its electricity supply. Capacity went up from 8.6

billion kwh in 1970 to 48 billion in 1988, 73 billion in 1993 and 95 billion in 1995. There are only 19 countries in the world that generate more electricity than Turkey. Only six of these are EU members, and among EU candidates only Poland produces a little more than Turkey does.

The foundation for Turkey's iron and steel industry was laid in 1930. The first raw steel production took place in 1939 in Karabük, a town in the Black Sea region. Turkey is a latecomer to this field when compared with the West; however, in recent years she has achieved remarkable results. Today Turkey's capacity in raw steel production is 19.3 million tons, with 5.6 million tons of this produced by the public sector and the remainder in private sector facilities. Considering that this capacity was only 2.6 million tons back in 1981, the significance of this development becomes even more evident. Turkey, which then ranked 32nd in the world, now ranks 12th. Only four EU countries place higher than Turkey: Germany, France, the United Kingdom and Italy. Spain's production equals Turkey's, whose production is more than twice that of Sweden, which is world-famous for its steel production. None of the candidate countries for EU membership produce as much steel as Turkey.

Turkey ranks 18th in the world in pig iron production. Only five EU countries produce more: Germany, the United Kingdom, France, Italy and Belgium. The Netherlands' production equals that of Turkey, while Poland produces more.

Turkey fares better in cement production. Monthly production went up to 3.8 million tons in January 1997. Turkey ranks the sixth in the world in this category. None of the EU countries produce more than Turkey, whose production is twice as much as France's and four times that of the United Kingdom.

Turkey ranks 22nd in automobile manufacturing, considered a leading indicator of industrialization. According to the latest UN figures, Turkey's monthly car production is

18,256 vehicles. This number is taken as the basis for comparison, although there have been years when Turkey produced even more. In 1993, for example, the monthly production level was up to 28,598. In the EU, only seven countries produce more cars than Turkey, and among EU candidates only Poland's output is higher. However, in commercial vehicle production such as buses and trucks, the Turkish production rate exceeds that of Poland and Belgium, both of which produce more cars than Turkey.

In industrialized countries the automotive sector is widely regarded as the locomotive of the economy. In the United States, the United Kingdom, France and Italy car manufacturing began in the early 19th century and since then has advanced significantly. Turkey entered this sector half a century later than these industrialized nations. The first investment in this field in Turkey was a jeep assembly plant established in 1954. In 1955 trucks and in 1963 buses began to be assembled. In the three years that followed car assembly as well was initiated. Later, more and more parts started to be produced locally, and cars began to be manufactured rather than merely assembled. Turkey produced 167,556 cars in 1990, jumping to 348,095 in 1993. Although there was a decline in the following year, production levels later picked up. In 1993, 30,796 trucks, 19,766 vans, 12,084 minibuses, 1,933 small trucks and 547 tractors were manufactured.

The total number of vehicles in Turkey went up from 1.5 million in 1985 to 4.3 million in 1996, i.e. one vehicle for every 14 persons. When compared with the figures for previous years this indicates an increase in Turkey's standard of living. Yet when compared with other Western countries, the Turkish automobile industry and auto market still have a huge potential.

The figures above show actual production; capacity, however, has become much larger thanks to recent investment in this sector. In 1995 production capacity was 495,000 cars per year. In the years to come, especially with investment from the United States, Japan, South Korea and other Far Eastern countries, this should soon reach 1 million cars per year.

Tire manufacturing is another important sector. Turkey ranks 14th in this field, and in January 1997 her monthly production reached 1.1 million. Among EU countries only Germany, France, the United Kingdom and Italy produce more tires than Turkey. Poland's output is equal to that of Turkey.

Paper production is significant as well. With 10,000 tons per month, Turkey ranks 22nd in the world. There are only seven countries in the EU that produce more paper than Turkey, and none of the EU candidates do so.

With the implementation of the planned economic programs, the petrochemical industry has also developed rapidly. Two factories established during the 1970s still meet most local demand and export their output as well. There are seven factories producing fertiliser. Oil refineries are able to fill domestic consumption needs, and they too export their excess production.

The first large-scale machinery production in Turkey began in the 1930s at the Kırıkkale Army Factories. In 1950 the name was changed to the Machinery and Chemicals Industry, which is still a public sector company. It was not until the 1960s that the private sector entered this field. Turkey made important advances in this area, particularly during the time of the second Five-Year Plan. The Turkish machinery industry can now produce spare parts for almost all of its products, with 80-85% of all production being done locally. Today there are 360 firms that employ 25 workers or more producing machinery.

The textile and garment sector now accounts for 10% of total Turkish industry. From January to September 1997 capacity usage was 82.6%. In the first 11 months of 1997, 1,082 new licenses were issued for investment in this sector. During the same period $3 billion worth of machinery was imported for textile production. Cotton fibre production is the mainstay of the textile industry. Turkey ranks fourth in the world in this field; no European country produces as much or comes even close to Turkey's production levels. Turkey ranks fourth in wool production as well, and only the United Kingdom produces more wool than Turkey among European countries.

Especially after the late 1980s the Turkish electronics sector has shown rapid development, with 120 companies in operation, some of which manufacture their goods under license from other countries.

In flour production Turkey had reached a monthly average of 172,000 tons by May of 1997, boosting her to 11th position in the world. In Europe, only Germany produces more.[75]

Refrigerator production was 500,000 in 1985, 1,663,000 in 1995 and 1,778,276 in the January-October period of 1997. Again during the same years television production went up from 819,000 to 1,860,000.

Washing machine output was 223,500 in 1985. In the first 10 months of 1997 it increased to 1,332,874. These products are now among Turkey's main export goods.[76] As a result of the great advances made by Turkey, only a few examples of which are given above, Turkey ranks ninth in the world for increases in industrial production.[77] Capacity usage in industry has also increased significantly, reaching around 50% in the 1980s and approaching 75% within a decade. It was 81.3% in manufacturing in October 1997. Among OECD countries there were only two countries with an uninterrupted increase in employment between 1980 and 1997: Japan and Turkey.[78]

According to the Brussels-based European Research Center's numbers, which are calculated using World Bank and

[75] UN Monthly Statistics, 1997.
[76] Ekonomik Forum, 15 Şubat 1998.
[77] World Competitiveness Yearbook, 1996.
[78] OECD, Economic Outlook, Paris, June 1997, p. A.23.

World Labour Organization figures, in the 1990-1995 period, Turkey follows Hungary and Poland in increase in labour efficiency, at 3.52%. Figures for some of the EU countries are as follows: Germany, 3.41%; Italy, 2.44%; UK, 2.01%; and Greece, 0.62%. Within the same period, efficiency in Russia declined by 6.91%. It must be stressed, however, that these are increases in efficiency. Turkey still has a long way to go in order to catch up with the most advanced nations in the world in efficiency. Having said this, there are important differences in efficiency among the most industrialized countries. According to one research institute, as of 1998 labour efficiency in the United States was 25% higher than that in France and Germany and 37% more than in Britain.[79]

Increased production naturally resulted in increased consumption. This is a sign of increased prosperity. However, it does not mean all strata of society have benefited equally from this increased well-being since there are important problems regarding income distribution. This dimension of the issue will be revisited in later sections.

In private consumption increase Turkey ranks among the highest in the OECD. For example, Turkey achieved 5% growth in real consumption during the 1970-1979 period. The corresponding figure for the OECD average was 4%, and the EU average for the same period was 3.6%. The same trend continued in later years; between 1980 and 1996, with the exception of six years, Turkey attained higher rates than the OECD average, ranking first in some years.

Turkey's achievements within the last 20 years in production, investment, employment and exports helped to visibly improve the living standards of the people. Despite the fact that some problems continue to exist, to which we will refer to in later sections, generally speaking there has been a significant improvement in per capita goods and services available to the public. For example, in the 1975-1996 period

---

[79] The Economist, 3 October 1998.

per capita energy consumption doubled. Between 1974 and 1996 the number of TV sets per thousand went up from 11 to 240.[80] In 1976 there were 29.2 refrigerators per100 families; this rose to 95.7 in 1990. During the same period families that owned washing machines increased from 11.8% to 53.1% of the total number of families. In 1970 there were four cars per thousand; in 1996 this exceeded 40 per thousand. While the total number of cars, domestic and foreign, sold in Turkey was 178,631 from January-October 1996, this went up to 257,796 during the same period in 1997, and the number of commercial vehicles sold jumped from 42,000 to 78,000.[81]

The same development took place for telephone services. While there were 1.9 million phones in Turkey back in 1984, this number rose to 12.3 million in 1994 and to 14 million in 1996. By the end of 1997 there were 17 million phone lines in Turkey, i.e. one phone per 3.6 people. This number does not include cellular phones, which are rapidly gaining wide acceptance. There were 800,000 cellular phones in 1996, reaching 2,000,000 by the end of 1998.

Parallel to these developments in the industrial sector, there have been important increases in the output levels of agricultural production and mining. In 1997 wheat production exceeded 18 million tons; it had been 10 million tons in 1970. Barley production climbed from 3.2 million to 8.2 million tons. During the same period cotton production doubled from 400,000 tons to 795,000 tons. Tobacco production also doubled, from 149,000 to 300,000 tons. The rate of increase in commercial crops is even more significant. During the same period sunflower production went up from 375,000 tons to 900,000. In all these areas there have been significant increases in per hectare yields. Mechanization also has helped the increase in productivity. There were 40,282 tractors in Turkey in 1955, jumping to 874,995 in 1997.

---

[80] L'Etat du Monde 1998.
[81] Executive's Handbook, op. cit., p. 71.

While some branches of mining have seen increased production, others are on the decline. The most significant increase can be seen in lignite production. While 8.7 million tons of lignite was produced in 1970, this number reached 57.5 million tons 1997. Iron production went up from 2.9 million tons to 6.2 million tons. Chromium jumped from 772,000 tons to 1.2 million tons. Yet coal production decreased from 7.6 million tons to 3.5 million tons. In 1970, 3.5 million tons of oil was extracted. Although this number declined in later years, by 1997 it had returned to the same level.[82]

That this dynamic development in Turkey far exceeds expectations is mentioned in OECD reports. The OECD expects Turkey to be among the fastest growing countries in the world. The forecasts made for the 1999-2003 period foresee a 5% annual growth rate for the Turkish economy. The 1998 world economic crisis that started in the Far East was felt in Turkey and kept the Turkish GDP growth rate at around 4% for 1998. Yet even this figure is one of the highest among all OECD members.

There are only four other OECD countries expected to perform similarly: South Korea, Ireland, Poland and Mexico. However, it remains to be seen whether South Korea manages to stay on this list, considering the 1998 financial crisis experienced in the Far East. During the same period, the EU is expected to grow by 2.6% per year. That is to say, Turkey is expected to grow at double the EU rate. There are organizations predicting that the Turkish GDP, which is currently estimated to be $200 billion at 1997 market prices, will become $350-$400 billion, with foreign trade volume expected to reach $80-$100 billion by 2010. According to these estimates EU exports to Turkey alone will be around $50 billion.[83] However, in addition to the negative effects of the

---

[82] State Institute of Statistics, October 1998.
[83] La Turquie Dix Ans Après sa Demanda d'Adhésion a l' Union Européenne, CRE, op. cit., p. 52.

Far Eastern and Russian crises, an unprecedented earthquake in August 1999 devastated cities, killing more than 15,000 people and affecting a large industrial area. New estimates, therefore, put the rate of growth for 1999 much lower than predicted before.

Foreign Trade

In the years that followed World War II international trade showed a dramatic increase. From 1948-1997, 6% was the yearly average increase in world trade which expanded 14 times over during the same period. This figure is much larger than the increase in production, which grew 3.7% per year within the same time frame, resulting in an expansion of 5.5 times. While international trade accounted for 7% of the world's GDP in 1950, it accounted for 23% in 1997, and by 2020 it is expected to reach 50%. Therefore, while analyzing economic developments one must keep in mind this trend of increased importance in foreign trade.

The production and consumption increases, for which we gave a few examples above, also influence foreign trade. Turkish foreign trade continued to improve after 1980. In 1974 the total volume of Turkish foreign trade was $5.31 billion, with $1.53 billion in exports and $3.78 billion in imports; exports coverage of imports was 40%. In 1996 the foreign trade volume grew to $66 billion, with exports totalling $23 billion and imports $42 billion. These figures do not include what is referred to as the "suitcase trade," which is not included in the official figures. When added to export numbers, the true value of Turkish exports is closer to $32 billion, while foreign trade volume is in the vicinity of $74 billion.

The following table gives statistics for Turkey's foreign trade, categorized by country and year.

Turkey's Exports ($ billion)

	1991	1992	1993	1994	1995	1996
TOTAL	13.6	14.7	15.3	19.1	21.6	23.1
OECD	8.8	9.3	9.1	10.7	13.2	13.9
EU	7.0	7.6	7.2	8.6	11.0	11.4
EFTA	0.6	0.6	0.5	0.2	0.3	0.3
Other OECD	1.2	1.1	1.2	1.8	1.8	2.1
Other Europe	1.1	0.6	1.8	2.3	3.5	3.8
Other Countries	3.6	4.7	4.4	4.9	4.8	5.2
Share of EU (%)	51.8	51.6	47.4	47.6	51.2	49.7

Source: Sadi Uzunoğlu, Zeitschrift für Türkeistudien, 2/97

According to State Institute of Statistics and Foreign Trade Office figures, Turkey's exports reached $26 billion in 1997. Compared to 1996 this represents a 12.5% increase. In 1997 exports to the EU went up by 5.5% and to the United States by 21%.

Looking at the table it is clear that in 1997 the EU's share of Turkish exports went down to 47% from its previous level, which had been above 50%. The signing of the customs union agreement in 1996 did not bring about significant increases in Turkish exports to the EU. On the other hand, there have been significant increases in exports to other OECD as well as non-OECD countries. In the first category the United States and in the latter Russia stand out as Turkey's most important commercial partners.

In recent years the structure of Turkey's exports has also changed. As mentioned in the sections above, this change that started in the 1970s continued at a more rapid pace in the 1980s and 1990s. Agricultural products accounted for 13.6% and industrial products for 84.9% of Turkish exports in 1994. Almost half of all industrial exports go to the EU. Two-thirds of all textile exports, which account for 38.7% of total exports, go to Europe.[84]

The import figures for Turkey present a different picture. The following table gives the statistics for Turkish imports within the same period.

Turkey's Imports ($ billions)

	1991	1992	1993	1994	1995	1996
Total	21.0	22.8	29.4	23.3	35.7	42.4
OECD	14.0	15.4	19.9	15.3	23.6	29.1
EU	9.2	10.0	12.9	10.9	16.8	22.3
EFTA	1.2	1.4	1.6	0.6	0.9	1.2
Other OECD	3.6	3.9	5.7	3.8	5.8	5.6
Other Europe	2.0	0.9	3.4	2.5	4.5	3.9
Other Countries	4.9	6.4	6.1	5.3	7.5	9.3
Share of EU (%)	43.8	43.9	44.0	46.9	47.2	52.5

Source: Sadi Uzunoğlu, Zeitschrift für Türkeistudien, 2/97

The State Institute of Statistics and Foreign Trade Office figures show that Turkey's imports reached $46.6 billion in 1997. The same-year increase in imports from the EU was 5.9% and from the United States, 22%.

The EU's share in Turkish imports is 52.8%. With the customs union agreement in 1996 the trade balance has moved further toward the EU's benefit. The trade deficit with the EU moved from its 1995 level of $5.8 billion to $11 billion in 1996. Therefore, the imports coverage by exports fell within a year from 65.7% to 51.4%. In the first half of 1970 this figure was more than 70%. Yet in total trade volume the EU's share has declined to 47.6%. Another point of interest is that while Turkey's overall exports went up by 6.6% in 1996, exports to the EU increased only by 3.6%. The reverse is true for Turkey's imports from the EU: While overall imports went up

---

[84] TUSIAD EU Office Documentation, 1998.

by 18.9%, imports from the EU increased by 32.4%. In 1997 imports from and exports to the EU increased by the same proportion. The great gap in favour of the EU, however, still persists. Trade deficits can prove to be a major problem, not only for Turkey but also for economically well-developed countries. The US trade deficit just for the month of August 1998 was $16.8 billion. The estimated figure for the whole of 1998 is around $165 billion.[85]

The freedom of movement for goods and services in the EU is the main reason why trade among EU members has gone up so quickly. This also accounts for the rapid development experienced by member countries. Various subsidies also helped boost the EU's share of world trade to 37.4%, followed by the United States with 13.5% and Japan with 7.1%. Among EU members, Germany has the largest share, with 9%, followed by France with 5.3% and the United Kingdom with 5.1%. Turkey's portion of world trade was 0.15% in the 1980s. In 1996 this went up to 0.44%, i.e. it tripled. EU member Greece's share is 0.3%. With 1.8% Turkey ranks 11th in the EU's imports, and at 2.8% she ranks eighth in its exports.[86]

The 1963 Association Agreement and the 1971 Additional Protocol gave some advantages to Turkey. In particular, Turkish industrial goods were allowed entry to EU markets without paying import duties. Yet probably when the EU realized Turkey's competitive strength in sectors such as textiles, they immediately imposed restrictions and protectionist measures against imports from Turkey. Article 60 of the agreement allows parties to take some measures so as to protect their own industries. The EU wanted in particular to restrict textile imports from Turkey. In the face of Turkey's objections the EU settled the matter in the 1980s with the private sector and imposed quotas. This situation lasted until

---

[85] IHT 21.10.1998.
[86] TUSIAD EU Office Documentation, 1998.

the implementation of the customs union in 1996. Restrictions were also imposed on some other items, and anti-dumping rules were exercised relentlessly against Turkey. Unofficial commercial restrictions were also resorted to.

Even more restrictions were imposed in the agricultural sector. During the customs union discussions agricultural products, services and social benefits were left out of the agreement, due to the objections of a few countries and despite Turkish protests.

While EU members benefited from the advantages of a single market, Turkey was pushed for a long time to wage an uphill battle in her commercial relations with the EU.

As stated above, the customs union agreement increased the trade deficit with the EU by another $5 billion, i.e. there has been the transfer of a sum of this magnitude from Turkey to the EU. While the agreement called for financial assistance to compensate to a certain extent for this deficit, internal problems within the EU, in particular the objections of one member and rejections by the European Parliament, prevented this from actualizing, and Turkey had to make up for this trade deficit by relying solely on her own resources. Following the customs union agreement Turkey was unable to increase her exports to the EU as much as expected. That most of Turkey's imports from the EU are investment goods such as machinery suggests that increases in exports in coming years may be seen.

In 1996, after she started to implement the customs union agreement, Turkey's exports to non-EU member countries increased by more than her exports to the EU. The situation deserves further investigation, when one considers that in 1996 textile quotas were eliminated for the first time. Only the next few years' results will enable a final verdict to be reached on the benefits or losses of the customs union with the EU for Turkey.

The above information concerns only trade in goods. When goods and services are taken under one heading, however, it can be seen that Turkey has a more significant place in world trade vis-a-vis a comparison based on trade in goods alone. The table below gives 1995 figures for the service sectors in Turkey.

Turkey's Services Trade in 1995

Sector	Exports ($ million)	Imports ($ million)
Freight	1,712	1,412
Travel	*4,957	**911
Construction	1,863	4
Insurance	20	42
Financial Services	201	350
Other Services to Firms	3,440	557
Personal, Cultural and Entertainment Services	2,282	1,378
Total	14,475	4,654

Source: IMF Balance of Payments
*Tourism income
** Tourism expenditures

In 1995, 60.3% of Turkey's $36 billion in goods and services exports were goods and 39.7% were services. The same year Turkish imports totalled $40 billion, of which 88.3% comprised goods and only 11.3% was services. Turkey ranks third in the share of services in exports, at double the world average of 19.7%. Shipping occupies an important place in commercial services. Turkey has improved her shipping sector in recent years and now handles 40% of all cargo with her own ships. The target now is to increase this proportion.

The share of services in Turkey's imports is half the world's average.[87]

When Turkey entered into a customs union with the EU in 1996, exports of goods and services to the entire world

---

[87] Organisation Mondiale du Commerce, Rapport Annuel, 1997, vol. 2, p. 6.

increased by 21.7%. Increase in imports was 29.6%. These numbers for a single year can be considered exceptions. Yet from a broader perspective the increase in Turkey's international trade in goods and services has been above the world average. For the 1992-1996 period Turkey's exports of goods and services went up by an average of 12.7% per year, while imports of goods and services increased by an average of 14.7% per year. These are OECD figures and are based on State Institute of Statistics data.[88]

As stated above the difficulties that were to arise due to the customs union with the EU were anticipated prior to the signing of the agreement. In particular, it was a well-known fact that in the short run the trade balance would shift in favour of the EU. However the customs union was seen as a stepping-stone for full EU membership. Leaving aside its political implications, the EU's Luxembourg Summit in 1997 caused great damage to the Turkish economy as well as creating unfair competition between Turkey and other candidate countries by putting their applications ahead of Turkey's. Although it may be argued that relative to the Central and Eastern European countries Turkey gained some commercial privileges vis-a-vis the EU, in reality the trend is just the opposite. It is clear that with the privileges to be granted to these countries in the near future, whatever relative advantages Turkey might have due to the customs union will soon disappear. The "pre-accession strategy" implemented uniquely for these countries not only created special financial support and lines of credit for them but also strengthened their competitive power in EU markets.

Customs union with the EU affected not only Turkey's trade with the EU, but by imposing EU tax rates in her trade with the rest of the world Turkey also lost income from custom duties on imports from other countries. The cost to the Turkish Treasury is estimated to be $2.5 billion. Only the

---

[88] OECD Statistical Yearbook of Turkey, Paris, 1997.

trade dimension of the question was touched upon here, but the subject of the EU will be revisited in later chapters.

Parallel to the developments in external trade summarized above, the share of international trade in national income has also gone up.

Between 1980 and 1990 Turkey's exports increased by an average of 16.1% per year, and imports have gone up by 10.9% annually. Within the same period the share of external trade in the GNP reached 19% from its level of 10%.[89]

Turkey has become the most important commercial power in the Mediterranean, after some EU countries, in fact more important than EU members Portugal and Greece. The following table shows to what extent international trade has grown in various countries.

Growth of Foreign Trade in Selected Countries

Country	1974		1996		
	Exports	Imports	Exports	Imports	Total Increase (%)
Turkey	1.5	3.8	23.1	42.4	1.128
Spain	7.1	15.4	102.0	121.0	891
Italy	30.5	41.1	250.8	206.9	539
UK	38.2	54.2	259.9	287.0	467
France	46.5	52.9	289.8	247.8	468
Germany	89.4	69.7	521.0	456.3	514
USA	99.4	110.9	624.8	817.9	586
Japan	55.5	61.9	410.9	349.1	547
S. Korea	4.5	6.9	129.8	150.2	2,356
Brazil	7.9	14.2	47.8	56.9	373

*Import and Export figure: L'Etat du Monde 1998

[89] The Implementation of the Customs Union in Turkey and its Macroeconomic Effects, Sadi Uzunoğlu, Zeitschrift für Türkeistudien, Essen, 1997, Heft 2, p. 1998.

The above table gives a good picture of the rapid development in international trade. In the last 20 years mid-sized economies as well as the industrialized countries have improved their international commercial activities. Among the countries listed above South Korea, has had the most rapid expansion in foreign trade. Turkey is next. With the exception of South Korea, none of the countries with GNPs larger than Turkey have shown a more rapid increase in international trade than Turkey. The difference between the industrialized countries and Turkey is fast disappearing. While in 1974 Italy's foreign trade was 13.5 times that of Turkey, in 1996 it dropped to 7.9 times. During the same period while Germany's foreign trade was 30 times larger than Turkey's, this came down to 17 times in 1996; the difference between the United States and Turkey decreased from 40 to 25 times, with Japan going from 22 to 13 times. So in proportional terms Turkey is catching up.

The only exception to this is again South Korea. While that country's foreign trade was twice Turkey's in 1974, the difference quadrupled in 1996. The enormous economic and financial problems faced by South Korea today show that its rapid economic development has not been without its associated costs. For the 1970-1979 period Turkey lagged behind the OECD average increase in exports, but later her performance became higher than the OECD average. In particular, each year after 1992 her exports increased at a faster rate than the OECD average. In some years after 1981 Turkish exports jumped by as much as 63.5%. For five years within this time frame Turkey ranked first in the OECD for increase in exports.

OECD statistics show that from 1986-1995 Turkey's exports of foodstuffs doubled, while exports of machinery and vehicles expanded six-fold. While in 1985 Turkey had exported $415 million worth of machinery and vehicles, in 1995 this rose to $2.4 billion. In imports, too, machinery and vehicles constitute a large portion and increased to $11.5 billion in 1995 from its level of $4 billion in 1985.

In order for these numbers to be more meaningful Turkey must create more capacity in those products with an export potential as well as in products that add value to the country's economy. At the same time adding variety to export items would also contribute to Turkey's competitive strength. Concentrating on a few goods only will leave Turkey exposed to the risk of exports dropping when the demand for such products goes down.

Turkey's domestic trade also has improved significantly. She comes first in Europe in retail sales increase. The average yearly increase for the 1990-1994 period in Turkey was 5.84%. The increase in Poland, which comes second after Turkey, was half as much, and there are smaller growth rates in seven EU countries.

Recently Central and Eastern European countries, equipped with investments that are heavily subsidized and supported with financial aid, have been entering the EU market as Turkey's competitors. EU firms that employ the cheap labour in these countries are using this advantage and improving their competitiveness relative to the Turkish firms in EU markets. Compared with 1989, in 1995 Poland increased its exports to the EU by 162.6%, Hungary by 127.6% and the Czech Republic by 273.5%. Most of the goods exported by these countries are competing against Turkish exports by benefiting from EU subsidies. Despite this Turkey's rate of growth in international trade has been larger than the Central and Eastern European countries.

The Davos competitiveness list of 1997 puts Turkey in 32nd place, leaving behind some EU countries as well as all candidates for EU membership. It can be seen that Turkey is able to balance her trade even with extremely competitive countries like Germany, with which she even had a surplus in 1991 and 1994. Of course Turkish workers and businessmen living in Germany played a role in achieving these results.

Turkey's success in foreign trade does not stem only from her cheap labour, as it may seem at first glance. Turkey's competitors in textiles, which are considered to be the locomotive of Turkish exports, have cheaper labour costs. Despite increased wages in this sector Turkey has preserved, and even improved, her competitiveness. While the hourly wage of a textile worker in Turkey was $2.31 in 1992, in China it was $0.24. Despite this difference Turkey is able to compete with China in EU markets. According to 1995 figures Turkey supplied 10.3% of the EU's textile and garment imports. China, India and Hong Kong follow Turkey in that order.[90]

A look at the distribution of Turkey's exports to different sectors gives the following results:

• Textile and garments are Turkey's prime exports. In the January-December 1997 period Turkish exports in this sector reached $10.2 billion, $7.3 billion of which was in garments and $2.9 billion in textiles. This sector accounted for 37.6% of Turkish exports.

• Turkey's garment industry has a 3.9% share worldwide, putting her in fifth place. If it is remembered that her portion of this sector was 0.3% back in 1980, her development in this area can be better appreciated.

• While Turkey exported 6,846 cars in 1993, this went up to 33,224 in 1995. In the same year total exports of transport vehicles topped 37,296.

• Those industries that supply parts to the automotive sector have also developed, with exports of $323 million in 1992. This number more than doubled in 1994, growing to $705 million. From January to October of 1996 total exports from the Turkish automotive industry together with exports of

---

[90] Astrid-Marina Lohrman, Der Textil-und Bekleidungssektor in der Türkei und die Auswirkungen der Zollunion mit der Europaeischen Union, Zeitschrift für Türkeistudien, 2/97, p. 211.

factories that supply parts to this sector reached more than $1 billion.[91]

• In 1980 Turkey exported $34 million worth of iron and steel. By 1995 this had become $2.2 billion. Iron and steel's portion of total exports is 10.4%, putting it in second place after textiles.

• Turkish chemical product exports were $1.28 billion in 1995. Turkey exports 20% of her chemical industry production.

• Turkey exported $331 million worth of machinery in 1992; this went up to $691 million in 1995. More industrialized countries are the primary customers for Turkish machinery, with 23.4% going to Germany, thus demonstrating the technological level attained by Turkey.

• Electronics industry exports totalled $662 million in 1992; by 1995 they had increased to $994 million. For example, exports of colour TV sets grew by 32% to $202 million. A parallel development was seen in the telecommunications sector, whose exports had reached $365 million by 1995.

While analyzing such positive and promising developments, the Turkish economy's problems must not be trivialized. Like any other country Turkey also has economic as well as social difficulties. These problems should be scrutinized by looking at whether or not other countries also have similar problems and if so, the weight of these problems and whether countries considered more developed than Turkey had to grapple with similar situations.

---

[91] Executive's Handbook, p. 74.

Problems and Expectations

The purpose of this study is not to generate solutions to problems faced by Turkey, but rather to investigate the external dimensions of some of these problems and ascertain whether or not other countries have ever found themselves in similar circumstances.

Among the most important of Turkey's economic difficulties are high inflation rates, inequitable distribution of wealth, budget deficits and internal as well as external debt burden. Inflation being foremost, Turkey fares much worse than the OECD and EU averages in economic criteria such as interest rates, devaluation, trade deficit and current account deficits.

Inflation

High inflation is the foremost economic problem facing Turkey. Since 1980, the rate of inflation has once exceeded 100% and was very close to that on several other occasions. The OECD average was 1.9% in 1995 and 2.1% in 1996. However, while taking a look at inflation rates in various countries and comparing them to one another, some facts must be kept in mind. First of all, inflation rates vary with time. For example, in the past 25 years there were times when inflation in Turkey was less than 5%. In the early 1960s the rate of inflation in Turkey was fairly low. In the 1960-1964 period the yearly average was 3.5%, less than the OECD average for the same period. In later years it went up a little: Between 1965 and 1969 the average annual inflation rate in Turkey was 7.4%, which was somewhat higher than the OECD average.

The real jump comes in the mid-1970s, when Turkey initiated extensive investment in her infrastructure and accepted the risk of increased inflation that comes with increased expenditures. Therefore, it can be said that giving priority to rapid economic development has been one of the underlying reasons behind increased inflation.

Could high-level economic development have been achieved while keeping inflation under control at the same time? Some countries have managed to do so. They did it as long as they could find financing at attractive rates and keep other economic balances in check. On the other hand, there were also countries like China that started to adopt a liberal economic system without really fully implementing its rules. Yet in Turkey, where democratic as well as liberal policies are in force, it is no easy task to keep the rate of inflation low, particularly when it has been extremely difficult to obtain financing to realize the necessary investment for the country. Many other countries that had set out with the same objective also experienced high inflation: Mexico, Argentina and Brazil during the 1980s and early 1990s, and Far Eastern countries like South Korea and Indonesia in 1998.

It is not possible to defend inflationary policies for any country. The social problems caused by inflation are well known. Its adverse effects on the distribution of income are also obvious. Was it really necessary for the Turkish people to go thorough all the sacrifices they did, in particular after the 1980s, in order to have Turkey attain its current level of development, which made Turkey's economy comparable to those of the advanced nations in the world? Specialists in the field will ponder questions like these for years to come. Naturally, it would be better if such analysis were to be done keeping in mind the amount of aid supplied by developed countries as well as international institutions to countries that are in situations similar to Turkey.

In EU countries an inflation rate of 3% is reason enough to sound the alarm. But it must not be forgotten that not so long ago these countries also had high inflation. In 1975 the rate of inflation in the United Kingdom had gone up to 24.2% and was brought down to 18% only after five years had elapsed.[92]

During the same period France also faced a similar situation. The rate of inflation, which was 11.8% in 1975, had gone up to 13.3% in 1980. In Italy conditions were even worse; its inflation rate was 17.1% in 1975 and in 1980, 21%. There have been similar situations in the United States as well, where inflation soared to 13.5% in 1980. In earlier days, during the economic crisis that came after the end of World War I, inflation rates in Western European countries were at mind-boggling levels.[93]

We can also give examples from other parts of the world. According to IMF figures, the average rate of inflation in developing countries was 62.5% in 1990. The Latin American average was even higher; in 1985 it was 127.5% and in 1990, 438.6%. But thanks to corrective measures taken, inflation had gone down to 19.5% by 1996.

It is worth remembering that in some of the Eastern European countries that have been accepted as candidates for EU membership, inflation rates were around 300% and even higher only a few years ago. Later, due to anti-inflationary policies as well as the foreign aid they have received, this rate of inflation was brought down to reasonable levels.

Latin American and East European countries have been successful in combating inflation, but the same cannot be said for some of the Far Eastern countries that have had high growth rates with low inflation. Indonesia, for example, right after its latest economic crisis, had an inflation rate of 32% for April 1998 alone. In South Korea, the January 1998 consumer price index had gone up by 8.3%, and in February the increase was 9.5%. Wholesale prices jumped by 17.7% for the same month.[94]

---

[92] l'Etat du Monde, Paris, 1998, p. 213.

[93] Ramses, 1997, op. cit., p. 161.

[94] IHT, March 3, 1998.

The goal here is not to down play the importance of the high inflation rates in Turkey by bringing to mind the problems faced by other countries. There is no one in Turkey who supports growth through inflation. Everyone is fully aware of the harm done by inflation to the economy as well as to the social order of the country. Yet it would not be correct to judge the economic condition or strength of a country by only looking at its rate of inflation.

Just like the unemployment rate, the inflation rate shows variations at different times. Trying to decrease the rate too rapidly may lead to a shrinking of the economy, resulting in unemployment and its associated social costs. Advice given by some foreign experts to quickly decrease inflation and rearrange macroeconomic balances in line with Western norms may fail to take into account social balances unique to a country, thereby leading to social unrest.

The basic causes of high inflation rates should be analyzed in detail. Here, public deficits are often singled out as the prime reason. However one must ponder on the economic, social and even political reasons leading to public deficits. To give an example, the GAP (Southeastern Anatolia Project) will contribute to Turkey's economic development as well as help remove regional differences. It is one of the largest regional projects in the world and has been financed from the government's budget, which leads to the conclusion that it also has been one of the important factors giving rise to public deficits. Yet one must think why a project of this magnitude was financed or had to be financed from budgetary sources instead of long-term financing with attractive interest rates. Couldn't this project, costing $32 billion, have been financed with international funds as similar projects in other countries have been?

The oil crisis of the mid-1970s, resulting in high inflation rates in most countries including Turkey, and the effects of this inflation on these countries should also be researched. Likewise, adverse developments in Turkey's debt structure and borrowing rates and their effects on inflation should be considered. Is tying the high inflation rates only to high public expenditures and budget deficits the most accurate way of researching the underlying causes of inflation in Turkey? The answers to some of these questions are discussed below. In particular, it can be seen that relative to other European countries, Turkey is not in bad shape and even fares better than some regarding public expenditures and budget deficits.

Defence expenditures also put inflationary pressures on the economy, but for a strategically located country like Turkey such expenditures are inescapable. Turkey, a latecomer to the economic development race, cannot refrain from making infrastructure investments, especially in the fields of education and health, when it still has a relatively high population growth rate, despite positive signs that this rate is declining. It should also be kept in mind that Turkey first decreased then abolished altogether the import taxes on EU goods and started imposing EU rates for imports from third countries, resulting in lost revenues of $2.5 billion per year. Naturally, these also contributed to the high inflation rates currently being experienced. Finally, the EU's failure to fulfil its financial obligations since 1981 and the significant decline in US economic and, in particular, defence aid strained the budget further and exacerbated the problem. Among the causes of inflation are also psychological factors, rapid increase in demand and the expectation of speculative gains; yet it can hardly be said that these played a determinative role on their own in the high inflation rates experienced in Turkey.

In summary, it would not be justified to see the high inflation rates in Turkey as stemming only from internal sources. External as well as internal reasons behind this problem must be looked into.

Unemployment

While inflation tops the list of economic problems in Turkey, it is unemployment that has been the most important, difficult and urgent economic problem in Europe. Today, some European countries are experiencing their highest rates of unemployment since World War II. The average unemployment rate among the 11 countries that adopted the euro was 11.1% in 1998.[95]

The unemployment rate in Germany is about 12%, with 5 million people unemployed. The levels in France, Italy and Spain are also close or even higher than this figure. Spain's rate of unemployment is about 20%. This rate is even higher among foreigners living in these countries. Unemployment not only has a high cost to the economy but also results in serious social problems. In this respect Turkey is in a better position than the EU average.

OECD figures show the unemployment rate in Turkey as less than 6%. Its latest numbers give the proportion of unemployed in the working population as 5.5%. According to the same statistics, this figure for 1998 was 12.3% in Belgium, 12% in France, 11.5% in Germany, 12% in Italy, 9.8% in Greece and 19.5% in Spain.

Unemployment rates in other Western countries are not as high as Western Europe's. In the United States, for example, it is at its lowest level in 30 years, around 5% in early 1998. Japan's unemployment rate is extremely low as well. Obviously unemployment is not a problem engulfing Western economies all at the same time. The level of unemployment experienced by a country depends on the economic and social policies it pursues.

---

[95] The Economist, 31 October 1998.

Unemployment Rates in Turkey and
Some OECDCountries

Country	1985	1990	1995	1996	1997
Spain	21.5	16.3	23.2	22.7	22.1
Belgium	12.4	8.8	13.1	12.9	12.7
France	10.2	8.9	11.5	12.4	12.6
Italy	8.6	9.1	12.0	12.1	12.1
Germany	8.0	6.2	9.4	10.3	11.1
Turkey	7.1	8.0	7.5	6.5	6.6
UK	11.0	5.8	8.1	7.4	6.1
USA	7.2	5.6	5.6	5.4	5.0
OECD Average	7.6	5.9	7.6	7.5	7.3
EU Average	10.2	7.9	11.2	11.3	11.2

Source: La Turquie en Mouvement
OECD Economic Outlook, June 1997

The above table shows the levels of unemployment in some Western and EU countries in which it is considered to be the most important economic and social problem. Countries other than Germany also have worrisome unemployment levels. Spain, for example, has three times more unemployed than Turkey has. The OECD's forecast for Turkey for 1998 is 6.5%, while the EU's rate is expected to be 10.8%.

Except for the Czech Republic, the EU candidates also have high unemployment rates.

That Turkey, which not only has more people than all the EU countries save Germany but which also continues to experience population growth, had relatively low levels of unemployment over a long period of time should be carefully studied.

Having said this, it is possible to make more flexible evaluations regarding this issue when one considers things such as seasonal unemployment as in the agricultural sector, or unregistered unemployment. In scientific research on this matter the variations among the methodologies used by different countries in calculating their unemployment rates should also be taken into consideration. However, as in other fields, taking the OECD's comparative tables as the basis for such analysis seems to be the best way to determine Turkey's place in the world as far as unemployment is concerned.

Public Spending

When Turkey's problems, especially the causes of inflation, are analyzed, high public spending is one of the areas that people focus on the most.

Actually this issue is one of the most debated issues everywhere. The amount of public spending and whether or not this spending is appropriate is followed closely by the public. In Turkey, laws and rules regulate public spending. The most important of these is the budget, which has to be approved by Parliament. This legislative body also has the responsibility for political oversight of the government. Yet in the final analysis, it is the duty of those in government to determine the priorities of this spending.

That aspect of the issue will not be gone into in this study, and the analysis will be confined to a comparison of the size of public spending in Turkey vis-a-vis other countries and the ratio of this spending to GDP.

As of 1993, public spending in Turkey was TL 258 trillion, whereas private spending totaled TL 1,369 trillion. That is to say, public spending is less than one-fifth of private spending.

In the same year Swedish public spending was half as much as private spending. The ratios in other Scandinavian countries were also similar to that of Sweden. In France, the ratio of public to private spending is a little less than one-third, still much higher than that of Turkey. The ratios in Germany, the United Kingdom and Italy are close to that of France. Spain is also not far off. All of these and most other European countries have higher public spending ratios than Turkey.

However, an even more interesting result presents itself when the ratio of public spending to GDP in various countries is looked at.

GNP-Public Expenditures Proportion in Turkey and Some Western Countries

Country	Share of public spending in GDP (%)
Denmark	25.1
UK	21.4
Germany	19.5
France	19.3
Italy	16.3
USA	16.2
Belgium	14.8
Turkey	10.8
Japan	9.7

Source: Etudes Economiques de l'OCDE, Turquie 1997

In none of the EU countries is public spending a smaller proportion of GDP than in Turkey. In the OECD there are only three countries in this position: Japan at 9.7%, Mexico at 10.6% and South Korea at 10.4%; however, these figures are fairly close to that of Turkey at 10.8%.

The table above shows public expenditures only on goods and services. But there are public expenditures on items such as salaries, transfer payments, subsidies, interest payments and capital expenditures. Therefore, total public expenditures are much higher than those indicated in the table. As an example, public expenditures in France had reached 54.1% of GDP in 1997. Germany's public expenditure was close to that rate also: 47.7%. In some Scandinavian countries this rate reached and even exceeded 70%.[96]

---

[96] The Economist, 3 October 1998.

Looking at this table, it is not possible to claim that relative to the size of her economy public expenditure in Turkey is higher than it should be.

Another topic widely discussed in Turkey is the public deficit, better known as the budget deficit. It is a widely held view that the budget deficit is what is driving inflation and other economic problems in Turkey. As a general rule it is not possible to argue against this. That there is a serious budget deficit in Turkey is a fact. But how about budget deficits in other places, especially in other Western countries?

The answer to this question is given below for the year 1995, in dollars and as a percentage of budget deficits to budget revenues:

Budget Deficits in Turkey and Some Western Countries (1995) ($ billion)

Country	Revenues	Expenditures	Deficit	Deficit/ Revenue(%)
Japan	595.0	829.0	234.0	39.3
Sweden	109.0	146.1	36.7	33.5
Italy	339.0	431.0	92.0	27.1
Spain	96.8	122.5	25.7	26.5
Austria	65.0	75.8	10.8	16.6
USA	1,258.0	1,461.0	203.0	16.1
UK	388.9	447.6	58.7	15.0
Turkey	30.2	35.0	4.8	15.0
Germany	690.0	780.0	90.0	13.0
France	220.5	249.1	28.6	12.9

Source: OECD Economic Outlook, June 1997

The table above compares Turkey's budget deficit, in absolute and proportional terms, with those of the most powerful economies in the world as well as countries like Spain and Sweden that have a higher per capita GDP. In proportional terms, the Turkish budget deficit is smaller than most of those of Western countries. In countries like Italy,

Sweden and Spain the proportion of the deficit is almost double or even higher than in Turkey or even more. Japan's deficit is larger than all others.

Budget deficits are among the most serious economic problems faced by many countries, including Turkey; therefore, this problem should not be seen as unique to Turkey. All countries aim to lower their budget deficits. Yet considering their social and economic goals as well as social responsibilities, most Western nations choose to tolerate a certain amount of deficit. The Maastricht criteria regulate the monetary union in the EU and set limits on the amount of debt and budget deficit a member country may have. Therefore, a common goal of the EU members now is to comply with those criteria, lower their deficits and discipline their economies. However most of the EU countries, despite the fact that they have been members of this organization and enjoyed its benefits, have had to live with budget deficits for a long time.

When comparing budget deficits to GDP a similar situation is encountered. As an example, in 1996 the Italian deficit had reached 6.7% of GDP. In 1994 it was even worse at 9.6%.

The situation in France was slightly better than Italy. In 1994 her deficit was 5.6% of GDP, and a year later, 4.2%. In Germany, it was 5.6% in 1995 and 5.8% in 1996. In Turkey this figure was 5.5% in 1995. During the same year the consolidated budget deficit was 4.1%. The OECD predicts that these numbers will increase.[97] However even if Turkey's deficit reaches 9% as the OECD predicts, this would still be smaller than the Italian percentage in 1994.

So, neither in the ratio of budget deficits to public revenue nor in the ratio of budget deficits to GDP does Turkey exhibit a worse situation than other Western countries in the last few years. Having said this, in order to do a comprehensive and scientific comparison, one must study the structure of the budgets of these countries. Whatever the results of such comparisons, however, Turkey, like any other country, must

---

[97] OECD Economic Outlook, June 1997.

expend more effort to decrease her budget deficit. It would be fruitful to analyze the causes of these deficits when looking at the numbers. Without any question, the basic reason is an insufficiency of tax revenues. In 1998 a law was enacted by the Turkish Parliament that would reform the tax system of the country and raise the tax rates to the level of Western European countries. But this law was revisited in 1999 and some adjustments were made to alleviate the financial burden on companies and to encourage investment. The tax system, which is Turkey's greatest drawback with regards to public finance entering the new millennium, is expected to have a more contemporary structure.

If this can be done, then Turkey will be able to make more public funding available for things such as health and education, making up for her current deficiencies. This is one of Turkey's most important targets. Three percent of her GDP today is spent on health and 2.7% on education. The total money spent on education and health is little more than the money put aside by the government to repay the public debt and interest. Whereas, if a further 1% of the GDP could be spent on health and education, then the life expectancy of Turkish citizens would go up by a year, and child deaths would go down by 24 points.[98] Therefore, no one can argue that Turkey does not have a budget deficit problem. To the contrary, there are many problems to be solved, and to accomplish this, reforms are needed. What needs to be stressed here, however, is the fact that public deficits are a problem all around the world and that the deficit ratios in some developed countries are worse than Turkey's.

---

[98] OECD, Turquie, 1997.

Unregistered Economy

When evaluating the numbers of the Turkish economy, one should not ignore the existence of an unregistered economy, which according to the OECD is estimated to be around 30-50% of the overall economy.[99] Other countries also have unregistered economies, yet the ratio in Turkey is among the highest. The effect of this fact on tax revenues and the economy in general is obvious.

The following table gives the percentages of unregistered economy to GDP in EU countries and Turkey.

Unregistered Economy Rate in Turkey and Selected Countries

Country	Unregistered Economy/ GDP (%)
Turkey*	30-50
Greece	29-35
Italy	20-26
Spain	10-23
Belgium	12-21
Netherlands	5-14
Germany	4-14
France	4-14
UK	7-13
Ireland	5-10
Austria	4-7
Sweden	4-7
Denmark	3-7
Finland	2-4
Portugal	No data
Luxembourg	No data
EU Average	7-16

Source: Target, ITKIB, May 1998, p. 44 (EU Commission Declaration)

---

[99] OCDE, Turquie 1997.

The table above shows that the existence of an unregistered economy is not unique to Turkey. Even in countries where economic discipline is at its highest levels, the entire economy cannot be registered. The unregistered economy in Turkey is larger than any other in Europe. The drawbacks of this situation are clear. The fact that there is such a large unregistered economy shows the need for better rules and regulations. This is one of the goals of the 1998 tax reform. Although some parts of this tax reform bill were later modified, the main goals remain the same. When the true size of various economies, i.e. including the size of the unregistered economy, are compared, Turkey's relative standing would appear to be better off as compared to rankings done based on official statistics. Another result of this study is the fact that if Turkey is able to pull down the level of her unregistered economy to the EU average, then her statistical GDP will increase by 23-34%. Per capita income would then have to be adjusted by this amount as well. This would also result in increased tax revenue.

If the lower OECD estimate of 30% of GDP is taken for the Turkish unregistered economy, then using the ppp method her real GDP should be around $530 billion. If the higher estimate of 50% were used, then this would amount to $612 billion. This is around the Spanish GDP of $557 billion; however, one would of course have to add the amount of the Spanish unregistered economy to this figure. If the same calculation were made for per capita GDP, then using the lower-end estimate it would amount to $8,295 while the upper-end figure would result in a real per capita income in Turkey of $10,071.

These numbers confirm those presented by the then head of the State Institute of Statistics, Professor Orhan Güvenen, at a speech he gave at the European Conference in Brussels October 30-31, 1991. There, Professor Güvenen stated that using ppp, per capita GDP in Turkey was estimated to be

$6,816 in 1990.[100] Taking this number as the base, it becomes clear that the upper estimate of the OECD would more accurately reflect the size of the Turkish economy in 1997.

Another aspect of the unregistered economy is unregistered exports. As mentioned in the foreign trade section above, a new form of export has evolved under the name of the "suitcase trade," which is not reflected in any official figures. Although it has decreased to a certain extent in recent years, such exports were estimated in the mid-1990s to be around $8-10 billion per year. This is one of the reasons why there have been unexpected increases in Turkey's foreign currency reserves.

Internal and External Debt

One of the most hotly debated issues regarding Turkey's economy is the size of her internal and external debt. There is no doubt that this is a real problem. More than half of the budget is spent on debt repayment. Lowering the amount of debt and improving its terms have always been among Turkey's chief economic targets; however, there are other countries with similar problems as well. Internal and external borrowing is a source of financing widely used by Western countries; however not only Western nations but also the whole world borrows in order to finance development. It would be very difficult to find a country with no debt. What is important is the amount of this debt and its size relative to the country's GDP as well as its terms and duration, whether or not it has been used in productive sectors and to what extent it has managed to add value to the economy.

Since the early days of the Republic, external debt has been high on the agenda of the country. After managing to remove the capitulations in Lausanne, the young Turkish Republic was faced with the Ottomans' huge debts. She paid these all despite

---

[100] Turkey and the European Community, Brussels, 1991.

the economic as well as financial difficulties of the time.
Therefore, Turkey, as a country that knows very well the
political costs of external debt, and having been closely
acquainted with them since the last century, has had adequate
experience with global financial circles. Since the 1950s,
however, it has been clearly understood that rapid
development can take place only through using external
sources together with internal savings. Therefore, in particular
in financing her investments, Turkey has had to resort to
external borrowing. In the 1980s there was a significant
increase in Turkey's external debt. While in 1975 the total
amount of external debt was $5 billion, in 1985 it grew to $26
billion, in 1991 $50 billion, in 1996 $79 billion and in 1997
$84.5 billion.

Overview of Turkish Foreign Debt ($ billion)

	1988	1990	1992	1993	1994	1995
Total	40.7	49.0	54.7	67.3	65.6	73.2
Medium/ long- term debt	34.3	39.5	42.0	48.8	54.2	57.5
Short-term debt	6.4	9.5	12.7	18.5	11.3	15.7
Creditors Public	32.8	37.7	39.0	42.8	48.1	49.9
Private	1.5	1.8	2.8	6.0	6.1	7.6
Payback Amortization	4.4	4.0	4.9	4.4	6.0	7.5
Interest	2.8	3.3	3.2	3.5	3.9	4.3
Payback/GDP	10.1	6.6	7.2	4.6	7.6	7.0
Payback/total foreign currency revenues	35.6	27.4	27.5	25.2	30.1	28.0
Short-term debt/ total debt	15.8	19.4	22.8	27.5	17.2	21.4

Source: Yakup Kepenek, Nurhan Yentürk, Türkiye Ekonomisi, Istanbul,
1996

The table above shows that has there been an increase not only in external debt but also in the ratio of short-term debt to the overall debt structure. Within a five-year period of time the share of short-term debt went up from 15.8% to 27.5%. There were ups and downs in later years as well, when Turkey made yearly payments of $7-11 billion, principal plus interest, against her debt. However, due to an increased GDP the proportion of these payments in the country's GDP dropped from 10.1% to 4.6%, after which it went up again slightly.

In later years Turkey's overall foreign debt rapidly increased, and in 1998 it reached $95 billion. In the 1991-1996 period short-term debt went up from $9 billion to $20 billion. Here, there is a point that deserves more attention: The public sector share of medium- to long-term debt has declined. While in 1991 it was 54.3%, in 1996 it went down to 44.2%. In the same period, the KITs' share which had been 10.3%, went down to 5.7%. The Central Bank's share increased by only 1%, from 12.9% to 13.9%. The real increase has been with the private sector; its portion went up from 4.5% in 1991 to 11.5% in 1996. It seems that it is the private sector that is driving the need for external financing.

The exorbitant amount of short-term debt and its high interest rates made repayment an enormous burden on the government budget. Almost one-third of all foreign currency earnings, 28% to be exact, is spent on paying back external debt. This is one of the underlying reasons behind economic bottlenecks experienced from time to time. When Turkey's position is compared with that of other countries, the situation becomes even clearer.

Comparative Data on Foreign Debt of Turkey and Selected Countries (1995)

Country	External Debt ($ billion)	External Dept/GDP (%)
Indonesia	107.8	47.7
Mexico	165.7	52.3
Brazil	159.1	20.0
Russia	120.5	36.3
China	118.1	15.8
South Korea	93.7	19.0
Argentina	89.7	30.4
Turkey	73.8	39.2

Source: L'Etat du Monde 1998

The table above gives the figures for Turkey together with some countries having high external debt. In absolute numbers, Turkey's debt seems to be smaller than the rest. Yet when we look at the ratios of external debt to GDP at current prices we see a different picture. Countries such as South Korea and Brazil seem to be doing better than Turkey. Indonesia and Mexico have higher external debt to GDP ratios.

The international media reported the total foreign debt of South Korea, Thailand, Malaysia and Indonesia after the last economic crisis as $400 billion.

Most of the figures given in the table are from 1995. However, there have been rapid developments since then, changing these numbers. Turkey's external debt increased to $90 billion. The debt of some of the other countries listed in the table also increased.

Far Eastern countries such as South Korea, which stood in a better position than Turkey in the table, suffered a financial crisis due to problems with their banks and had to borrow heavily once again. It became evident that some large investment projects did not have sound financial sources.

Governments and banks were unable to pay back their debts. The IMF organized a $60 billion aid program. Inflation in these countries increased rapidly, and their currencies depreciated sharply. Despite the efforts of international aid agencies the problems are not yet fully resolved.

Most of the numbers given in the table are from 1995. However, there have been rapid developments since then, changing these figures and ratios. Turkey's external debt increased to $90 billion, and the debts of some of the other countries listed in the table increased as well.

Far Eastern countries such as South Korea, which was in a better position than Turkey in the table above, experienced financial crisis due to problems with their banks. They had to borrow heavily again. It became clear that some of the large investment projects did not have sound financial sources. Governments and banks could not pay back their debts. The IMF organized a $60 billion aid program. Inflation in these countries increased rapidly, and their currencies depreciated sharply. Despite the efforts of international aid agencies, the problems are not yet fully over. It should be emphasized once again that some of these countries had a higher standing than Turkey.

The size and ratio of external debt reflect only a part of the picture of a country's debt burden. Yet external debt is not the only source tapped into by governments to finance their deficits. Those countries with higher savings and stronger financial resources as well as stronger banks rely more on internal borrowing. Therefore, in order to have a better grasp of a country's debt burden, both its external and internal debt must be considered. Giving an absolute number for these debts would not be adequate either; their ratio to the GDP of the country must be looked at. Only in this way can the debt of a country relative to its wealth be judged.

The table below compares Turkey with the most advanced nations in the world and gives per capita debt burden for each of these countries.

Ratio of Foreign Debt to GNP in Turkey and Selected Countries (1997)

Country	GDP With Current Prices ($ billon)	Population (million)	GDP/ gross public dept(%)**	Total public dept ($ billion)	Dept per capital($)
USA	7.817	268.2	62.8	4.909	18.303
Japan	2.594	125.0	73.1	1.890	15.168
Italy	1.145	57.5	121.6	1.392	24.208
Germany	2.100	92.2	61.3	1.282	15.596
France	1.383	58.6	57.7	797	13.600
UK	1.282	58.9	53.3	683	11.595
Spain	534	39.3	69.3	370	9.438
Turkey	189	62.6	***43.8	91	1.453

Source:*Eurostat
**OECD
***Etudes Economiques de l'OCDE, Turquie 1997 (year of 1995)

The public debt quoted in the above table is given as gross debt in international statistics. Public receivables must be looked at as well in order to obtain a correct balance sheet. Having said this, these gross numbers also give a good idea about where countries stand relative to each other. As compared to the developed countries on the list, Turkey's debt relative to her GDP is smaller.

The ratio of external debt to Bulgaria's GDP is three times that of Turkey. The ratios of Hungary and Poland are also larger.

When the analysis is focused on the share of internal debt in GDP an interesting fact can be seen. In 1995 this figure for Turkey was 18.0%. In 1997 the total amount of Turkey's internal debt was $30.614 million, which was equivalent to 15% of that year's GDP. Apart from Luxembourg, the only EU members with smaller figures than Turkey were Finland and Germany. The French ratio of internal debt to GDP was double that of Turkey, Italy's was 3.5 times and Belgium's was 5.5 times larger.

From time to time the Turkish press publishes the amount of debt a Turkish child is born with. The total amount of the country's debt is ivided into the population to find per capita debt for each Turkish national. According to these and considering the numbers above, each Turkish child is born owing $1,453. But according to the same approach each Spanish child is born with $9,438 worth of debt. German, American and Japanese children owe more than $15,000 at birth. It is clear that such calculations are misleading, however, since each newborn also has a share of the total wealth of the country as well.

Insufficiency of Public Revenue

According to OECD statistics, budget revenues are 25.1% of the GDP in Turkey. This figure is well below those of other countries. The following table gives the percentages for some of the OECD numbers for 1996.

Ratio of Public Revenue to GNP
in Turkey and Selected Countries

Country	GDP/public revenues (%)
Denmark	51.9
Germany	38.2
France	45.7
Italy	43.5
Canada	37.2
Spain	33.7
UK	35.3
Japan	28.5
USA	19.1
Turkey	25.1

Source: OECD Main Economic Indicators, January 1998

As can be seen from the above table Turkey's proportion of taxes to GDP is much smaller than all other industrialized Western nations, with the exception of the United States.

Here one of the basic sources of economic problems facing Turkey is encountered. Turkey has engaged in bold moves to catch up with developed nations and has indeed achieved exemplary results. However, lack of public revenue has been an important factor that has prevented Turkey from achieving even better results. Whether or not revenues from the privatization of state-owned companies are included does not really matter, as this would not significantly change the results of this comparison.

Although Turkey's percentage of public expenditures to GDP is smaller relative to most other countries because her revenues are also small, now and then she enters into economically difficult periods that prevent her from devoting resources to areas such as education and health to the extent other developed countries do. The obligatory defence expenditures imposed by her geographic location are comparable to those spent by other Western countries, and are even more than is spent by some. This makes it necessary to obtain funds from internal and international sources in order to undertake the required infrastructure and social investments. A sizeable portion of this borrowing takes the form of short-term loans. The share of short-term debt in Turkey's external borrowing is on the rise; hence, a large part of the already inadequate public revenues go to pay for these debts. This is one of the primary reasons why the budget deficit reached 8.2% of GDP in 1996.

This situation has led to cutbacks in public spending and investment. For example, the amount put aside for debt repayment in the budget is as large as the sum of money reserved for health and education combined. Moreover, these calculations do not take the unregistered economy into account. Other countries also have unregistered economies but particularly in the EU, strict controls decrease their proportion of the overall economy. Rules and regulations in the United States pull down this figure as well. In this respect, if the unregistered economy is also taken into account, then the ratio of public revenues to GDP in Turkey will go down even further, increasing the gap between Turkey and other countries.

The following calculations make the point clearer: What would happen if the ratio of public revenues to GDP in Turkey were at the same level as in other Western countries?

Even leaving aside countries like Sweden and Denmark, which have very high levels of public revenue, Turkey's achieving a level of taxes to GDP equal to countries like Italy or Spain would enable her to engage in substantial developments in the economic and social structure of the country, not to mention increased ability to reduce the amount of her debt. For example, for Turkey to reach Spain's figure of 33.7% calculated at current prices would put her public revenues at $63 billion. If she could achieve Italy's proportion of 43.5%, then her tax revenues would equal $81.3 billion. Considering that according to the OECD Turkey's tax revenues were $46.9 billion in 1996 using current prices, it is clear just how much a tax reform would add to Turkey's potential. Reaching Spain's level, Turkey would earn further revenue of $16.1 billion, and using Italy's percentage the added revenues would be $34.4 billion. With such extra revenues the state would be able to spend an additional $250 per person. In these calculations Turkey's 1996 GDP has been taken as $187 billion, using current prices. Had the ppp method been used, much larger numbers would emerge.

The only way to obtain these results would be by reforming the overall system. One of the goals of the tax reforms recently initiated in Turkey was to increase the level of public revenue to levels seen in other Western countries.

All this data shows inadequacies on the one hand and on the other, the huge potential of Turkey. Prior to becoming an EU member Spain's economic and financial situation was not much different from that of the Turkey of today. After EU membership Spain was able to significantly develop its economy, lifestyle, education and health services. Hence, while Spain's GDP was $161.5 billion at current prices before joining the EU, i.e. less than Turkey's current GDP, it increased to $586.2 billion in 1996. The increase in public revenue played an important role in this substantial economic development.

Distribution of Wealth

A big portion of criticism levelled against Turkey focuses on problems associated with the distribution of wealth. This has serious connotations for the social situation not only of Turkey but also of many countries with similar concerns. One of the primary goals of any state is to decrease differences in wealth to acceptable levels. Yet while criticizing Turkey for her shortfalls in this respect, it must not be thought that Western countries have managed to solve this problem altogether.

Injustices stemming from the inequitable distribution of wealth are a prime source of concern for all countries.

From a global viewpoint the unjust distribution of wealth is striking. Sixty-seven percent of total income in the world goes to seven industrialized countries, commonly referred as the G-7, i.e. the United States, the United Kingdom, France, Germany, Japan, Italy and Canada. Taking this a step further it can be seen that 43 wealthy countries representing 20% of the world's population have 84% of all its income. The share of the poorest countries, constituting 70% of the world's population, is only 10%. The difference between Switzerland, which has the highest per capita income in the world, and Mozambique, which has the lowest, is 275 times. Swiss per capita income is $26,716 whereas Mozambique's is merely $95.[101]

If the existing uneven distribution of wealth within countries is added to the above picture, then the magnitude of the economic and social problems created by this situation can more easily be grasped. OECD specialists indicate that the distribution of wealth in Turkey differs from the norms in the West. However, they point to the difficulties in making an accurate estimate and stress that not enough research has been done in this regard.

OECD documents mention two recent papers on Turkey concerning this matter dated 1987 and 1994, covering 24,000 families from towns and villages.[102]

The OECD compared the data collected from this research with studies conducted in other member countries and concluded that Turkey ranks second from the bottom, just above Mexico. The calculations on the distribution of wealth are done according to a measure called the "Gini coefficient." According to this measure, theoretically speaking, if the wealth of a nation is shared equally among all citizens, then the coefficient for that country is assumed to be "0." Again theoretically speaking, if all the wealth in a country is in the hands of a single individual, that country's coefficient would be "1." According to this method Turkey's coefficient is 0.49.

---

[101] World GDP and Population Data.

[102] OCDE, Turquie, 1997.

Other Western countries also exhibit differences in distribution of wealth, but the figures there are better than in Turkey. Finland seems to have the most equitable distribution of wealth, with a coefficient a little above 0.20, followed by other Scandinavian countries and Belgium. Germany ranks sixth. In the OECD the last three countries are the United States, Turkey and Mexico. The United States coefficient is close to 0.35. Switzerland and Italy are also among those with a relatively poor distribution of wealth.

In Turkey both the State Planning Organization (DPT) and the State Institute of Statistics (DIE) have carried out studies on this subject. Various Turkish scientists also have conducted research and presented their estimates.[103]

There is no significant difference between 1973 DPT estimates, regarded as the most credible source, and 1994 DIE research. If the 1987 and 1994 research done by DIE is used as the basis and these results are compared with numbers for Germany and Portugal, the following picture presents itself:

Income Distribution in Turkey, Germany and Portugal (%)

Members Of Family	Turkey (1987)	Turkey (1994)	Germany (1983)	Portugal (1973-74)
1st 20%*	5.2	4.8	6.8	5.2
2nd 20%	9.6	8.6	12.7	10.0
3rd 20%	14.1	12.6	17.8	14.4
4th 20%	21.2	19.3	24.1	21.3
5th 20%**	49.9	54.8	38.7	49.1

*Lowest income segment
** Highest income segment
Source: Yakup Kepenek, Nurhan Yentürk, Türkiye Ekonomisi, Istanbul, 1996

[103] Kongar, op. cit., p. 637.

Looking at this table it is obvious that relative to 1987 the distribution of wealth in Turkey in 1994 became more uneven. Turkey's 1987 distribution looks similar to that of Portugal before it became an EU member. Germany's distribution of wealth looks more equitable than the other two but is still far from ideal. For example the wealthiest 20% in that country receive 38.7% of total income, i.e. double their numerical size. Despite having the extensive resources of a welfare state, rules and regulations on unemployment insurance and social benefits as well as funds from the EU to eliminate regional differences, Germany's distribution of income is not at ideal levels.

Yet it is also clear that Turkey has a serious problem regarding distribution of income. Before looking at the reasons for this, it would be useful to draw attention to some interesting points in various countries on this issue. The United States is the wealthiest and most powerful country in the world. The Income, Poverty and Health Insurance Office in the U.S. Department of Commerce has researched this topic, with the following results: In 1996 the number of Americans considered to be below the poverty line was 36.5 million. This was 13.7% of the population. The measure of poverty was taken as $16,036 annual income for a family of four. Those who received less than $4,000 per year, i.e. $333 per month per person, are considered as being poor. In this country where per capita income is $26,980 those who receive less than the above-stated average are considered as belonging to the "poor category."

A large majority of these poor people do not qualify for social subsidies. Fully 11.3 million of this group of 36.5 million do not have health insurance, and 10.6 million of those younger than 18 are not insured. These numbers for the United States cannot be considered merely as estimates; The

U.S. Bureau of the Census conducts 100 studies on the topic per year.[104]

The situation in the United States does not reflect the overall situation among OECD countries. There are much better examples. While getting wealthier, Germany managed to shrink differences between social classes and achieve a more even distribution of income. The middle class got larger. Almost 60% of the population is considered to belong to this group; yet among them are those who are richer, just as there are those who are poorer. Forty percent of the population comprises the lower middle class, while 10.7%, i.e. around 8 million people, are considered to be at the lower end of society. Below these are a further 2.2%, around 1.7 million people, who are considered to be in the poorest group.[105]

These numbers are from the pre-unification period of East and West Germany. In order to balance the lower income level of the former East Germany, billions of deutsche marks have been invested in that region. Yet up until now the healthy balances of the pre-1990 period among the different levels of society have not been able to be re-established.

Germany is not a perfect example. The situation in the Scandinavian countries is much better. Thanks to their governments' social benefits system there is almost no one who can be considered as being below the poverty line. Social security is widespread. For this reason in fields like health and education they have managed to achieve higher standards than some of the richer European countries. In some Scandinavian countries such as Denmark the necessary infrastructure has been put in place to enable all children to attend pre-school. In order to achieve this, the ratio of public revenue to GDP has been increased to levels much higher than those found in other European countries. Taxes are very high, with income above a

---

[104] U.S. Department of Commerce, Economic and Statistics Administration, Public Information Office, September 1997.
[105] Facts About Germany, 1989, p. 248.

certain level taxed so much so that almost all of it goes to the state. Moreover, as their budgets were not sufficient to attain this advanced level of equitable distribution of wealth and equal opportunity for all, they resorted to borrowing which, considering the scale of their economies, can be judged as a policy of heavy borrowing.

With these policies they not only achieved per capita incomes which are among the highest in the world, they also managed to have an exceptionally enhanced system of redistribution of wealth. However, here it must not be forgotten that the largest of these countries is Sweden, with a population of only 8 million, a figure which is not increasing. Can larger countries use systems of income redistribution that have proven to be so effective for such small countries? Does the size of population play no role in the fact that the United States ranks next to Turkey in poor distribution of income? Why hasn't the United Kingdom, a country that has made maintaining social justice and balances a primary policy goal, been able to attain the standards reached by the Scandinavian countries?

Certainly these cannot be used to excuse the great inequality in income distribution in Turkey. This is an issue that Turkey must deal with, and she is sparing no effort to remedy the situation. The large investments made in the underdeveloped regions of the country are cases in point. Comparing taxes paid to investment received from the government by different regions gives hard evidence to that effect. For example, taxes paid in 1996 by regions in the southeastern part of Turkey totalled TL 15.9 trillion, yet they received TL 101.6 trillion in subsidies from the government. However, the Istanbul region, the richest in Turkey, paid TL 849.9 trillion and received only TL 190.1 trillion.[106]

Despite all these efforts Turkey's income distribution situation continues to be a serious problem. Turkey will be

---

[106] Kongar, op. cit., pp. 314-315.

able to correct the inequities in the distribution of income so far as she can bring the ratio of public revenue and social transfers to the levels seen in other Western European countries. But it must be remembered that although problems with distribution of income remain, any increase in GDP will have its relative impact on all income levels. A calculation made using the ppp method shows that despite income distribution problems, the income of the bottom 20% increased from $836 in 1985 to $1,500 in 1996, while that of the upper 20% increased from $8,060 to $17,000. Accordingly, the average income of the wealthiest 12.5 million people is much higher than in Spain, Portugal and Greece, while the income of the poorest 12.5 million is at par with the average income in the Kyrgyz Republic.

In order to eliminate injustices in distribution of income, Western European countries implement comprehensive programs within the context of the EU. A major part of the EU budget is devoted to eliminating economic differences among countries as well as among regions within countries. Therefore, while criticizing Turkey for the existence of disparities between her regions as well as problems in distribution of income, it must be kept in mind that so far, Turkey has not benefited at all from the vast pool of funds that EU members benefit from to correct such problems. What are the sources available to the EU? How does it use such funds for these and other similar purposes? To what extent does it help those countries that are not EU members? The answers to these questions contain elements that will shed light on EU-Turkey relations.

TURKEY AND THE EUROPEAN UNION: PAST, PRESENT AND FUTURE

Evolution of the EU

The EU can be considered a product of the conditions that came into being after World War II. Within a period of 25 years Europe had experienced two world wars. While people were trying to develop ideas to prevent the repetition of such wars, the French minister of foreign affairs, Robert Schumann, made an interesting suggestion: Coal and steel production, which constitute the base for countries' war capabilities, should be controlled by a supra-national organization. The idea found substantial support. With this goal in mind, the European Coal and Steel Community was established on April 18, 1951. In later years this cooperation was broadened. On March 25, 1957 Euratom was founded to cooperate in the nuclear field. Later agreements establishing the European Economic Community were signed. In the following years these three institutions merged and became the European Community. With the signing of the Maastricht Treaty in 1992 the European Community assumed its current shape and became the European Union.

When the European Economic Community was first established, the economies of member states were still suffering from the effects of World War II. Despite the aid received through the Marshall Plan, their economic strength was incomparably lower than it currently is. In 1960 the GDP of EEC member Germany and non-EEC member Britain was $72 billion in current prices. In the same year the United States GDP was $518 billion, or seven times that of Germany

and Britain. That same year Turkey's GDP was estimated at
$13.6 billion.

Membership in the EEC was the crucial factor enabling the
rapid economic development of these countries. Using
calculations made with current prices, in the 1960-1995
period the GDP of founding members Germany and the
Netherlands increased 26-fold, Italy's GDP went up 23 times,
and the GDPs of France, Belgium and Luxembourg increased
by a factor of 20. During the same period, the GDP of Britain,
which became a member of the EEC 14 years after its
establishment, increased 13-fold. Being a member of the EU
also changed the economic balances among the greater powers
of Western Europe. In the span of 35 years a large gap came
into being between the German and British economies, which
had been at par in 1960; in 1996 the economic power of
Germany was twice that of Britain. The balances between the
United States and EU members also changed. In 1960 the US
GDP was seven times larger than that of Germany; in 1995 it
was three times as much. Meanwhile Japan entered the world
stage as a new economic power. While these changes in
economic balances were taking place, within the same period
Turkey's economic strength increased 13 times, identical to
the British rate of increase. While making these calculations
the depreciation in the value of the U.S. dollar must be taken
into account. Calculations made using fixed prices give
somewhat different results. Relative to estimates prepared by
using current prices, GDP adjusted using the ppp approach
decreases the difference between Turkey and other European
industrialized nations. However, the general trend is as
mentioned above. Those countries that became EU members
earlier on gained an advantageous position. Germany in
particular widened the gap between herself and her
competitors.[107]

---

[107] Economie Européenne, Rapport Economique Annuel pour 1995,
Commission Européenne, Bruxelles, 1995.

The European countries owe this rapid development to implementing the Treaty of Rome and realizing the goal of establishing a common market together with structural reforms. The treaty called for the abolition of customs duties among member states and the implementation of a common custom code for imports from non-members, as well as achieving freedom of movement for people, goods, capital and services. There are two requirements for EU membership: being European and democratic.

It took 12 years to establish the Common Market. Meanwhile the Common Agricultural Policy (CAP) was devised to iron out regional differences in agriculture thorough heavy use of subsidies. Common policies were determined to achieve fair competition among the companies of the member states. The European Monetary System was adopted in 1979, and the currencies of each state were, to a certain extent, tied to each other. In 1987 the Single Act was adopted, and as mentioned above, the EEC, Euratom and the European Coal and Steel Community were merged and the decision was taken to form the single market of the EU. This took place in 1993. Moreover, it was decided to establish structural funds to help the less developed regions of the Union. One of the EU's most important decisions has been to move into a monetary union and replace national currencies with a single currency. The criteria to join this system were specified in the Maastricht Treaty. Among these are caps on long-term interest rates, limiting budget deficits to 60% of GDP and having made no devaluation in the two years prior to joining the system. The 11 member countries that decided to become a part of the system in 1998 adopted the single currency in stages, starting on January 1, 1999 and finalizing the process by July 1, 2002. Hence, for the first time in Europe the use of a single currency has been accepted. Greece, which was unable to meet the criteria, as well as the United Kingdom, Sweden and Denmark, countries that chose not to join at that stage, will be out of the system for the time being. The move into a single currency is an important one that will influence the future of the European Union. To view the implications of this only from an economic or financial point of view would not give the full picture. Currency is an important symbol of sovereignty. By adopting a single currency, those countries that already have surrendered a part of their sovereignty by being members of the EU are taking a further step in that direction and taking their interdependence up one more notch. To balance this, each member country is given the right of veto; however, this right can not be exercised in all circumstances.

The Maastricht and 1997 Amsterdam treaties gave the EU a new form and depth. Apart from economic integration, steps were taken and mechanisms put in place to establish a common foreign and defence policy. The European Parliament was given more powers.

Various European Union decisions make up a document of tens of thousands of pages, which are collectively called the "Acquis Communautaire." Countries that aspire to be members of the EU must adopt the Acquis, accept the Treaty of Rome and fulfil the membership criteria in order to join. Provided, of course, that all of the current members also consent to it... In 1970 the Britain, Ireland and Denmark joined the EU. The United Kingdom's entry was not a smooth one. During de Gaulle's presidency, France twice vetoed British membership; however the French governments that came after de Gaulle abandoned this policy. In 1981, with the second wave of enlargement, Greece became a member, followed by Spain and Portugal in 1986. In the fourth wave Austria, Sweden and Finland became EU members.

However, while analyzing the distance the EU has come in the past 40 years since its establishment, it would not be satisfactory to mention only the achievements summarized above. On a global scale there are many areas where the EU has not been so successful. According to a 1998 report by UNICE, an umbrella organization for the largest private sector corporations and most influential businessman in Europe, which also counts TUSIAD (Turkish Industrialists' and Businessmen's Association) as a member, the EU ranks behind the United States and Japan in competitiveness. The problems listed in this report are as follows:

• The standard of living in Europe is regressing. Taking the standard of living index as being 100 for the United States, Japan's would be 90 and the EU's would be around 70. Since the 1970s Japan has overtaken Europe in welfare.

• In the 1975-1995 period the rate of increase in the EU's GDP is less than that of the United States.

• Relative to 1970 the EU's share of world trade has decreased by 7%. Since 1991 there also has been a 15% decline in foreign investment in the EU.

• In 1980 the unemployment rate in Western Europe and the United States was around 6-7%. In Japan it was 2%. In 1996 the EU unemployment rate doubled, in the United States it fell below 6% and in Japan it remained below 4%.

• Compared with the United States, EU energy prices are 47% more expensive, land transport is 40% higher, connecting to the Internet costs 200% more and international calls are 300% more costly.

• The percentage of money spent on research and development in EU GDP is less than that of the United States and Japan.

• In the United States there are 400 PCs per thousand; in the most advanced nations of the EU there are 200.

• In most EU countries state intervention in the economy occurs more often than in other developed economies.

• In the 1996-1997 period public spending in EU countries was almost half of GDP, whereas in countries like the United States and Japan it is less than one-third.

• EU tax rates including social benefit payments in 1996 were, on average, around 42.5%. In the United States and Japan they were less than 30%. The EU has the highest levels of tax rates in the world.

• In the EU, employees' share in taxes and social security is around 57% of gross income. This proportion is around 37%

in the United States and 33% in Japan. (The report mentions that this figure is 25% in Turkey.)

• The public sector share in employment is around 18% in the EU. In Japan this is 10% and in the United States, 15%.

UNICE says all these adverse developments are putting even the most competitive companies of the EU into a difficult position and calls upon the EU to reform itself in these and similar areas.[108]

It was necessary to mention some of the deficiencies of the EU, using the reports of the EU private sector, before engaging in an analysis of Turkey-EU relations and the EU's criticism of Turkey. It seems that despite all the positive results and efforts of many years, the EU should not be viewed as a perfect organization that has resolved all its problems. Turkey was aware of these shortcomings when applying for EU membership.

However, taking a historical perspective, Turkey has long put integration with Western Europe as a national policy goal. Despite the difficulties mentioned above EU membership would still benefit Turkey economically and socially, and it also must not be forgotten that in the long run the EU can assume a pan-European defence dimension. That is why in the last 40 years cooperation with the EU has been high on Turkey's agenda. The subject of Turkey-EU relations will be touched on in the following sections. In order to better understand those sections, the workings of the economic and financial cooperation mechanisms of the EU and benefits gained by EU members will first be looked at.

---

[108] Benchmarking Europe's Competitiveness: From Analyses to Action, UNICE, Brussels, December 1997.

To Be a Member of the Union

The main sources of income for the EU are a share from the VAT tax revenues of member states, members' contributions according to their GDP level, a portion of customs duties and taxes on agricultural products such as sugar. These revenues are first used for the economic and social development programs of the member states, and some portion of it is allocated as foreign assistance.

The EU's budget is between 2% and 4% of the sum of national budgets of member countries and should not exceed 1.2% of their total GDP of EU member countries. The 1997 budget was 87.6 million ECUs. Germany is the main donor. Germany's contribution is 31.5% of VAT revenues and 24.4% of contributions based on GDP.

The resources in the EU budget are used in various projects prepared for different purposes. For example, at the Edinburgh Summit of 1992, it was decided to spend 146 billion ECUs by 1999 in order to improve economic and social harmony among EU members. There is another program to eliminate regional differences. If the income of a region is less than 75% of the EU average, then funds are provided for this region to reduce the disparities. All of Greece, Portugal and Ireland are considered regions to be supported. At 28%, Spain receives the largest share of these funds. Greece is next with 15%, followed by Portugal with 14.8%. Germany also receives substantial funds to develop areas that were part of East Germany before reunification.

Another source is the Structural Funds established by the 1992 Maastricht Treaty. The economically weaker members benefit from these funds. For the 1993-1999 period these countries were scheduled to receive 15 billion ECUs. Spain will receive 52-58% of these funds, while Greece and Portugal will get 16-20% each.

In addition to these, there are funds available through the European Investment Bank. Since 1994, 38 projects designed to develop certain regions of Greece, Ireland, Portugal and

Spain have been financed through these funds. There is a fund valued at 326.5 million ECUs used to increase cooperation among different regions. Technical aid is funded from separate sources. Expenditures in areas such as agriculture, forestry and the fishing industry are also paid for from the EU's budget. In addition there are many projects to support industry, science, the environment and medium- and small-sized companies as well as entrepreneurs.

EU-supported education projects carry a particular importance. There are comprehensive programs such as the Socrates, Leonardo and Youth for Europe III. Moreover, not only the youth of EU member countries but also young people from countries like Iceland, Liechtenstein and Norway benefit from these programs. These programs are also now made available to Malta and Central and Eastern European countries as well as to the Greek Cypriot administration. And what about Turkey? Will Turkish youngsters also benefit from these programs? No. Up until now suggestions to that effect have not taken the form of official cooperation programs and have not been implemented.

The media and information sectors have not been left out either. For the 1996-2000 period 310 million ECUs were budgeted for use in these sectors, and it was decided to support 147 projects in the cultural field.

An interesting project is the Sister Cities Project, which aims to bring the people of Europe closer together. In this project, too, in addition to EU members, cities from Albania, Bulgaria, Croatia, the Greek Cypriot administration, the Czech Republic, Estonia, Hungary, Lithuania, Latvia, Malta, Poland, Romania, Slovakia and Slovenia are included. How about Turkish cities and Sister City projects that would draw Turkish people closer together to Europe? They do not exist; no one has thought about it.

There are many other projects, from health to sports, from transportation to energy. All of these are financed from the EU's budget.[109]

Greece, which became an EU member in 1981, received 275 million ECUs that year. A year later this went up to 875 million ECUs. The total amount of aid received by Greece in the 1981-1996 period was 44.2 billion ECUs, i.e. 4,416 ECUs per person. Portugal, which became a member in 1986, had received 22.2 billion ECUs by 1996. During the same period, Spain received 64.6 billion ECUs. These figures change from year to year. As an example, the net contributions received by Spain from the EU budget totalled 7.945 million ECUs in 1995, i.e. $8.5 billion. Accordingly, EU support for each Spanish citizen had reached 205 ECUs. During the same year Greece received 351 ECUs and Ireland 522 ECUs per capita. Of course the contributions of these countries to the EU budget should also be taken into consideration. The table below shows the contributions and amounts received by member countries for the year 1996.

---

[109] Grants and Loans from the European Union, Luxembourg, 1997.

Contributions of EU Countries to the EU Budget and the
Funds They Received (million ECU) (1996)

Country	Contributions to the Budget	Received from the Budget	Difference
Spain	4,538	10,511	5,972
Greece	1,107	5,039	3,932
Portugal	906	3,680	2,774
Ireland	710	2,970	2,260
Denmark	1,359	1,553	193
Finland	961	988	27
Luxembourg	163	83	-79
Austria	1,872	1,600	-272
France	12,410	11,951	-459
Belgium	2,743	1,996	-746
Sweden	1,957	1,204	-752
Italy	8,935	7,532	-1,402
UK	8,227	5,951	-2,276
Netherlands	4,435	1,988	-2,446
Germany	20,766	9,872	-10,894

Source: Europaeisher Rechnungshof and the Research Center of Turkey.

As indicated in the table above, nine EU countries, in
particular Spain, Greece, Portugal and Ireland, received
substantial amounts from the EU budget. Here lies the key for
the integral development of the EU. During the last wave of
enlargement three new members were accepted, while Turkey
was left out. A lack of funds in the EU budget and the fact that
Sweden, Finland and Austria would be net contributors were
given as reasons why such a decision was made. However, as
can be seen from the above table, two of the aforementioned
three countries are net receivers, although the amounts they
received are not that large. That Turkey would receive large
sums of money in the event she becomes a member is an oft-
quoted remark. How much, exactly, would Turkey receive
from the EU budget? The answer to this question is revealed in
later sections.

Preparations for the Enlarged Family

In addition to aid supplied to its own member countries the EU also supplies sizeable funds to non-member countries. The Central and Eastern European countries that were recently accepted as EU candidates benefited extensively from such funds. These countries received substantial assistance from sources other than the EU budget as well.

The aid given through the PHARE program was in the form of grants, whereas that supplied through the European Investment Bank (EIB) was in the form of loans. Until the end of 1996, 6.6 billion ECUs were given in aid through the PHARE program. During the 1995 Cannes Summit a decision was made to increase the annual budget of the PHARE program from 1.2 to 1.5 billion ECUs by 1999. A part of the EU aid package to the Central and Eastern European countries was done under the macro-financial aid framework. These countries received 1.2 billion ECUs from this program during the 1990-1994 period. Hungary was the largest recipient with 870 million ECUs.

During the 1992-1996 period the EIB also supplied the Central European countries with 4.3 billion ECUs in loans, 27% of which went to Poland, 25% to the Czech Republic and 15% to Hungary.

With regards to donors, Germany is by far the largest, supplying 14.6 billion of the 32.6 billion ECUs given by the EU through bilateral agreements. France ranks second, but her 6.1 billion ECUs is not nearly half as much that of Germany. Britain's contributions remained at 836 million ECUs.

By the end of 1995 the total amount of funds they had received from EU as well as non-EU sources had reached 86.5 billion ECUs. This amount does not include aid given to Russia or the republics of the former Soviet Union.

The breakdown of this money among the donor countries is
given in the table below.

Aid Supplied to the Central and Eastern European Countries by the End of 1995

Donor	ECU (billion)	%
EU	13.3	15.3
EU member Countries	32.6	37.6
USA	10.1	11.6
Japan	5.0	5.7
Other G-24 Members	4.0	4.6
International financial organizations.	21.4	24.7
Total	86.5	100

Source: Le Courier des Pays de l'Est no: 421, August 1997, p. 11

Turkey, considered by the EU to be behind these Central
and Eastern European countries, is in reality among those that
supplied aid to this region. As a member of the G-24 Turkey
provided 424.2 million ECUs to the countries of this region in
the January 1, 1990-December 31, 1995 period. The
recipients of this aid were the Czech Republic, Slovakia,
Hungary, Bulgaria and Albania.[110]

---

[110] Paul van den Bempt, op. cit., pp. 117-118.

The Czech Republic received 3 billion ECUs between 1990 and 1996. Other than that, the Czechs received 434 million ECUs under the EU's PHARE program.

During the same period the amount received by Hungary was 12.6 billion ECUs. Hungary also received $387 million from the IMF. The loans it has received from the World Bank since 1982 have amounted to $3.5 billion. Moreover, the European Bank for Reconstruction and Development (EBRD) also supplied Hungary with 1 billion ECUs. It also managed to receive $290 million from the International Finance Corporation (IFC) and EU aid totalling 582.8 million ECUs from the PHARE program, benefiting from multi-purpose funds in the amount of 491 million ECUs from the same program.

Hungary spent 111.5 million ECUs on education from the funds it received from the PHARE program alone. Poland also benefited from these sources. During the 1990-1995 period it received 1.2 billion ECUs in aid from the EU as well as 839 million ECUs from the PHARE program. Again from PHARE they were the recipients of 2 billion ECUs between 1990 and 1999. By 1994 the European Investment Bank had already supplied them with 886 million ECUs.[111]

As indicated in the above table, just like the financial aid supplied by the EU, the bilateral aid given by individual EU member countries is also at a significant level. From the distribution of these funds one can clearly see where the priorities of these countries lie. For example, between 1989 and 1995, 78% of all aid given by Germany went to Poland, the Czech Republic, Hungary and Slovakia. The German aid is not confined only to this. After the end of the Cold War some of the Eastern European countries applied to the Paris Club to defer their debts. One of these was Poland. The greatest support to this country came from Germany, which gave Poland DM 4.5 billion in aid and deferred its debt of DM 5

---

[111] The European Union, EU-CEES Relations, Spokesman's Service of the European Commission, Memos 97/43, 96/124 and 96/97.

billion. This support amounted to one-third of all aid supplied by those who were members of the Paris Club and had joined this deferred debt schedule.[112]

Starting from the early 1990s large sums of foreign investment have also gone to the Central and Eastern European States (CEES). This to a large extent has helped the recent increases in production and exports seen in these countries. It would be useful to have a look at foreign investment in the Czech Republic, Poland and Hungary, three countries considered to be at the front of the line for EU membership.

Foreign Investment in the Czech Republic, Hungary and Poland

Country	Investment ($ million)			Comulative Investment ($ million)	
	1994	1995	1996	1995	1996
Czech R.	862	2,562	1,428	5,943	7,371
Hungary	1,146	4,453	1,983	11,394	13,777
Poland	542	1,134	2,741	2,751	5,492

Source: Le Courier des Pays de l'Est, no. 421, August 1997

In earlier sections we gave examples from around the world regarding the extent to which governments support private firms in their countries. It is a well-known fact that these subsidies are also used to direct the foreign investment of these firms. Private firms that engage in investing abroad are insured against political and commercial risk by state banks or state-owned finance institutions set up specifically for this purpose.

---

[112] Henning Tewes, German Politics, vol. 6, no. 2, August 1997, pp. 106-107.

Using this tool, states may lead their companies to invest in specific countries that in their view would serve their own economic and political interests. The fact that Poland, the Czech Republic and Hungary, the largest three of the five Eastern European countries, started to receive so much foreign aid as well as foreign investment from the early 1990s seems to be the result of policies of donor countries encouraging such investment as well as from the creation of a hospitable environment for investors following the switch to a liberal economic system.

For example, Germany's foreign trade insurance organization, Hermes, plays an important role in that respect. Germany guarantees the receivables of firms in specific countries in the event those receivables cannot be collected.

In this way German firms are encouraged to invest in countries with political as well as commercial risks. It is the same for the exports of such companies. In 1992 the total exports by German firms to countries insured through the Hermes system against financial loss was DM 39.2 billion, with DM 12.1 billion going to the CEES, i.e. one-third of exports covered by insurance provided by Germany went to these countries.

Some of the organizations that supply funds for investment ask host countries to apply protective measures, such as high customs duties, and to create more favourable conditions for their companies, hence protecting their investments. This is often seen in the automotive industry. Perhaps due to this factor, import duty on cars in Poland is 35% and in Romania 30%.[113]

The effects of these large aid packages and investments on the Central and Eastern European countries have started to become visible in the trade of these countries with the EU. Since 1992 their average annual increase in exports to the EU has been around 20% (29% in 1994, 25% in 1995). In 1996,

---

[113] Alan Mayhew. P. 102

10.2% of all EU exports to non-members went to these
nations, and 8.1% of all imports from non-EU states came
from them as well. Yet the distribution of this increased trade
was not evenly distributed among EU members. The largest
share went to Germany, who in 1996 realized 42.6% of all
exports and 47.7% of all imports from the EU to and from
this region. It is interesting to note that the EU invoked anti-
dumping measures against the Central and Eastern European
countries in only a very few cases. For example, in 1992 only
0.36% of all imports from Central Europe was subjected to
anti-dumping regulations. During the 1990-1994 period anti-
dumping measures were applied to only 15 items imported
from this region.[114]

Yet as a result of these developments the Central and
Eastern European states started to have large trade deficits
with the EU, reaching 4.8 billion ECUs in 1994, 5.6 billion
ECUs in 1995 and double that in 1996, at 12.8 billion ECUs.
In parallel fashion, Germany's trade surplus with these
countries went up to 4.7 billion ECUs in 1996 from 1.5 billion
ECUs in 1994 and 1995. That is to say, although they do not
have a customs union agreement with the EU as Turkey does,
the total trade deficit of these countries has reached 1.5 times
that of Turkey.

While their trade with the EU has increased, commerce
among the Central and Eastern European countries has
declined considerably. While in 1989 the trade volume
between the Czech Republic, Hungary, Poland, Bulgaria and
Romania was around $37 billion, it later declined to $29
billion in 1990, $21 billion in 1991 and $3 billion in 1993.[115]

Under the Hermes system German firms operating abroad
are insured against the political risks of those countries in
which they do business. In 1990 the total value of this
insurance system was DM 10 billion, 15% of which was

---

[114] Ibid., pp. 75-77, 95.
[115] Ibid., p. 87.

reserved for European countries. The main beneficiaries of this system were Spain Yugoslavia, Hungary and Turkey. In 1994 the system underwent significant changes, and the amount to be guaranteed was increased to DM 16.4 billion. Poland, Hungary, the Czech Republic and Slovakia started to receive a larger portion from the system. Statistics show that the total amount insured in these CEES was DM 3.5 billion. While evaluating this development one should remember that during its turn in the EU's Presidency in the second half of 1994 Germany declared enlargement of the EU towards Eastern Europe as its prime objective.[116]

In general it can be seen that the CEES have taken significant steps forward, thanks to such generous foreign aid and investment.

Still, it would be helpful to bring to mind the size of these economies when analyzing these developments. In 1995 the sum of all the GDPs of 10 Central and Eastern European countries was only $234 billion. This is approximately equal to the GDP of Belgium and is equivalent to 4% of the GDP of the EU. Even when adjusted using the ppp approach, the average per capita income of these 10 countries is less than one-third of the EU average.[117]

Relative to their past performance these countries have started to obtain more positive results from their shift into a market economy. Yet realistically speaking, one cannot turn a blind eye to some of the difficulties they still face. To give a few examples, in 1996 the Bulgarian GDP shrank by 10%; the same year Hungary's economy grew only by 0.5%; according to the International Herald Tribune in 1996 the inflation rate in Bulgaria was 1,095% per year; and the unemployment rate in Poland in that same year reached 13.6%.

Also, one must not forget that 30-50% of the CEES' population is still living below the poverty line. In 1996 the

---

[116] Henning Tewes, op. cit., pp. 108-109, 112.
[117] Alan Mayhews p. 181.

total number of unemployed in these countries was around 6 million. In Bulgaria, which recently experienced a major economic crisis, the annual per capita income of 33% of the people was less than $120 per year.

The Bulgarian leva depreciated by 500% in 1996, and foreign currency reserves went down to $518 million, whereas just to pay pack debts due in 1997 they needed $1.313 billion. The internal debt of the country tripled and reached 60% of the GDP. The new Bulgarian government took economic measures to solve this crisis; however, the results of these reforms will only be seen in years to come.

Other CEES also face various economic problems. Hungary is the one country that has benefited the most from foreign investment; however, some sectors there are now totally dominated by foreign capital. In some manufacturing sectors the share of foreign capital is around 50%, even reaching 80% in some cases. The drawbacks of such a situation are obvious.

Poland is one of the most successful countries in Central Europe, but it too has problems. In 1996 the share of the private sector was only 36.8%. In that same year the current account deficit of the Czech Republic amounted to 7.8% of the country's GDP, and it was reported that there were 25,000 crimes categorized as "economic" in character.[118]

As can be seen, these countries too have many problems. EU membership is expected to help solve them. Yet these problems have not been considered obstacles to EU membership.

It seems that the decision to begin the accession talks with these countries is a result of political considerations rather than an objective economic evaluation. In fact, the total value added by the first five candidate countries into the EU will be around $255 billion, i.e. only 3% of the EU's GDP. The total population of these countries is 63 million, equivalent to 17%

[118] Le Courrier des Pays de l'Est, 1997, no. 421, p. 18; no. 419, pp. 3-4, 11, 29, 39, 46.

of the current EU population. The fact that those who feel concerned about granting freedom of movement to approximately the same number of Turks do not feel the same towards these countries and that neither do they feel concerned about the effects on the current recipient members of the billions of dollars these countries will get from Common Agricultural Policy (CAP) funds can only be explained by saying that for them this is basically a political choice.

Turkey, Distant Relative

Turkey established official relations with the EEC soon after the establishment of the Community, on June 30, 1959.

These relations resulted from the signing of the Association Agreement in Ankara on September 12, 1963. From then on Turkey was an EEC partner, and full membership was set as the target, clearly indicated in Article 28 of the agreement. That is to say the question of Turkey's full membership was taken up on a political level at that time and in principle received a positive response. This general policy, which was binding on both parties, has influenced Turkey's economic policy and even her political choices for the last 35 years. All this time Turkey prepared herself in accordance with the goal of full membership, trying to adapt her laws and regulations to EU norms. That is why the efforts of some to question the premise of Turkey's full membership seem odd.

It is also odd to state Turkey's eligibility for full membership in the declarations that are made at the end of some EU meetings. As pointed out by Foreign Minister İsmail Cem, the fact that Turkey is a European country is self-evident; there is no need to question it and try to prove it over and over again. When the Turkey-EU Association Agreement was to be signed, the senior officials of the EEC defended the same view. These are the words of EEC Commissioner Walter Hallstein: "Today we are witnessing a historic event. Turkey belongs in Europe. Here lies the significance of this event. This is an expression of reality rather than a summarized geographical fact or the historical events of the past few centuries." At that time there was no one contemplating or expressing the view that EU was a "project of civilization that would exclude Turkey forever." While developing her polices towards Europe for the past 35 years, Turkey believed that Europe's viewpoint vis-à-vis Turkey was as stated by Hallstein.

The Ankara Agreement foresaw a three-stage process for full membership: First, a preparatory stage in which the Turkish economy would be strengthened to be able to shoulder the responsibilities that were to come. The second phase would be one of transition. Here, mutual steps would be taken to achieve customs union, and economic policies would be harmonized. In the last stage coordination of economic policies would be intensified and customs union would be achieved. Article 28 as mentioned above refers to Turkey's full membership in this last phase.

In order to achieve all these goals an Association Council at the foreign minister level and an Association Committee at the technical level were established. In 1965 the Association Council decided to form a Joint Parliamentary Commission composed of Turkish and Euro members of parliament. Later a Joint Consulting Committee was formed with the participation of representatives from labour organizations, employers and independent professional institutions from Turkey and representatives of the Economic and Social Committee of the EU.

An Additional Protocol was signed between Turkey and the EU in 1970, and a timetable of 22 years was set to move into customs union. Turkey started to receive financial aid under certain programs, and there were developments in other areas as well. Until 1980 EU-Turkey relations progressed smoothly, despite difficulties faced from time to time and delays incurred in fulfilling mutual obligations. However, some of the Turkish expectations did not materialize. During the fourth Five-Year Plan Turkey sought the EU's assistance to stabilize her economy, which was trying to cope with the adverse effects of the world oil crisis. Within this framework, Turkey asked for a postponement of her obligations under the Additional Protocol, the facilitation of agricultural trade, the removal of barriers on textile exports and an increase in the amount of assistance provided by the EU under the financial protocol to $8 billion. In May 1979 the commission accepted only the delay of Turkey's obligations; the rest of the requests were rejected. Although Turkey was reflecting her true needs, some circles viewed Turkey's request of $8 billion as exaggerated. Turkey could not receive assistance from the EU to deal with her economic problems, which, to a large extent, stemmed from international economic developments.

Following Greece's entry into the Union in 1980 practically all relations between Turkey and the EU, and financial cooperation in particular, came to a halt. The fourth Turkey-EU financial protocol has not been implemented despite the fact that it has been 18 years since it was signed.

In 1980 Turkey seriously considered applying for full EU membership. According to press reports, between 1976 and 1979 some high-ranking European officials who were friends of Turkey, such as Emil Noel, suggested that Turkey apply for EU membership at the same time as Greece. There was even a statement made by the then Turkish Minister of Foreign Affairs, Hayrettin Erkmen, that the application would be made in autumn of 1980. However, with the coup of September 12 this issue dropped off the agenda for a long time. Meanwhile, Turkey engaged in substantial economic reforms, removed protectionist barriers, started to implement the liberal economic system to its full extent and entered into a period of rapid economic development, the result of which she applied for full EU membership in April 1987.

Immediately following this application a campaign of heavy criticism against Turkey was initiated in European countries and institutions. With a resolution it adopted on June 18, 1987, two months after the application, the European Parliament took its criticism back to the period of the "Young

Turks" government of the pre-World War I era. They referred to Turkey's disputes with Greece, the Cyprus problem and some of Turkey's problems with critical language hitherto unprecedented in foreign affairs and claimed that "there is no real parliamentary democracy in Turkey." The exaggerated expressions used in this European Parliament declaration have for many years been employed against Turkey on different occasions.

The European Parliament refused to convene the Turkey-EU Parliamentary Commission until April 1989, nine years after the September 12, 1980 military intervention, despite the fact that Turkey had returned to parliamentary democracy with the general elections of 1983. Perhaps they thought that by refusing to meet Turkish parliamentarians they would do a greater service to Turkish democracy. Six years elapsed from the time Turkey actually returned to parliamentary democracy, however, before the commission was allowed to convene.

During the same period significant differences of opinion surfaced between Turkey and the European Union regarding freedom of movement for Turkish workers. According to Article 36 of the 12th Protocol of the Ankara Agreement, starting from December 1, 1986 Turkish workers should have been granted freedom of movement in EU countries. The EU failed to comply with this commitment, claiming that the agreement's language did not imply a clear obligation. The EU Court of Justice concurred with this view.

It took two-and-a-half years for the EU to prepare its reply to Turkey's application for membership. According to the view made public on December 18, 1989 Turkey was "eligible" for full membership; however, due to reasons stemming in part from the EU's internal problems and partly from Turkey, the conditions were not ripe to initiate accession talks. There were structural differences between Turkey and Europe in agriculture and industry; protectionism in industry was too high; there were macroeconomic imbalances; and significant differences in the level of development existed between

Turkey and the EU. The view of the EU Commission also pointed out political "deficiencies." The parliamentary system was close to EU norms, but the rights of labor unions were not adequate, and improvements were needed in the fields of human rights and democracy. Turkish-Greek relations and the Cyprus question were also important factors.

When the EU Commission's views on Turkey and other candidate countries are analyzed together, interesting differences of approach surface. If differences in the levels of development of agriculture and industry between Turkey and EU countries were obstacles for opening accession talks as claimed by the 1989 commission opinion, then how can the Central and Eastern European states, which are far behind Turkey in those areas, start accession talks today?

To give an example, while the proportion of people working in farming is 3.2% in Germany, 4.9% in France and 2% in the United Kingdom, this ratio is 27% in Poland. Only 160,000 of the 2 million farms in Poland are capable of competing with European farms. Yet these factors did not prevent Poland from being included in the EU accession process.

If protectionism is an obstacle, Turkey today is among those countries with the least amount of protectionist measures in the world, whereas the Central and Eastern European countries are generally far behind Turkey in this respect. Trade union rights might not have been up to European standards in 1989, but looking at improvements made since along with agreements signed with the International Labour Organization (ILO) makes it impossible to ignore the rights these unions have acquired in Turkey. As a result these arguments have lost their validity.

Coming to the issues of democracy and human rights, a comparison between Turkey and Western European countries will be made in later sections. Let it suffice to say here that on this issue too a double standard is used between Turkey and the rest of the candidates.

For example, when the opinion regarding the Spanish application was issued on December 1, 1978, only three years had elapsed since that country's move into democracy. This development was praised, and the need for support was mentioned. Whereas by the time the opinion on Turkey was issued, it had been 69 years since a parliament with Western standards deriving its power from the people had been established, and 43 years since the switch to a multi-party system. It had also been six years since democratic elections had been resumed following the military intervention of 1980. In the opinion issued by the EU Commission regarding Portugal's application on May 19, 1978 it was said, "Democracy has now been established in Portugal." At that time Portugal had had democracy for only three years and a democratic constitution for two.

The Commission said: "The Community should not exclude Portugal from the European integration process. Otherwise the disappointment this would create would be too serious, resulting in enormous difficulties." There is no mention of such concerns in the view on Turkey. Therefore, it can be understood that the Turkey's disappointment was not seen as something that would lead to undesired developments, or even if it did these developments would not be something that would cause concern for the EU. The opinion on Greece was issued on January 26, 1976. It had only been one-and-a-half years since the military junta was unseated and democracy established. The view of the commission was as follows: "As one of the goals of the Community set forth in the Association Agreement was the re-establishment of a democratic system in Greece, without a doubt the Community should give a positive reply to Greece's application for membership." There are no such comments in the opinion on Turkey.

Coming to relations with Greece and the Cyprus issue mentioned in the opinion on Turkey, the EU followed a balanced path between Turkey and Greece until 1980. Nor did the EU change this policy during the Greek application for membership in the mid-1970s. The EU Commission's view dated January 29, 1976 on Greece states: "The membership perspective of Greece will surface the disputes between this country and Turkey. Turkey too is a partner of this Community, and the goal of this partnership is Turkey's membership. The Community is not and should not be a party to the disputes between Greece and Turkey. Until now the Community's relationship with the two countries was defined with the equal partnership status of both and although with different timetables, both have full membership as the final goal. The membership of Greece inevitably brings in a new element to this balance. The Commission believes that in order to materialize its decision not to let the Greek application for membership influence EU-Turkey relations, that there will not be any changes in the rights granted to Turkey under the Association Agreement, the Council should take special measures."

Was this balance looked after in practice? Did Greece's membership in fact not influence Turkey's relations with the EU? It is not possible to give positive responses to these questions. Moreover, the commission, which did not see the Turkish-Greek disputes as an obstacle to Greek membership, while mentioning them in its view on Greece, had this to say in its 1987 view on Turkey: "The political analysis of Turkey's membership would be incomplete if it ignored the dispute between Turkey and one of the member countries of the EU." Did the EU assume a similar attitude in other enlargement processes? For example, in the view on the Spanish application was the dispute over Gibraltar with the United Kingdom, which was already a member country, ever mentioned? No, there is no mention of this in the December 1, 1978 opinion on Spain.

It seems that much happened in the EU between 1976 and 1989. The Turkish-Greek disputes were not seen as an obstacle to EU membership for Greece, but they now may prevent it for Turkey. That was the message. The Cyprus issue prevented the initiation of accession talks with Turkey, but as

put forward by the December 1997 summit, it will not prevent
accession talks from being conducted with the Greek Cypriot
administration. It is inevitable for those reading these decisions
to conclude that the Greek Cypriots had no blame regarding
the Cyprus problem and that all the responsibility lay with
Turkey. Is this the truth? The EU's balanced approach in 1976
between Greece and Turkey, the commitment that Greek
membership would not impinge upon EU-Turkey relations
remain part of the "Acquis Communautaire," if anyone ever
reads or remembers them.

In recent years the most important development in Turkey-
EU relations has been the customs union. As stated earlier, this
was a goal that had been jointly established in 1963. What was
negotiated in 1990 were the terms, content and compensation
Turkey would receive against her losses due to the agreement.
Regarding commercial issues, the major contribution of the EU
was only the removal of the quotas on Turkish textiles that
had existed for years. Other than that the most significant
contribution was the financial aid to be given to Turkey.
Following lengthy negotiations, agreement was reached.

The March 6, 1995 decision of the Turkey-EU Association
Council was approved by the European Parliament on
December 13, 1995 and became effective as of December 31.
All mutual commitments remained in place for about one
month. While preparations for implementation were still going
on, Greece used the Kardak incident as an excuse and vetoed
the EU financial aid it had approved only a few months earlier.
Hence, the EU's financial commitments arising from the
customs union died or were frozen. The effects of the customs
union on Turkey-EU relations will not be repeated here, since
this topic is discussed in the external trade section. However,
taking a general perspective, it is clear that the balances
achieved through customs union negotiations could not be
protected due to the EU's failure to fulfil its obligations. The
efforts of some EU countries to correct this situation did not
yield any results until mid-1999.

Mutual obligations written in texts and the implementation of these constitute only one dimension of the issue. However, in looking at the approaches exhibited against Turkey and towards the other candidates as well as the declarations made, a totally unbalanced picture emerges.

It would not be incorrect to say that when it comes to membership, Greece, Spain, Portugal and the Central and Eastern European states are seen as close relatives whose membership in the European family should be supported; whereas Turkey is viewed as a distant relative whose membership, although it cannot be prevented in the long run, should not be rushed.

This impression comes not only from the views of the commission but also from EU summits, EU Parliament decisions, declarations of EU member countries on Turkey and other candidate countries and articles published in the media. It does not go unnoticed that while other candidates' positive aspects and achievements are pushed to the forefront, Turkey's "imperfections and mistakes" are stressed on every occasion in order to sway public opinion in that direction. For some reason those who frequently stress that "the Eastern borders of Germany cannot be the EU's final borders" shy away from saying the same thing about the eastern borders of Greece.

This different approach shows itself in practice as well and becomes evident when the financial assistance extended to Turkey is compared with that accorded other applicants.

When the Association Agreement was signed in 1963, the EEC had promised to give financial aid to Turkey. In return Turkey agreed to gradually decrease its customs duties on imports originating from the EEC. What were the financial obligations of the EEC and to what extent have they materialized?

Turkey-EU Financial Cooperation (ECU Million)

	Date	Period	Credits From the Budget	EIB	Donation	Total	Actual
1st Financial Protocol	1963	1963-1969	175	-	-	175	175
2nd Financial Protocol	1970	1971-1977	195	25	-	220	220
Supplementary Protocol	1973	1971-1977	47	-	-	47	47
3rd Financial Protocol	1977	1979-1982	220	90	-	310	310
4th Financial Protocol (1)	1981	1982-1986	325	225	50	600	0
Special Cooperation Fund	1980	1980-1982	-	-	75	75	75
Total			*962*	*340*	*125*	*1,427*	*827*

Within the Contex of the Custom Union

	Date	Period	Credits From the Budget	EIB	Donation	Total	Actual
Budgetary Sources (3)	1995	1996-2000	-	-	375	375	0
EIB (3)	1995	1996-2000	-	750	-	750	0
Macro economic aid (4)	1995	-	-	-	300	300	0
MEDA (5)	1996	1995-1999	-	-	375	375	103
EIB (5)	1997	1997-1999	-	300	-	300	95
Renewed MEDA (5-6)	1992	1992-1996	-	340	-	340	340
Special Financial Cooperation (7)		1996	-	-	2.9	2,9	2.3
Total			*1,390*	*1,053*	*2,443*	*540*
Overall Sum			**962**	**1,730**	**1,178**	**3,870**	**1,367**

1.   Was never activated
2.   Has been extended
3.   Could not be accessed due to the veto of one member country
4.   Estimated figure, will be used in case of difficulties with payments
5.   The fund to help Mediterranean countries
6.   Implemented between 1992-1996. Turkey used 130 million ECUs from this program
7. Could not be used due to a decision by the European Parliament

The total amount of assistance given to Turkey in 35 years is less than 1.5 billion ECUs. This is less than the total amount of aid given to Poland, Hungary and the Czech Republic in any single year. This, despite the fact that Turkey opened up its market to EU companies, resulting in a trade deficit of $10 billion with the EU. The other candidates do not have such obligations, as they still have not reached the level to be able to conclude a customs union agreement with the EU.

While withholding the aid it undertook to give Turkey, the EU is giving billions of ECUs to the Central and Eastern European countries and encouraging investment in those countries. Moreover, it supplies much more aid to Mediterranean countries whose relations with the EU cannot even be compared to the EU's relations with Turkey, deciding to give 4.7 billion ECUs between 1995 and 1999, 3.4 billion of which will be offered under the MEDA program. In fact, according to the customs union agreement, some of the aid planned for Turkey would have been supplied from the MEDA funds as well, but this was prevented. First came the Greek veto, and the entire MEDA program came to halt. Later a solution was found, and the veto was withdrawn in July 1996. However, there was one condition: The decision would be effective as of September. The European Parliament met that September and prevented the release of MEDA funds to Turkey, claiming that legal reforms in the fields of democracy and human rights had not been sufficient. Hence, Turkey could not benefit from this facility whereas other Mediterranean countries could. Which countries were these? The extent to which the Mediterranean countries have benefited from the fourth protocol prepared for the 1992-1996 period gives us a good idea: Egypt 27%, Morocco 21%, Algeria 17%, Tunisia 14%, Syria 8%, Jordan 6%, Israel 4% and Lebanon 3%. The fact that the European Parliament did not prevent these countries from receiving aid from the EU indicates that this Parliament views all these countries as more democratic and respectful towards human rights than Turkey.

These are not the only countries that receive aid from the EU. The candidates from the Central and Eastern European countries as well as Albania, Bosnia-Herzegovina and Macedonia all benefit from the PHARE program, which in 1996 had a budget of 1.2 billion ECUs. The former Soviet states benefit from the TACIS program, which has a budget of 600 million ECUs. Thirty-seven projects were realized in these countries with the help of the EU. The EU also has important aid programs for countries in Asia, Latin America and Africa.

Considering the feeble amount of aid given to Turkey since 1981 a troubling picture is faced. Turkey is the only country that has had an Association Agreement with the EU since 1963 as well as alliance ties with most of the EU member states. The EU that transfers funds to practically the entire world forgets just one: Turkey, the only country outside the Union that has removed all customs and trade barriers and opened up its markets to the EU.

The Brussels-based Center de Relations Europeennes (CRE) prepared a comparative study between the economies of Turkey and the Central and Eastern European states, the results of which have been published in a 200-page report. It was decided at the Copenhagen Summit to use the following three criteria to determine which countries could be considered candidates for EU membership:

•Does the candidate state have institutions that respect and guarantee democracy, supremacy of law, human rights and minority rights?

•Does it have a market economy that has the capacity to stand against the competitive forces within the EU?

•Does it have the competence to adopt the obligations of membership, in particular the EU's political, economic and financial targets?

Focusing on the economic dimension of the issue, the CRE study gives the following results:

•The process of removing the protectionist measures on Turkish industry has been completed successfully. Following the implementation of the customs union agreement the level of protectionism in Turkey has fallen below the levels that exist in the EU in the form of non-tariff protections and governmental subsidies.

•Differences in average income and standards of living remain despite rapid development in economy. Differences in industrial and commercial development have dropped, and today Turkey is somewhere between the most developed EU countries and less developed members like Greece and Portugal.

•Although macroeconomic balances are strained due to monetary imbalances, results obtained in GDP growth, job creation, budget deficits and public debt are relatively better than those of EU countries.

•Differences in the social security field between Turkey and the EU remain, though at lower levels due to improvements in Turkey's level of development and a less protective system in Europe since the end of the 1980s.

•The methodology used by the commission while giving its opinion on Turkey in 1989 is debatable, the reason being that the commission compares Turkey's performance with those of some EU member states, whereas the commission did not use such a method while giving its opinion on the applications of Greece, Spain and Portugal.

•The following can be said in determining the extent to which Turkey fulfils the 1993 Copenhagen criteria: Turkey completely fulfils the first criteria. The market economy in Turkey is much more viable than that of the Central and Eastern European states, and it has been that way for a long period of time. As compared to all other candidates Turkey is ahead of all the rest in this respect. The only country that can be considered at par with Turkey is the Czech Republic.

•The verdict with respect to the second criteria is also positive. The Turkish economy has proved its ability to compete with Europe. In this respect too Turkey can be considered as standing at the top of the list.

•Coming to the third criteria, here the overall evaluation on Turkey is again positive. Turkey is capable of fulfilling three of the five political, economic and monetary targets of the EU within a short period of time. Turkey can comply with the economic policies called for by the single market, the Common Agricultural Policy and defence and foreign relations but not with the European Monetary Union or Europe's social policies.

•In conclusion, based on all of the three criteria put forward in Copenhagen, Turkey is in a good position relative to candidates from Central and Eastern Europe.

These are the evaluations of the CRE. That is to say, from the economic point of view and based on the criteria determined at the Copenhagen Summit there is no reason to consider Turkey as being behind other candidates.

If Turkey Were a Member

According to a study by the Essen-based Turkish Studies Center, had Turkey joined the EU in 1996 prior to any changes in EU legislation, she would have received 11.7 billion ECUs from the EU budget. Her contribution to the budget in that same year would have been 1.9 billion ECUs. Therefore, the net amount she received would have been 9.8 billion ECUs, equivalent to 11% of the total EU budget and around 0.15 % of the EU member states' total GDP. Other studies estimate the annual amount that would have been received by Turkey from the EU as 6-8 billion ECUs. It seems that those who claim that Turkey's membership in the EU would bring an extraordinary burden are not justified in their arguments.

There is also the other side of the coin: 9.8 billion ECUs almost equals the amount of Turkey's trade deficit with the EU. In this way the transfer of funds from Turkey to Europe that has been going on for years would be balanced to a certain extent. What's more, as the Spanish case shows, full membership would boost the Turkish economy and general welfare, thereby allowing the Turkish contribution to the EU budget to increase in a relatively short time. It would be realistic to assume that in the near future the balance between Turkey's receivables and payables in the EU budget would be similar to that of Spain. A balance of mutual interest among the EU member states is maintained. For example, although Spain receives around 6 billion ECUs from the EU budget, most of its $20 billion trade deficit stems from her trade with the rest of the EU. Through their contributions to the budget, the larger members of the EU help the development of the less developed members; however, in this way they benefit from the freedom of movement of goods, Labor and capital and gain free access to a market of 300 million, giving them sizeable gains. That is to say, the EU should not be viewed as a philanthropic institution in which the rich help the poor.

There are avenues of cooperation outside the EU between developed and developing countries. It would be useful to take a look at Turkey's position in this respect as well.

Every year the Development Aid Committee (DAC), comprising of the richest countries in the world, gives out around $60 billion in assistance to various countries. In 1995 this amount was $58.8 billion, which is equivalent to 0.30% of the GDPs of contributing countries. From these sources Turkey obtained $268 million in 1992, $406 million in 1993,

$163 million in 1994 and $303 million in 1995. Egypt, on the other hand, received $3.6 billion only in 1992. The aid she received in later years has varied between $1.6 and $2.5 billion, and the amount received by Israel is close to these figures as well. Aid received by China has never fallen below $3 billion. Turkey, a country that is receiving a limited amount of aid herself, has extended help to developing countries through the same program, despite the fact that she is not a member of the DAC. The aid given by Turkey went up from $83 million in 1991 to $245 million in 1993. These amounts showed variations in later years. The IMF comes first among the sources most often used by countries seeking external funds. Yet we see large differences among the funds supplied by the IMF through its standby or other financial assistance formulations. The table below compares the quotas of some countries with the IMF and the actual funds they received.

Funds Obtained by Various Countries from the IMF as of September 30, 1998 (Million SDR*)

Country	IMF Quota	Loans	Financial Aid
Argentina	1,537	3,934	6,820
Brazil	2,170	7	6,835
Indonesia	1,497	5,087	13,007
South Korea	799	13,325	16,355
Mexico	1,753	6,417	17,199
Russia	4,313	14,089	18,238
Turkey	642	333	1,060

* Special Drawing Rights
Source: IMF Treasurer's Department, Accounts and Financial Reports Division

The table above gives an idea of the amount of IMF support received by these countries. The loans to Turkey were given after 1984. More IMF funds, exceeding those mentioned above, were granted to Indonesia, South Korea and Brazil after

·this table was published. The amount of funds received by Brazil in November 1998 under the auspices of the IMF was $41 billion. When compared with other developing nations, the amount of loans received by Turkey from the IMF or IMF-led syndicates is clearly at low levels. This proves two things: First, that Turkey has never faced economic problems as serious as those faced by countries she is compared with; and second, she overcame periods of economic downturn by relying for the most part on her own resources.

The conclusion reached from these figures is as follows: In recent years both the member states and the EU as an institution have made large contributions to countries whose eligibility for membership is compared with that of Turkey. With her own contributions Turkey too joined these donor countries. The same rich countries gave billions of dollars in aid to many nations, including China, Egypt and Israel, and within her limits Turkey has contributed to these efforts as well. But when it was Turkey's, turn excuses and obstacles abounded and she received almost nothing. Turkey's performance is now held up against those that have received so much in aid, and still in most respects she manages to outperform all of them, despite the EU's quotas on Turkish textiles that have lasted for years, anti-dumping policies and non-tariff obstacles. It's here where Turkey's economic power becomes apparent.

TURKEY AND THE GLOBALIZATION: A NEW CENTER OF ECONOMIC DYNAMIZM

The developments summarized above give a comparative analysis of the overall position of the Turkish economy, its evolution and its development process. The resulting picture is as follows: Turkey began its economic development and industrialization later than most other Western countries. There are internal as well as external reasons for this. A lack of financial resources has been one of the reasons why the reforms initiated during the period of decline of the Ottoman Empire could not take place as fast as they should have or did not yield the desired results. One of the reasons why the Ottoman Empire fell behind in industrial and general economic development was the capitulations that maintained the import tax revenues, which were among the main sources of income, at minimum levels. It must be remembered that Abdülhamit II had to struggle for seven years just to be able to increase tariffs by 3%.

In the early days of the Republic it was only natural to face economic difficulties, since World War I had devastated the country. Most of her economic resources were now outside the new borders of the country, and a part of the already limited number of educated people and a sizeable portion of the active population had been lost in the war. Moreover, due to restrictive articles in the Lausanne Treaty tariffs could not be raised during the first five years of the Republic, not to mention the fact that the new state had agreed to repay all the debt owed from the Ottoman period. In those days Western countries that had traditionally been Turkey's main trading partners were in turmoil. French and Belgian occupation of Germany's Ruhr region had forced the German economy into bankruptcy. England was still recovering from the effects of the war. When the Great Depression that had originated in the US economy and subsequently engulfed the whole world began, the Turkish Republic was only five years old.

Despite all these drawbacks, Turkey embarked on a reform process, laying the foundations of a strong economy, building her infrastructure and educating her people. She kept her currency strong and followed a balanced budget policy, having a trade surplus almost every year. At a time when some Western countries such as Germany were experiencing hyperinflation, the Turkish economy was stable and had a very low inflation rate. Turkey's economic development began in those years. What's more, Turkey received almost no foreign aid, support or investment to help in this process.

By staying neutral during World War II Turkey saved herself from another economic devastation. In that period there was almost no Western country that could preserve its pre-war economic power and infrastructure. By not participating in the war Turkey was able to protect her trained manpower.

One must be fair when examining the past and present economic rigours experienced by Turkey. Countries that today look better than Turkey went through periods of hardship and sacrifice as well. Relatively speaking, Turkey had an easier and more stable time between the two world wars as well as during World War II. The main reason for this, of course, was the fact that she did not enter World War II.

During the early days of the Republic, Turkey had just gotten rid of the capitulations and gained her economic independence. She started to establish a modern, contemporary state structure from scratch and meanwhile was trying to complete her infrastructure. During that period she was considered to be among the developing nations. She needed protectionist measures. Her economy was not yet ready to fly under its own power. That is to say, she did not start the race with the Western Europeans at the same starting point or with the same accumulation of resources. Looking at it from this angle, while examining Turkey's efforts for economic development as well as the results obtained, one must take a holistic approach and commend Turkey's dynamism, power and ability to mobilize this power. One must also laud the economic achievements obtained through the joint efforts of her people, workers, businessmen and government officials, and the public as well as private sectors.

The years following the war were a time of moving into a multi-party democratic regime and to a liberal economic system. During that period Turkey reshaped her economic policies in order to be able to benefit from the Marshall Plan. This without doubt accelerated her economic development. However, experts and representatives of foreign economic and financial institutions advised Turkey not to invest in heavy industry and instead try to develop as a country of light industry and agriculture.

Budget deficits, trade deficits and foreign debts all started in those years. Nevertheless, Turkey took major steps in agriculture, transportation and in particular the construction of roads, dams and hydroelectric power plants. The foreign aid received during those years helped in the development of the infrastructure and some industrial sectors, but at the same time increased Turkey's dependence on such assistance. Due to the lack of capital accumulation in the private sector, the public sector continued to play an important role in the economy despite the liberal economic policies adopted. The Turkish private sector, however, started to make headway in those years.

In the 1960s when Turkey moved into a planned economy, a mixed economic system was adopted, and the public sector had to assume a leadership role again. By resorting to protectionist policies the government tried to shield domestic industry from the damaging effects of foreign competition, and through an import substitution policy it encouraged the local production of imported goods. In the mid-1960s Turkey had managed to attain high growth rates with low inflation. Ever since then Turkey has been following a policy of rapid economic development in order to catch up with the most industrialized nations. However, two oil crises in the 1970s shook the Turkish economy just as they did other economies.

The rapid increase in oil prices not only increased the share of oil expenditures in imports but also raised inflation in Western countries, which in turn increased the cost of imported goods, initiating the ongoing period of high inflation in Turkey. For this reason external factors play a role in the increase of the Turkish inflation rate, which even today is one of the foremost economic problems of the Turkish economy.

Another factor influencing the rate of inflation has been the rapid change in the structure of foreign debt seen since the mid-1970s. It is worth looking at the reasons why the share of short-term debt in the total amount of foreign debt jumped while at the same time the duration of long-term debt decreased and the interest burden of these debts doubled. What can be said now is only the fact that Turkey had a very difficult time then obtaining the necessary economic and financial resources to overcome the problems.

Economic problems, which to a large extent stemmed from external factors, gave rise at the end of the 1970s to shortages in oil and other basic consumer goods. This led to the belief that these problems were in general due to misguided economic policies. Turkey may in fact have made mistakes and experienced shortfalls, but it is difficult to assume that all problems were a result of these.

The big devaluation of 1980 and the economic reform package constituted the starting point of a new era for Turkey. During this period, policies such as import substitution, protection of domestic industry and protection of the national currency were all abandoned in favour of liberal economic policies. These policies enabled Turkey to globalize in terms of economic activities, giving her a dynamic market economy, opening the way for the private sector to develop and be more competitive in foreign trade. Within the same period, major investments in infrastructure were completed. Motorways were built, while Turkey became one of the most popular tourist destinations in Europe as well as constructing a world-standard project like the Atatürk Dam. Yet, this rapid development was not without its costs.

Inflation became nearly chronic, the Turkish lira depreciated to a large extent, problems with distribution of income could not be solved and the real increase expected in workers' and civil servants' earnings not only did not materialize, they even fell.

Turkey financed the majority of large infrastructure investments through her own budget. Although the Build-Operate-Transfer (BOT) system was used, the number of such projects remained limited.

As a result of her own efforts Turkey ceased to be a developing nation and became a moderately developed country, able to extend economic and technical assistance to other countries. But due to the unfavourable terms of external financing she became more and more burdened with external debt. The fact that some countries with more debt could find financing at more attractive rates and conditions prevented their economies from being as adversely affected as Turkey's. While the Central and Eastern European states benefited from foreign economic and financial aid packages as well as from internationally subsidized investments, Turkey showed a higher growth rate than any other European country, more or less by just relying on her own resources. As said previously, using the ppp system the Turkish economy now ranks sixth in size in Europe. Turkey's external trade has been one of the most rapidly developing in the world, and her foreign currency reserves have reached record levels. The customs union of 1995, a result of the 1963 Association Agreement, benefited EU countries, at least to begin with, and Turkey's trade deficit with the EU jumped from $5 billion to more than $10 billion. During this period the EU failed to fulfil its own obligations. Despite various incentive programs the amount of foreign investment coming into Turkey has failed to reach desired levels. International financial circles are not particularly encouraging foreign investors to come to Turkey. Whether there are political considerations behind this reality deserves a separate study. Despite these facts, the Turkish economy has managed to compete in the tough economic environment that came with customs union, and contrary to the expectations of some there have not been large-scale bankruptcies and collapses.

Within the same framework, Turkey has started to adapt her internal economic regulations, in particular those that relate to competition and standards, to those of the EU. At the same time, she has managed to maintain one of the largest armies in the world as well as modernize and strengthen it, and neutralize a terrorist campaign the likes of which have not been seen in post-war Europe.

Turkey's economic development stems from economic policies adopted and from new approaches to economic development as well as from the human element capable of implementing these policies, and not from natural resources discovered and operated by other nations. This socioeconomic change, which that had started during the Ottoman era and became much more pronounced in the Atatürk period, gave rise to a professional, technical manager group, the middle class. It is this middle class that gives life to and empowers Western democracies. [119]

While these are the realities of the situation, it is interesting that some foreign institutions, authorities and experts say that Turkey's current problems are all of her own making. To claim that Turkey's economy is not sufficiently developed for her to be included in the enlargement process of the EU has been particularly surprising.

---

[119] Bernard Lewis, Why Turkey is the Only Muslim Democracy, Middle East Quarterly, March 1994, p. 46.

When the enlargement process was in question, the EU chose to compare Turkey with the Central and Eastern European countries which it had recently been supporting with large aid packages and investment. Despite all criticism it is clear that Turkey's economy is well ahead of those of all other applicants, even ahead of some of those who are currently members of the Union. When this was understood, yet another argument was given: "You still cannot begin the accession process with the other applicants because you have problems with your democracy and human rights record. You are behind other applicants in that respect."

One must understand that some circles are surprised by Turkey's progress in economic and other areas, that they refuse to accept Turkey's achievements and try to portray Turkey as an unsuccessful country, since for a long time many had a dogmatic belief that Turks could never be successful. At the start of 1919 French Prime Minister Clemenceau said, "Not a single country developed nor culture progressed under Turkish administration."[120]

Turkey proved the opposite in economic and other fields. Now the question is to accept and digest the success of the Turkish people.

Those who fail to do this keep trying to put forward Turkey's shortfalls. Moreover, they do it by putting aside the rule of courtesy and mutual respect that is normally observed in international relations. In particular they try to propagate the image that democracy and human rights in Turkey are behind the standards of other Western countries. In the face of these claims that hurt the Turkish people, a comparative analysis between Turkey and other Western countries should be made to see where Turkey stands on these issues, what kind of an evolution is taking place and what progress has been achieved.

---

[120] Güvenç, op.cit., p. 284.

How and when did regimes based on democracy, freedom and understanding among people develop in other countries and in Turkey?

DEMOCRACY: IDEALS AND REALITIES

Whether or not Turkish democracy conforms to democratic standards has been a subject of frequent discussion in the local as well as foreign media, among the public and in political circles. When EU membership was put on the agenda, the claim that democratic principles are not fully respected in Turkey was put forward as an argument that prevented Turkey from being included in the accession process. It is also argued that other applicants are well ahead of Turkey in the field of democracy.

Before explaining the structure of the state, the process through which democratic thought and government arrived in Turkey and how the mechanisms of democracy work there, it would be useful to analyze the definition of democracy and see how it works in its places of birth, its evolution in those places as well as its current status and problems. In particular, without a comparative study of how parliamentary regimes, people's sovereignty and democracy developed both in Turkey and Western Europe during the past 75 years since the birth of the Turkish Republic, it will not possible to understand Turkey's current state structure and political order based on the will of the people.

"Democracy" is a word of Greek origin. Its dictionary definition is "government by the people." Throughout history, various definitions have been given for the concept of democracy. One of the most often used is "the rule of the people, by the people and for the people." Democracy is also defined as a system of government by the people exercised either directly or through representatives elected with free elections.[121]

There are more detailed definitions. These distinguish the difference between direct and representative democracies. In another definition democracy is explained as "the rule of the majority within constitutional borders protecting the minorities' individual and collective rights." There are also definitions that state that social and economic democracy is a political and social system that aims to minimize the inequalities arising from private ownership.[122]

Bernard Lewis gives a simpler and clearer definition of democracy. According to him democracy is a constitutional and representative system of government where those in government can be changed with known and internationally accepted methods, without the use of force. Samuel Huntington thinks that if the government changes hands twice with this method, then democracy in that country may be considered as established. The Europe of the 1930s and 1940s is filled with examples of anti-democratic governments coming to power by benefiting from democratic principles but refusing to step down from the government through the same means and instead establishing dictatorships. For example, Hitler came to power in democratic elections but did not agree to organize democratic elections again during his lifetime. Lewis gives these examples, then brings the discussion to Turkey and says: "Of the 51 sovereign state members of the Islamic Conference, some never tried democracy; some did but were unsuccessful and gave up on the idea; some are trying again by devolving the powers of the central government carefully and in restricted fashion; some of these have already passed the test of changing their governments by democratic means. But in modern times, only one country passed the test of changing its government with democratic rules twice, which is not only

---

[121] Webster's Encyclopedic Dictionary.
[122] The New Encylopaedia Britannica.

more difficult but also means that the government is ready to surrender itself to the will of the people. That country is the Turkish Republic."[123]

---

[123] Bernard Lewis, Why Turkey is the Only Muslim Democracy, op. cit., p. 44.

Political Life Until the French Revolution

The world's first democratic experiences were seen in the ancient Greek city-states. Their populations were usually no larger than 10,000, and women and slaves did not have the right to vote. Therefore, the democracy found in Greek city-states was much different from contemporary democracy, as was the democracy of ancient Rome. It took 2,000 years for modern democracy to evolve into what it is today.

In more recent periods we see examples of some Western European monarchs securing the approval of institutions or parliaments composed of different groups in society for some of their prerogatives, such as collecting taxes, thereby restricting their own absolute powers. The Scandinavian countries and England had such experiences. Although the date when such local parliaments were established in Scandinavian countries is not definitively known, it is believed that they existed in A.D. 600.

In the old tradition of northern countries the right to rebel against a king who would not abide by the rules did exist. In the 12th and 13th centuries laws granting such rights were enacted in Norway, and there were occasions when monarchs were dethroned and executed.[124] Yet such ancient traditions did not prevent these countries from being ruled by absolutist monarchies. Just like anywhere else in the world, those were the centuries of sovereign kings and power struggles between monarchs and the Church. It would be appropriate to accept the French Revolution and the US Constitution, which incorporated a Bill of Rights of people and citizens, as the starting points for contemporary democracy. If one considers

---

[124] Erik Allard and others, Nordic Democracy, Copenhagen, 1981, p. 21.

the developments that took place in the centuries preceding the French Revolution, one can understand how it came to pass, and in the process provide a useful tool for the study the evolution of Turkish democracy.

The systems that gave people a voice in social affairs first developed in England. After a period of small Anglo-Saxon kingdoms in which the monarch had absolute power, an era emerged wherein the kings were elected by a court of elders. The first manifestations of the English system of government came in the 11th century, when William the Conqueror ruled over all of England. This was also when the Turks started to settle in Anatolia.

It was Henry II, ascending the throne in the mid-12th century, who first established a system of law that applied over the entire country. In even earlier times a Grand Council was periodically summoned; however only nobles could participate in these meetings. Therefore, it is not possible to draw a parallel with that council and today's parliaments. In those days the main goal of the nobles was to prevent the king from turning into a despot. In 1215, as a result of pressure from the nobles, the Magna Carta was accepted, and the authority of the king was curbed. Actually, the goal was to protect the rights of the noblemen but rules such as meting out punishment according to the crime committed had an effect on all strata of society.

Although it is not an example of a democratic system as it is known today, by restricting the king's authority the Magna Carta was a major step towards democracy. Again, in the mid-13th century, the Grand Council began to be called "Parliament." At the end of the century King Edward I convened the "Model Parliament." This was not a parliament elected by the people but rather appointed by the king. In the beginning, the Parliament would meet in three groups: the lords, the religious leaders and the commoners. At the end of the 14th century the lords and religious leaders merged, and a

Parliament with two houses called the House of Lords and the House of Commons was formed.

The establishment of a parliamentary system in England set an example for other countries. Yet one must not assume that this system has continued uninterrupted in England since then. For example, during the time of the Tudor dynasty in the 15th century the kings were so powerful that the era was known as the reign of the House of Tudor. The Parliament gave in to the king and obeyed his will on every occasion. During the Stuart reign that followed the king and the Parliament experienced conflict. The struggle that began to reinstate the rights of the Parliament gave rise to a civil war, which resulted in the trial and execution of the king.

During the Cromwell period, England had the brief experience of being a republic, after which the kings took over once again. The king was dethroned in 1688. Prince William III of Orange became king at the invitation of the Parliament and in 1689 accepted the Bill of Rights. This bill is a turning point in the establishment of democratic thought in England.[125]

Four hundred years had elapsed between the Magna Carta that restricted the king's rights and the Bill of Rights that paved the way for the acceptance of democratic principles. In between there were periods of absolute sovereigns, dethronements and even royal executions. Moreover the level of democracy in 17th century England was still far from the current understanding of the concept. The people had to wait for another 200 years in order to obtain the right to vote.

The United States of America was one of the firsts in the world to accept and implement democracy. But there too the evolution of democracy was not without its difficulties. For the greater part of the 18th century America was comprised of colonies. July 4, 1776 is the date when these 13 colonies declared independence from British rule. Their goal was to

---

[125] Manfred C. Vernon, Devlet Sistemleri, translated by Mümtaz Soysal, Ankara 1961, pp. 7-10.

develop a system of government that would respect the will of the people and man's natural and inalienable rights. Until that time, the governors sent by the colonial powers had represented the sovereign. There were some local legislative bodies, but the real authority rested with the governor. Through the Declaration of Independence the former colonies left the administration of the new United States to the Continental Congress. Each state had one vote in the Congress. Declaring war and making peace as well as conducting foreign affairs was under its authority, and those rights that were not delegated to the Congress were retained by the states. The Constitution of the United States of America was drawn up at a convention held in Philadelphia in 1787, and the Congress put the Constitution into effect in September 1788. This is the oldest written constitution in the world.[126] Yet one must not assume that by adopting this Constitution, which called for respect for human rights, freedoms and equality, that the United States immediately started enjoying the same kind of democratic structure it does today. In order to achieve that, it had to struggle for years to come.

The French Revolution of 1789, which today is seen as the symbol of modern democracy, turned the concepts of freedom, equality and brotherhood into a goal not only for France but for all peoples of the world. But in France rights and freedoms were established only after great difficulties. Like England, France also went through turbulent years, and following the French Revolution France lived through two empires, several constitutional kingdoms and five republics.

During the 16th and 17th centuries tremendous struggles had taken place between the kings and the clergy of France. Following these conflicts, the Protestants gained their freedom with the Edict of Nantes in 1598. However, not even a hundred years had passed before King Louis XIV in 1685 withdrew the rights granted by the edict. Most Protestants fled

---

[126] Ibid., p.116.

the country, and Louis XIV ruled the country as an absolute monarch.

Prior to the period of revolution the country had economic and social problems as well. The nobles and the clergy benefited from exemptions and did not pay taxes. Philosophers like Montesquieu, Voltaire and Rousseau were struggling for individual freedom, claiming that sovereignty should rest with the people. In this atmosphere the Estates-General, a three-party representative assembly that had not met since 1614, was convened in 1789. They were unable to achieve much, but the Third Estate declared itself the National Constituent Assembly. The "Declaration of the Rights of Man and of the Citizen" had turned into a burning torch for all peoples struggling for democracy.

Democratic Struggle after the French Revolution

Fight for Democracy in its Cradle

The Constitution that was accepted in France in 1791 curtailed the authority of the king, and a constitutional monarchy was established. But when the king tried to flee the county, the Constitution was abolished, as it had become obsolete. The king and queen were beheaded. The new Assembly fell into the hands of radical elements led by the Committee of Public Safety. The First Republic was initially entrusted to the control of a Directory comprising five members, a system that existed for only four years. Later, under the influence of Napoleon, the Council of State was formed. Napoleon declared himself consul for life, abolished the Republic and in 1804 declared himself emperor. So, the Republic established by the French Revolution was able to survive only 14 years. Some of the revolutionaries were then executed by those in power.

Napoleon was not a strong believer in the ideals of freedom fought for during the revolution. But he believed in the equality of man and did not permit the discrimination of the old regime to resurface. He strengthened French unity and established a new judicial system, putting a new legal code in place. He also reformed education and administration of the state. At the same time the Ottoman Sultan Selim III was also undertaking reformist moves. During the reign of the Bourbons, who followed Napoleon, French democracy was unable to progress. To the contrary, in line with requests of the nobility, the clergy were given back their old privileges.

With the revolution of 1830 the Bourbons were ousted from power, and the privileges of that period were abolished.

The Orleans dynasty, which replaced the Bourbons, raised the hope for democracy; however, not much could be done to that effect during that period. The right to vote was granted only to a selected few. The people, who were also struggling with economic problems, rebelled in 1848. The king was forced to flee the country. Once again, France returned to the status of a republic, known as the Second Republic. However, its existence was even more short-lived than the previous one. The right to vote was extended to cover more people, and it was agreed that they would elect the president. The French chose Napoleon's nephew, Louis Napoleon Bonaparte, as their president. He drafted a new Constitution in 1851 that designated him as president for 10 years, which the French accepted. But even this was not enough for Louis Napoleon because after a year, following in the footsteps of his uncle, he declared himself emperor. Faced with an increase in popular unrest, he announced that his would be a "liberal empire"; however, it was too late. The Constitution of 1870 bestowed authority on the people. The Franco-Prussian war that broke out that same year spelled the end of the empire, and once again a republican government was established. [127]

After the Prussian defeat of 1870, France tried to reform its political structure. Right after a cease-fire was declared, elections were held and the Assembly met in Bordeaux. But most of the elected representatives and a majority of the government were in favour of monarchy. President Louis Adolphe Thiers was also a known royalist. Meanwhile, the Assembly moved to Versailles. Republicans, socialists and communists feared that the Assembly would re-establish the monarchy. A large uprising began, and the Paris Commune was formed. Thiers ordered the use of force to put down the uprising, giving Marshal Marie E.P.M. de MacMahon the

---

[127] Ibid., p. 61.

responsibility to do so. Bloody street fights ensued for three months. For six weeks de MacMahon bombed the strongholds of the communes in Paris during which 20,000 people were killed, and 17,000 were either executed or deported to prisons in distant French colonies. Outside Paris in commune strongholds such as Toulouse, Lyon, St. Etienne and Marseilles, the rebellion was crushed in bloody fashion. De MacMahon, who had put down the rebellion by force, was elected president; however, he too was a royalist.

In such an atmosphere a fierce struggle took place in the Assembly between the royalists and the republicans in 1875. The republicans won by a single vote, thus establishing the Third Republic. A Constitution was drafted. All men were granted the right to vote. This was a significant improvement, but women still had no electoral rights. The Constitution gave extensive powers to the president; selecting ministers, proposing legislation, abolishing the Assembly upon the recommendation of the Senate were all under the authority of the head of state. This Constitution remained in place until 1940. The Constitution of the Third Republic was only one year older than the 1876 Ottoman Constitution.

The first 40 years of the Third Republic were filled with political turmoil. During this period France had 50 governments. The fact that royalists initially were the majority in the Senate created problems. After 1881, extensive reforms were undertaken, especially in the field of education, and later major steps were taken for economic development. Coal and iron production increased rapidly. New railroads were built. New legislation was drawn up to give more social rights to workers and women. However, within the same period, France expanded its colonies. In 1881 it invaded Tunisia, which had been under Ottoman rule for a long time. A few years later the French occupied Madagascar. The colonization of Indochina, which had begun during the reign of Napoleon III, continued with more vigour. These territories remained under French rule until defeat against the forces of Ho Chi

Minh in 1954. The ill treatment of the local colonial populace by French authorities drew heavy criticism at home, led by Clemenceau, a radical left-winger. In this period the socialists began to play an increasingly important role in French political life, and in the elections of 1893, 45 socialist representatives managed to get into the Assembly.

Despite all the turmoil France kept the Third Republic alive, tried to improve her democracy and engaged in reforms; but she continued to be a colonial power. The rights of people living in the colonies was another matter.

Towards the end of the 18th century in England the Irish Catholics, who were demanding freedom and democracy, were not allowed to become members of parliament. Their fight to obtain equal rights went on for many years, until 1828. The British Parliament passed legislation that banned the slave trade as late as 1807. Secret ballots are not sufficient to make a proper democracy, and at that time tampering with election results, buying votes and pressuring voters were common practice in Western countries. In order to prevent such occurrences an "Impropriety and Prevention of Illegal Practices" act was adopted in Britain in 1883. In 1920 legislation with similar purposes was passed in the United States as well.

In the first half of the 19th century reformist laws were passed in England. With the reforms of 1828, some sections of society, but not all of it, were granted representative rights in Parliament. Workers, artisans and a part of the middle class still had no voting rights. Efforts to develop democracy continued well into that century. Legislation that allowed for secret ballots was passed in 1872.[128] The 1884 law also expanded voting rights to a certain extent. As a result landlords and tenants who paid more than a certain amount of rent could vote. This meant giving electoral power to an additional 2 million people, an important piece of progress. Yet there too women still did not have the right to vote. They

---

[128] Peacock, op. cit., p. 5.

would have to wait for years, well into the 20th century. Having said this, democratic progress in England was less painful relative to other European countries.

In 1887, with the support of some European nations, Britain invaded Egypt, which was Ottoman territory, thus securing the route to India. During Chamberlain's tenure as colonial secretary, British sovereignty in its colonies, in particular those in Africa, was reinforced. As the result of a local war in 1899 the British broke the resistance of the Boers in South Africa, and the South African Union was established in 1910. It too was under British sovereignty. There were insurrections in Ireland. While agitation continued in the colonies, reforms were implemented at home, new social rights were granted and the economy was developed. The human rights of those living in colonies were a different issue.

Fight for Equality in the United States

Until 1820 only property owners had the right to vote in the United States, and not all of them, at that; only white males could take part in elections. In later years significant reforms were made. The years between 1830 and 1850 are known as the reform period of the United States. In 1830, except for the blacks, then called Negroes, and Native Americans, or Indians, all white males in almost every state were granted the right to vote. In those days one of the most hotly debated issues was the abolition of slavery. Associations and political parties were established, and calls were made for the unconditional abolition of slavery, saying that it was contrary to the principles of democracy. Yet, it was not easy to obtain results toward that end, and years of struggle were necessary. It was easier to abolish slavery in the northern states, but the Southerners put up resistance. In 1830 there were 347,525 slaves in those states that had not abolished slavery. A total of 1,800 people owned more than 100 slaves each; these were large plantation owners. The slaves organized mass revolts in 1800, 1822 and 1831, the last of which was put down forcefully. At the end of the 19th century the United States endured the trauma of a civil war. The southern states in particular were almost totally devastated. Approximately 600,000 soldiers died from the North and the South during the Civil War.

The Constitution was amended to prohibit slavery and forced Labor in 1865; however, "black codes" restricting the rights of blacks were passed in the southern states. According to these they could not own property, could not trade, could not be jury members and could not vote.

Meanwhile, it had been 26 years since the Tanzimat Fermanı, an imperial edict at the time of Sultan Abdülmecid that accepted the principle of equality of all the citizens, and nine years since the Islahat Fermanı that expanded on these rights. The principle of equality of all people had been accepted in Turkey before it had been in some US states. However, a system of representative government developed in the United States before it did in Turkey. The first Ottoman Parliament was established 100 years later than independence was declared and a democratic Congress was established in the United States. The Ottomans, who were latecomers to democracy, were ahead of the Americans in accepting the equality of all men.

American democracy developed towards the end of the 19th century, but it was still not possible to remove all the obstacles barring the way to a true democracy. Following years of struggle slavery was abolished with the 13th amendment to the Constitution, but the southern states were reluctant to comply. To the contrary, with the "black codes" they prevented blacks from owning land, working in specialized professions, serving on juries and, most importantly, from voting in elections. Congress reacted harshly to this development. With the 14th amendment to the Constitution the legislative body had guaranteed that no state can put restrictions on the rights of US citizens. This law does not explicitly mention that blacks too had the right to vote, but it stresses that in the event voting rights are restricted Congress will be able to take corrective action. The Southern states were unable to withstand the pressure much longer, and they accepted the 14th amendment as well as the 15th. The problem seems to have been resolved from a legal point of view, but the situation was quite different in practice. Large plantation owners and their supporters, who wanted to prevent the blacks from exercising their rights and keep them as second-class citizens, began to form underground organizations, the most notorious being the Ku Klux Klan. This organization spelled terror to blacks who wanted to exercise their constitutional rights and put the local courts under pressure. It became difficult for blacks to secure their rights through legal means. As a result the number of black voters in the South remained extremely low. Congress took a dim view of this as well. In 1870 legislation dealing with the Ku Klux Klan was passed, and the president was given authority to declare martial law. Following the electoral defeat of President Andrew Johnson, who was known as a supporter of citizens' rights, pressure on blacks intensified in the elections of 1870. During this period a ruling by the Supreme Court facilitated the task of the racists. According to this ruling the 15th amendment did not give voting rights to everyone. In a sense, blacks could legally be prevented from voting, if it was proved that this was not done for racist reasons. In 1877 the Federal Army withdrew from the southern states, taking the black people's main protectors out of the picture. At the end of the century most African-Americans were still unable to effectively exercise their voting rights.

During the same period the situation of the Native Americans was not ideal either. Many white Americans were eager to farm the fertile land and operate the rich mines of the west. Settling in those areas was particularly attractive for large cattle ranchers, but their biggest obstacle was the Indian.

With legislation passed in 1851, Congress forced some Native Americans to live on reservations. However, in the years following the Civil War the Indians stepped up their resistance. Between 1869 and 1876 more than 200 clashes took place between the Federal Army and the Indians. This is the date of acceptance of the Ottoman Empire's first Constitution, calling for equal treatment for all irrespective of race or religion. The Indians' resistance ended with the Battle of Wounded Knee in 1890. At the beginning of the century, there were only 250,000 Native Americans left in all America; the first law protecting the rights of Indians wasn't passed until 1934.

After that, Congress passed various pieces of legislation that abolished the restrictions on blacks and ethnic groups' rights to elect and be elected. One of these was the Election Reform Act of 1950. But more progressive legislation was passed in 1965. Called the Voting Rights Act, this abolished literacy tests for voters as well as restrictive articles in the tax laws of some states connected to voting rights and gave the federal government the right to inspect new legislation passed by the states so that it would not infringe upon suffrage rights.

Progressive ideas developed between 1901 and 1914, and some social rights were secured in the United States. The US took positive steps in this field during the presidency of Theodore Roosevelt, who was elected after President William McKinley was assassinated in 1901. However, during the same period the United States tried to extend its influence to Latin America and the Pacific region, using as an argument "helping the underdeveloped people of the Pacific and the Latin America." [129]

---

[129] Ibid., pp. 71, 80.

Germany: Late Democracy

There were important developments in Germany as well. Otto von Bismarck, who united smaller German states under the leadership of Prussia and won the war against France, established the German Empire in 1871. He held the position of chancellor, i.e. prime minister. Bismarck gave priority to achieving internal union and industrial development and was not particularly interested in giving the people a voice in the government. A constitution was drawn up, but the real authority rested with the emperor, the army, the bureaucracy and Bismarck. A two-house Parliament, comprising the Bundesrat and the Reichstag, was established. Representatives from all the states were in the Bundesrat; however, the Prussian representatives dominated. The Reischtag's members were elected, but its authority was restricted. All males could participate in elections, but only males. The imperial government was not responsible to either of these houses; it answered only to the emperor. The emperor could consult with the Bundesrat and abolish the Parliament whenever he wanted. Bismarck sometimes struggled with the Church, sometimes with the socialists and sometimes with the liberals. He restricted the activities of the Church; in 1872 the Jesuits were thrown out of Germany, and in 1873 thousands of Catholic priests were jailed or expelled from the country. The battle between the state and the Church in Prussia was referred as a "cultural battle" or a "civilization battle." Later Bismarck made peace with the Church, reinstating some of its former privileges and benefiting from their support in dealing with the socialists, whom he viewed as enemies of the empire.

Despite Bismarck's efforts the socialists won half a million votes in the elections of 1877. They put 12 members in Parliament. In the meantime two attempts were made on the emperor's life. Bismarck used these as an opportunity to pass state of emergency laws through Parliament. According to these laws the government would be able to declare martial law whenever it saw reason do so, and when there was a Labor uprising in Berlin the government invoked this right. The police prohibited socialists' meetings and confiscated their publications. Fifteen hundred members of the Socialist Party were put into prison, and many were exiled. When the leaders of the Ottoman freedom movement were exiled, the German socialists were either imprisoned or exiled as well. Despite these pressures the socialists continued to get stronger; in 1890 they increased their votes to 1.5 million and in 1914 to 4.2 million.

During the Bismarck period the German government, along with the business community, pursued a colonial policy. In 1884 Bismarck, who was against this idea in the beginning, organized a conference in Berlin of all the great colonial powers. They divided up the colonies in "Central Africa" among themselves and established spheres of influence. Southwestern Africa, Togo, Cameroon and Tanganyika fell to Germany.

Bismarck also chaired the Berlin Congress of 1878, right after the Turco-Russian war in which a large portion of Ottoman territory in the Balkans was lost.

In fact the history of colonialism dates back even further. Leaving aside ancient times, colonialism can be seen as starting as far back as the 16th century. It rapidly expanded during the 17th century in Central and South America, and Africa and Asia. In the early 18th century 70,000 slaves per year were brought to America to work on plantations. By the early 20th century the colonies of Great Britain covered 20% of the world and had 400 million people.

Emperor Wilhelm I died in 1888. Shortly afterwards Wilhelm II was crowned, and Bismarck, who was unable to agree with him on many issues, had to resign. The new emperor too was a supporter of colonial policies. To this end he strengthened the German Navy. It was Emperor Wilhelm II who accepted Enver Pasha's offer of an alliance with the Ottoman Empire. During that period Germany made enormous expenditures to strengthen its army and navy. After the elections of 1912 the Socialists became the largest political party; they had 110 members of parliament but were not in a position to control the government. Germany's population reached 65 million. A large industrial movement took place. Steel production reached twice that of Britain, and the armaments industry was developed. Germany entered World War I with great confidence, dragging with it the Ottoman Empire as well.

Political Life In Russia

Russia at that time was one of the greatest powers in Europe, but the internal political struggles there were quite interesting. From the early 19th century onwards reformists and anti-reformists clashed with each other. Czar Alexander II was supportive of reform. During the reign of his predecessor, Czar Nicholas I, the rebellion of the serfs had been one of the country's most serious problems. With a law he passed on March 3, 1861 Alexander II freed all serfs, affecting 44 million people. In 1850 the Russian population numbered 50 million, and in 1897, 82 million. This means that until then, more than half the Russian population had had the status of serf. Yet, this law did not solve all the problems; during the reign of Alexander II 15% of all peasants were in reality living under conditions of serfdom.

Serfs did not exist in the Ottoman Empire during that period. Peasants, called "reaya," were people who were dependent on the land. They could go to the "kadı," or local judge, to protect some of their rights. The Ottoman peasants' situation was quite different from that of the serfs, who had been working the land in Europe since the Middle Ages. The state did not leave the well-being of these peasants merely to the mercy of the "sipahi" or the owners of the "timar," two groups of local people who received land use privileges in return for paying taxes and helping mobilize local troops for the Ottoman Army. The general welfare of the peasants was the responsibility of the state.[130]

During the reign of Alexander II important reforms were enacted, in particular in the field of education. Ten thousand elementary schools were opened. Censorship was relaxed. The number of newspapers increased from six to 16. Judiciary reforms making judges more independent were carried out. However, those who were accused of political crimes were subject to separate proceedings. There were also separate courts both for journalists critical of the administration and for peasants.

Following the 1860s the Nihilism movement began in Russia, according to which everything connected to the past must first be destroyed in order to establish a new system. Its main targets were the czar and the Orthodox Church. In 1866 they made a failed assassination attempt against the czar, in response to which the czar tightened his authority. From then on only students who could be trusted were accepted into universities. During the final days of Alexander II the number of people arrested and exiled to Siberia increased significantly.

Meanwhile an underground organization called "The Will of the People" was formed. Its goal was to overthrow the government through violent and terrorist means. Between 1863 and 1874 150,000 people were sent into exile in Siberia. In 1881 the czar was assassinated by a bomb thrown by a terrorist.

During the period of Czar Alexander III, who succeeded Alexander II, autocratic methods were stepped up. His theory was that an elite group should lead the state. The universities were put under strict police control, and professors with liberal views were fired. Children of workers and peasants were not accepted into secondary schools. Fourteen newspapers were closed down for criticizing the government. Jews were allowed to live only in designated areas, and their

---

[130] Kongar, op. cit., p. 59.

children's right to education was also restricted. The views of Czar Nicholas II, who ruled from 1894 to 1917, were not that different from those of his father.

Lenin was one of the leaders of the Russian Social Democrat Workers' Party, established in 1898. Believers in Karl Marx's revolutionary theories, most of the party's leaders were arrested; those who escaped arrest fled the country. The government stepped up the pressure even further. The then minister of the interior, Plehve, who was seen as responsible for the anti-Semitic movements, was murdered in 1904. The czar's brother shared the same fate. On January 22, 1905 a large group demanding political freedom demonstrated at the gates of the czar's winter palace at St. Petersburg. Security forces put the demonstration down through a bloody intervention during which at least 100 people were killed. The czar could no longer withstand the pressure of the workers and the opposition and proclaimed a constitution. The Russian Parliament, known as the Duma, was established. However, the Duma's only role was to act as an advisory body; it did not have the right to pass legislation. In October 1905 the social democrats organized a general strike, and the czar was obliged to accept freedom of speech and various other democratic rights. But this, however, failed to calm the rebels. In December, workers' demonstrations in Moscow were violently dispersed. Once the government gained back control, the czar revoked some of the Duma's powers. At the same time, some groups who opposed a constitutional system engaged in terrorist attacks targeting the social democrats. Nationalist movements in the Ukraine were also harshly put down. In that period martial courts sentenced 4,500 people to death.[131] Jews were also under intense pressure. Efforts to establish a parliamentary system in Russia failed completely. The opposition went underground or fled the country. People's

---

[131] Peacock, op. cit., p. 66.

adverse reaction to the czar grew. It was under such circumstances that Russia entered World War I.

Democracy in Other European Countries

Democratic experiments were not unique to the great powers of the time. Smaller countries also made noteworthy attempts, and some were even more successful than those of larger nations. The Scandinavian countries can be considered cases in point. Yet there, too, it had not been easy to have the will of the people accepted. It took years of struggle. In Sweden, following a Bill of Rights, it took 400 years to come up with an appropriate form of administration. A constitution restricting the authority of the king was accepted in 1723; however, the power struggle between the kings and the Parliament continued even after that. For example, King Adolph Fredrick, who came to the throne in the mid-18th century, inspired by the French and Prussian examples, tried to establish an absolute monarchy. In 1772 King Gustav III declared himself the "Enlightened Despot," and that same year the Swedish Parliament accepted a constitution that gave almost absolute power to the king. The Parliament was abolished and could not reconvene until 1809. During the same period in Turkey, Sultan Selim III gathered the country's prominent people and secured their approval for his reforms, preparing the "Senedi İttifak" (Contract of Consensus) that reflected the agreement reached on this matter.

In Denmark, too, there were efforts to curb the authority of the king. However, the influence of the aristocracy was stronger there, in particular in the 16th and 17th centuries. In the 17th and 18th centuries there were absolutist regimes. Denmark was not much influenced by the French Revolution. At the beginning of the 19th century, pressure was intensified to restrict the powers of the king. Faced with this, the king established the regional consultative parliaments in 1834. He implemented a few reforms. When the Tanzimat restricting the powers of the sultan was declared in the Ottoman Empire in 1839, Denmark was still an absolute monarchy. In 1849 a constitution containing democratic elements was accepted. A two-house Parliament was established. There were a few restrictive rules that applied regarding the elections of the upper house, but all males were granted the right to vote. This promising start did not last long. In the second half of the 19th century, the king, together with the Upper House, whose members were under his influence, reduced the rights of the Lower House. This situation continued until 1890. In 1918 a more democratic constitution was designed, and a balance was achieved in Parliament. For the first time, women were granted the right to vote. On this issue, Finland was ahead of Denmark. Finland was the first country in Europe to grant voting rights to women. Finland's 1905 election law was a democratic revolution that increased the number of those eligible to vote 10-fold and accepted the right to vote of all citizens without any restrictions.[132]

Belgium too was among those that took steps in the direction of giving sovereignty to the people and restricting the power of the king. In this respect, the Belgian Constitution of 1831 played a leading role in Europe. But throughout the 19th and well into the 20th century, Belgium remained a colonial power. The rights of the people in its colonies were not that much different from those in other colonies. The ill treatment of the Africans in the Belgian Congo and methods used to coerce people into free Labor gave rise to strong reactions at home.[133]

In 1819, with the support of Czar Alexander I, a text known as the Carlsbad Decision was accepted in Austria. German and Austrian universities were put under the strict control of the government. Student unions were prohibited.

---

[132] Allard, op. cit., pp. 29, 31, 47.
[133] Peacock, op. cit., p. 87.

Censorship was stepped up. In reaction to pro-republican demonstrations in Hambach in 1831 and in Frankfurt in 1833, these measures were enforced with growing vigour. In 1848, a violent demonstration staged by the young and the intellectuals was harshly put down. But with the spread of the rebellion and the joining of the workers to the uprising, hard-line absolutist Prime Minister Metternich had to resign. Later, a relatively democratic constitution was drafted, and hence the regime was somewhat liberalized. But it is not possible to talk about democracy in Austria in the first half of the 19th century.[134]

---

[134] Encyclopaedia Britannica.

Reform Movements in the Ottoman Empire

Encounter with the French Revolution

The French Revolution had a major impact on the reform movements and the development of democratic thought in the Ottoman Empire. Actually the moves towards reform had started earlier in the Ottoman Empire, at the beginning of the 18th century. In a report presented to Sultan Ahmet III by İbrahim Pasha of Nevşehir in 1718 the need to catch up with the West was stressed.[135]

In relations with the West, the closest cooperation was with France. Selim III, considered to be the true leader of the reform movement aimed at Westernization of the country, was exchanging letters with Louis XIV. The Ottomans made extensive use of French specialists. The dethronement of Louis XIV and his subsequent execution was met with disbelief at the Ottoman palace. As a result of this, the Ottomans kept their distance from France for a few years. For example, while sending ambassadors to various European countries, they did not send one to France. However, the ideology of the French Revolution met with interest among Ottoman leaders and thinkers.

The Ottomans' first official contact with the administration stemming from the French Revolution took place four years after the revolution. A French citizen named Descorches, who would later be known as the Marquis of Sainte-Croix, arrived in Istanbul. His goal was to win the sympathy of the Ottomans

---

[135] Kongar, op. cit. p. 64.

for the French Revolution as well as disseminate its ideology within the Ottoman Empire. On July 14, 1793, the fourth anniversary of the French Revolution, two French ships anchored in Istanbul. They hoisted the Ottoman, French and American flags, which they referred to as countries that "pulled a gun on tyranny." They planted a tree of liberty in Istanbul during a public ceremony.

Two years later, in 1795, a publishing house headed by the president of the French National Publishing House was established in Istanbul on the premises the French Embassy. Here books and brochures promoting the ideas of the French Revolution were published and distributed to Turks who understood the French language. An association was formed at which both Turkish and French people could come together and freely discuss these ideas. The Ottomans saw the revolution as an internal affair of France in the early days. Even when the ideas of the French Revolution had spread to other neighbouring countries, causing wars and clashes, the Ottomans still viewed this as an internal matter among the Christians and never suspected that it could reach their shores. But when some of the Aegean islands that had belonged to Venice as well as parts of Greece and Albania came under French influence with the 1797 Campo Formio Agreement, France became Turkey's neighbour, and the Ottomans began to get worried.

These worries were exacerbated when the Ottomans learned that the French were spreading the ideas of the revolution among the Christian Ottomans in these territories, encouraging them to break ties with the Ottoman Empire. In the meantime news that the French were going to annex Peloponnese and Crete started to arrive. When information about the preparations of the French Navy at Toulon to occupy some Ottoman territory also became known, the Ottomans took a clear stand in opposition to the French Revolution. Skepticism and reaction replaced the optimism of the early days. Ahmet Atıf Efendi, the then minister of foreign affairs, presented a report to the government on how the French Revolution could jeopardize the interests of the

Ottomans. He referred to the French Revolution as a movement of infidels and recommended taking a position against it. When Napoleon attempted to occupy Egypt and Palestine by landing at Alexandria in 1798, Turkish-French relations were suspended for three years. The Ottomans distributed brochures that showed the French Revolution as an enemy of the faith.[136]

The Ottomans were by now strongly alienated from the French Revolution, seeing it as a hostile act. They foresaw that this ideology could potentially spread around the empire and incite independence movements. Subsequent developments proved that their fears were justified.

The goal of the reform movements in the Ottoman Empire was to give the country, in particular the army, a modern structure. Some of the developments taking place in the West, especially in the military arena, were followed with interest and used as examples by the Ottomans.

Abdülhamit I, who came to the throne in 1774, was quick to realize the need for reforms. He initiated the modernization of the navy and the artillery. Economic reforms were also made. Domestic production, especially textile production, was encouraged. Publishing houses were established and new books printed. These reforms were welcomed by the English, French and Dutch governments but caused concern with the Russians and the Austrians, who were worried about increased Turkish strength. With the 1774 Kaynarca Agreement Russia had secured special privileges for the Orthodox community living in Turkey and was now fearful that these modernization moves would infringe upon these rights. These countries started to secretly support anti-reformist conservative circles. Not all foreign powers wanted to see Turkey become a modern country. As a result of these efforts Sadrazam (prime minister) Halil Hamid Pasha was removed from his post, and foreign specialists helping the reforms were sent back to their countries.

---

[136] Lewis, The Emergence of Modern Turkey, London 1961, pp. 63, 67.

Period of Selim the Third: Hopes and Setbacks

Historians give the reign of Selim III as the starting point of the real reform movement in the Ottoman Empire. Selim III came to throne in 1789, the year of the French Revolution. He too began his reforms with the military, forming a modern army called the Nizamı cedid, with which he tried to replace the outdated Janissaries who had started to harm the empire more than benefit it. In 1795 he established a modern artillery school and tried to modernize the navy as well as the maritime school. He changed the financial structure of the state and continued to send ambassadors abroad.

During Selim III's time modest first steps were taken towards democratization. The sultan summoned civil and military leaders from all over the country to Istanbul and shared his views with them on the reforms he was planning, listening to their comments. On October 7, 1808, he and these local community leaders reached an agreement called Senedi İttifak, according to which these local leaders pledged their loyalty to the sultan and his grand vizier. In return the sultan agreed to collect taxes in a regular, rather than arbitrary, way and also agreed that the law would be respected. Local leaders promised to support the reform.[137] Yet it must be mentioned that the participation of local administrations in this agreement was low. At the time when these steps towards democracy were being taken in the Ottoman Empire, it had already been two years since the collapse of the republican regime of the French Revolution and the establishment of an empire in its place.

While these moves for reform were continuing in the Ottoman Empire, a large uprising began in Serbia with the support of Austria and Russia. The effects of the French Revolution were seen there too. This revolt continued until Serbia obtained restricted autonomy in 1812.

---

[137] Mantran, op. cit., p. 437.

Mahmud the Second and Fundamental Reforms

Faced with an uprising of the Janissaries, who were against the reforms, Selim III had to abdicate. His replacement, Mahmud II, accelerated the major reforms. He too started the job with the army. In place of the Nizamı cedid, which was established by his predecessor but later abolished due to pressure from the Janissaries and those against reforms, he established a new force called the Sekbanı cedid. Anti-reformists were very strong during his reign as well, including prominent provincial leaders and the clergy. Contrary to developments in Western Europe, rather than from the people, the pressure for reforms came from the sultan and statesmen who saw the inadequacies of the old structures and the necessity for reforms in all state institutions, in particular the military, in order for the empire to continue to exist in the changing conditions of the world.

During this period Russia tried to impose pressure on the Ottoman Empire to place the empire's Orthodox residents under its protection. The 1812 Bucharest Agreement gave some concessions to the Russians on this matter. But while Russia was applying pressure to protect the rights of the Orthodox community in the Ottoman Empire, millions of Russian Orthodox believers had the status of only a serf in Russia. As a result there is no way to see those pressures as stemming from humanitarian reasons.

During the reign of Mahmud II, a rebellion of the Janissaries against the reforms was forcefully put down. This spelled the end of the Janissaries, who had served the empire for centuries but had turned into a serious obstacle in the face of reform. In 1826 their unit was disbanded, and reforms were continued. In the years that followed modern units were formed, and new military schools were opened.

The reforms were not confined solely to the military. In 1830 serious structural changes were made within central as well as local administrations. These were not only bureaucratic changes. The entire approach to public administration was altered and rendered more modern. A ministerial system in state administration was established. One of the ministries formed in 1836 was the Ministry of Foreign Affairs. Foreign trade was also put under the responsibility of this ministry. From that day onwards, modern trade agreements were signed with other countries. In 1838 the Agriculture and Commerce Council was established.

That same year the Babıali Shura was established to study legislative proposals. Census and land registry studies were conducted. Civil servants were categorized, and their positions and salaries were determined using a modern approach. The structure of the army and its chain of command was updated according to contemporary standards. In addition to military schools, schools of law, literature and medicine were opened. When diplomats sent abroad returned home, they and their children used the experience acquired overseas and played an active role in the reform movement.

Between 1795 and 1828 printing companies were established, and they started to print newspapers in foreign languages. In 1831 the first Turkish paper, Takvimi Vekai, published its first issue. In 1840 the second Turkish newspaper, Ceridei Havadis, came out. The sultan himself adopted a European lifestyle, learning French and giving receptions. In 1814 he moved from Topkapı Palace to the Western-style Dolmabahçe Palace. Guisseppe Donizetti, brother of the famous Italian composer Gaetano Donizetti, was invited to Istanbul, where he organized concerts, operas and ballet in the palace. A military band in the Western style was formed. Western European fashion became popular.

Tanzimat and Reforming the State Structure

The most important of the reforms realized during the reign of Mahmud II was legislation restricting the powers of the sultan and protecting the rights of ordinary people. On November 3, 1839, a few months after the death of Mahmud II, his Grand Vizier Mustafa Reşid Pasha, in the presence of senior government officials and representatives of foreign countries, read out the text of the Gülhane Hattı Hümayunu or the Tanzimat Fermanı, named after its reforms in the judiciary, financial, administrative and military fields.

According to the Tanzimat, the principle of equality for all Ottoman citizens, irrespective of their religious or ethnic backgrounds, was agreed upon. Everyone would have the right to a fair trial by impartial courts, based on the laws of the country. Everyone would pay taxes in accordance with their income or wealth. Reading this in the presence of government officials as well as foreign representatives was considered a commitment on the part of the state to its people and the world at large. But some countries that wanted to take advantage of the weaknesses of the Ottoman Empire in order to divide it up were not pleased with these reforms.

During that period while Russia was trying to reach the Mediterranean, the British were also keen on dominating that region so as to control the road to India. The French also had ambitions in the Mediterranean. Using the protection of religious and ethnic minorities as an excuse, but more for the protection of their political and commercial interests, foreign countries were working to speed up the disintegration of the Ottoman Empire.[138]

The 1839-1878 period is known as the Tanzimat period of the Ottoman Empire. During this time important reforms called for by the Tanzimat Fermanı were carried out. The idea of liberty from the French Revolution found ardent supporters among Turkish intellectuals. They organized both inside and outside the country and engaged in a great political struggle to have the reforms render the country more democratic and

---

[138] Ibid., pp. 447-449.

respectful toward freedoms in addition to restricting the sultan's authority and restructuring of the government.

In the meantime, Ottomans of different religious and ethnic backgrounds started to publish their own newspapers, exercising their religious and social rights to the fullest. In 1850 15,000 Protestants received the right from the sultan to establish their own community. Religious rights were as extensive as any other place in Europe, if not more so.

In 1853 Czar Nicholas I of Russia said the following to British Ambassador Hamilton Seymour regarding the Ottoman Empire: "What we have in our arms is a very sick man. One of these days he may leave us, so we must take precautions for that day." This was a message about dividing up the lands of the Ottoman Empire. In March of the same year the czar's deputy, Prince Menchikof, arrived in Istanbul to relay the demands of the czar as follows: The question of holy places would be resolved as necessary by Russia. But that wasn't all: An agreement would be signed placing the Orthodox Church under the protection of the Russian Empire. Menchikof also gave an ultimatum: The Ottoman state must accept these demands within five days.

The Ottomans rejected the demands. In this incident the British and French were on the Ottomans' side. Russia showed its reaction by invading a few Romanian princedoms. The Crimean War erupted. The British and French had a precondition for fighting alongside the Ottomans: Measures must be taken to give people of different religious backgrounds equal treatment. This was fulfilled in the Istanbul Agreement of March 12, 1854, and a few days later France and Britain declared war on Russia. Hence, a Muslim country had allied itself with Christian countries and declared war on another Christian country, an event that received extensive coverage in the Western press. Bernard Lewis sees this as the victory of more or less democratic countries against totally undemocratic Russia.[139]

---

[139] Lewis, Why Turkey is the Only Muslim Democracy, op. cit., p. 42.

Russia suffered tremendously during the reign of Czar Nicholas I, who demanded that the Ottomans allow him to be protector of members of the Orthodox faith. The uprising of the serfs also occurred during his reign. As mentioned earlier the law giving freedom to serfs was passed in 1861, during the time of Alexander II, who came to the throne after Nicholas I. This, of course, was possible provided the serfs could pay the local authorities their emancipation fees.[140] However, serfdom continued for many years in actual practice. This was the situation of the Orthodox people in a Russia that was demanding to be protector of the Orthodox faithful in the Ottoman Empire.

France, on the other hand, wanted to be protector of the Catholics living in the Holy Land, then under Ottoman sovereignty. This was also dictated by France's domestic politics of the time, since Louis Napoleon had to gain the support of the Catholics.

Such was the situation of countries that demanded more rights for minorities in the Ottoman Empire and wanted to be their protectors.

Sultan Abdülmecid issued a new reform decree on February 28, 1856. With this decree full judicial and religious equality was established among Muslim, Christian and Jewish citizens. With the end of the Crimean War a month later, the Ottomans were accepted as part of the European Entente through the Treaty of Paris. However, the reference made to this decree in the agreement was interpreted by some Western countries to mean that all Christians in the Ottoman Empire were from then on under the "collective protection" of the treaty's signatories. Following the 1774 Kaynarca Agreement Russia had viewed itself as the protector of Christians in Turkey, but now, the signatories of the Paris Treaty saw themselves as such. As a result British diplomats in the Ottoman Empire

---

[140] Peacock, op. cit., p. 49.

considered themselves watchdogs for the rights of the Christians there. In a telegram to London, the British consul general in Izmir, Charles Blunt, reported that the position of the Christians was better than that of the Muslims.[141]

Before the Tanzimat period, while the government was trying to enact reforms and work on the basic elements of the Tanzimat, some sections of the empire were attacked and occupied. In 1830 the French occupied Algeria.

The reforms in the Ottoman Empire were carried out under such adverse conditions. On the one hand, the Ottomans were adapting to the modernization process taking place in the West in cooperation with Western countries while at the same time struggling to save its territories from Western occupation and preventing them from abusing the question of minorities. The structure of society in the Ottoman Empire was very different from today's Turkey. In the 19th century Muslims comprised only 68% of the population.

Towards the end of the century, with the loss of some of the territories that had Christian majorities the proportion of Muslims went up to 76% in the 1880s. Twenty-four percent of the people belonged to other religious groups. Foreign countries that wanted to dominate these minorities were actually seeking control of a quarter of the population. Some of these minorities obtained passports from these nations and came directly under their protection. Therefore, one should not view the minority problem in the Ottoman Empire as confined to a small community. Together with foreign companies, the non-Muslims in the Ottoman Empire controlled the most of the economic structure of the country. Piece by piece occupation of the empire by foreign countries or the secession of some territory due to ideologies fed by those countries increased suspicion and adverse reaction towards foreigners.

---

[141] Bilal Şimşir, British Documents on Ottoman Armenians, vol. 1, Ankara, 1982, p. X.

Almost no one clung to the naive view that foreigners were trying to protect Christians because of good intentions and humanitarian goals. The optimism of the Tanzimat era was replaced by scepticism. The people start to ask, "Can Europeans and Christian minorities be trusted?"[142]

What is referred to as "the eastern problem" was actually the problem of how to divide up the Ottoman Empire between Western countries and Russia. The claims that minorities were ill-treated or their rights not protected were a smokescreen for these policies, since none of these countries had fully implemented the liberties brought by the French Revolution at home. In fact the democratic moves inspired by the French Revolution were violently crushed in many places.

When the Tanzimat Fermanı was announced, neither France nor Russia nor Austria had democracies that could serve as an example to the rest.

During the second half of the 19th century ideas of freedom and people's sovereignty developed rapidly in the Ottoman Empire. Numerous Ottoman authors, poets and thinkers led these freedom movements, with Namık Kemal the most prominent among them. The 1860s were the days of the Young Ottomans movement. One of their leaders, Mustafa Fazıl Pasha, wrote an open letter to the sultan proposing the establishment of a constitutional form of government. During that period there were steps towards democracy in some regions of the Ottoman Empire. In 1861 the bey of Tunisia accepted a written constitution. In 1866 the hidiv of Egypt established an elected parliament. There were elections in Egypt in 1869, 1876 and 1881. During these years freedom movements rapidly developed within the empire. In some periods the leaders of these movements were arrested and exiled, later returning to continue their struggle. In the meantime reforms were implemented in government administration and the judiciary. New schools were opened,

---

[142] Mantran, op. cit., p. 525.

but none of this was enough for the Young Ottomans, who even viewed the Tanzimat as inadequate. There were those among them who saw the Tanzimat as a charade to satisfy Western powers. Switching to a parliamentary system and restricting the authority of the sultan became the primary goal of this group, which also included some Christian intellectuals among its ranks.

The First Constitution and the First Elections in Turkey

As a result of these struggles the Ottoman Empire underwent its first parliamentary experience. On December 23, 1876 the first Ottoman Constitution was approved.

Mithat Pasha was the drafter of this Constitution. All the preparations were conducted during the authoritarian period under Sultan Abdülaziz. They had also obtained the consent of Abdülhamit, who was then crown prince. This Constitution resembled those found in Western countries during that period. A two-house Parliament was envisaged. In one house would be members appointed by the sultan for life, and in the other would be representatives of the people. The government was also structured in a Western fashion. The sultan preserved most of his powers: convening Parliament or disbanding it, appointing ministers, declaring war or signing peace treaties were all within his jurisdiction. However, the Parliament had the authority to make laws, approve the budget and control the financial expenditures of the state. The Constitution gave equal rights to all citizens without discrimination. Individual rights would be respected and entry into public service would be open to all.

This was the first Parliament of the Turkish people. In 1875, Mithat Pasha had this to say to the British ambassador, Henry Elliot, about the primary goals of the Constitution: "The only way to save the country from a catastrophe is to draw up a constitution that will make the ministers accountable to the people's parliament. This parliament should not discriminate among different classes or religions and should be a true national parliament. Governors in the regions should also be controlled, and local governments should be strengthened. These are the prime targets of the constitution."[143]

The Ottoman Constitution was deeply influenced by the 1831 Belgian Constitution, the main difference being the fact that the sultan and not the Parliament approved the constitution. When the first Ottoman Constitution was accepted it had been 100 years since the start of the reform process. However, the idea of establishing a government based on the will of the people and having a liberal constitution could flourish only years later. The 1876 Constitution met with strong criticism. On the one hand conservatives reacted to this new development that changed the traditional ways; on the other hand freedom fighters like Namık Kemal and Ziya Pasha saw these changes as inadequate. Actually, with today's standards the Constitution was inadequate in many respects.

Following approval of the Constitution elections were held, and the Mebusan Meclisi (Parliament) met for the first time in March 1877. The Senate had 25 members and the Assembly had 120. This Parliament worked until July 28, 1877, when elections were held again. After these new elections, the Parliament met again on December 13, 1877. The election method used was different from that of its contemporaries. Despite this, the Parliament embarked upon some important tasks. The 120 regional representatives started to voice the mistakes, inadequacies and corruption in their areas. Ministers were strongly criticized. In February 1878 the level of criticism became severe. The Parliament called upon three ministers present their defence in view of the allegations against them. The following day the sultan abolished the Parliament. The

---

[143] Lewis, Why Turkey is the Only Muslim Democracy, p. 160.

first Ottoman Parliament had two elections and a life of 10 months and 25 days.[144]

Following this event, the Ottoman Empire entered into a 30-year period of authoritarian rule by Abdülhamit. The opponents of the regime and the proponents of constitutional order were exiled. The press was put under strict censorship. All the characteristics of an oppressive regime could be seen in the Ottoman Empire of that period. Two assassinations were attempted on Abdülhamit with the intention of replacing him with the former sultan, Murad V, a pro-reform monarch. Abdülhamid's oppressive regime was intensified following these failed attempts on his life.

Despite this, Turkey had had a restricted and brief experience with democracy and saw what constitutional rights and freedoms meant. No oppression could destroy these ideas.

During Abdülhamit's era the Ottomans continued to lose large amounts of territory. Following the 1877-1878 Berlin Conference, Romania, Serbia, Bosnia, Herzegovina, Bulgaria and Cyprus were lost. These regions constituted one-third of the Ottoman territory. Approximately 800,000 Turks in these regions that were either occupied or had gained their independence moved to Istanbul or parts of Anatolia. This exacerbated the burden on the empire. By the end of the century the population of Ottoman Empire had reached 27 million.[145]

Abdülhamit pursued some of the reform movements that had been in progress for 100 years. New railroads were built, schools opened and a telegraph system was established. But none of these reforms were as important as the Constitution that he had shelved.

---

[144] Lewis, The Emergence of Modern Turkey, op. cit., p. 165, Lewis, Why Turkey is the Only Muslim Democracy, op. cit., p. 42.
[145] Erich J. Zürcher, Turkey, a Modern History, London, 1994, p. 90.

Opposition Movements, Union and Progress

Organized opposition to reinstate the Constitution began in 1889. That year the İttihadi Osmani Cemiyeti (Union of the Ottoman Community) was established in the Military Medical School. Some members of this community later fled to Paris and established the İttihat ve Terraki Cemiyeti (Union and Progress Party) with Ahmet Rıza, the son of an ex-MP, as their president. They continued their opposition by publishing a paper called the Meşveret. This group later became known as the Young Turks. In 1902 they held their first congress in Paris. These were intellectuals with varying opinions and different ethnic origins. What united them was their hatred of Abdülhamit and a desire to return to constitutional order. In the declaration they issued after the congress, the Young Turks criticized the authoritarian regime of the sultan, defended the equality of all citizens and demanded the protection of the territorial integrity of the empire and reinstatement of the 1876 Constitution. In Turkey supporters of the Young Turks movement were growing in number in institutes of higher learning, and revolts against the established order were becoming frequent, with slogans like "Long live the Constitution" being heard. Especially after 1897, the sultan stepped up his efforts to silence the opposition movements that asked for more freedom. Some of the opposition members fled the country. In addition to Paris, the Young Turks movement opened up branches in London, Geneva, Bucharest and Cairo. But Paris remained the center for the proponents of constitutional order. Prince Sabahattin, who had first joined the group in the early 20th century, later fell into disagreement with them and formed his own group, called the Liberal Ottomans' Association. They saw nothing wrong with seeking the support of foreign countries to overthrow the sultan.

In the meantime, other associations defending freedoms and the Constitution were also established. One of these, known as Vatan ve Özgürlük (Country and Freedom), was established by young military officers. Serious conflicts surfaced among these associations, but in the end the İttihat ve Terraki group persevered as the main representative of the opposition.

In 1908 officers who were members of the İttihat ve Terraki revolted against the Ottoman government in Macedonia and occupied a mountain region with their loyal units, demanding that the Constitution be reinstated. Among the rebellious officers was one Major Enver, who would later play an important role in the policies of the empire. The sultan sent 18,000 men to put down this rebellion. But most of these troops joined the rebels. Under the directives of the İttihat ve Terraki the rebellion had spread, and hundreds of telegrams were sent to the palace asking for the Constitution to be reinstated. Soldiers threatened to march into Istanbul if their conditions were not met. Realizing he could not resist the pressures of the rebels any longer, Sultan Abdülhamit reinstated the Constitution on July 23, 1908. He declared that the elections would be held soon and that the Parliament would be convened after an interval of 30 years.

All of a sudden the political atmosphere in the empire changed. Officials who had oppressed the people for years had escaped, and those who could not flee were arrested. Censorship was removed, and many newspapers started to be published. From 1908-1909 there were 350 papers and magazines published in the Ottoman Empire.[146] Ideas could now be expressed freely. Freedom could be felt, not only in the political arena or in the media, but also in social life as well. Workers who were complaining about price increases and low wages quickly went on strike in more than 100 places.

---

[146] Mantran, op. cit., pp. 574, 585.

Parliamentary Regime in the Years Leading to World War I

While the winds of freedom were blowing in the country, developments abroad were taking place that would shake the empire. Three months after the reinstatement of the Constitution Bulgaria declared its independence. The next day Austria announced that it had annexed Bosnia-Herzegovina. That was followed by Crete stating that it had united with Greece. There was a big uproar from the people, and the İttihat ve Terraki declared a boycott on Austrian goods.[147]

The İttihat ve Terraki, which had put its stamp on this era but had worked underground, held a congress in the autumn of 1908 and assumed a true political identity.

Parliament opened its doors in such an environment on December 17, 1908. In his opening speech Abdülhamit pledged his loyalty to the Constitution. Ahmet Rıza, one of the leaders of the Young Turks movement, was elected speaker of Parliament. In order to reflect the idea of equality among religions that had been promised earlier by the supporters of the İttihat ve Terraki, minorities were allocated a large number of seats in Parliament; in fact Muslims occupied only a little more than 50% of its 288 seats. In addition to the İttihat ve Terraki another party had also taken part in the elections, the liberal-minded Ahrar Party. However, they won only one seat in Parliament.[148]

The move into a more democratic life had not been painless. There were strong critics against the İttihat ve Terraki, foremost among which was the İttihadı Muhammedi, an organization of Islamic fundamentalists. On April 13, 1909 (March 31 according to the Ottoman calendar, also referred to as the March 31 Incident) these fundamentalists launched an armed insurrection in reaction to the secular approach and Western-style reforms of the İttihat ve Terraki Partisi. Their

[147] Ibid.,p.580
[148] Zürcher, op. cit., p. 99.

goal was to bring back Sharia (Islamic law). The prime minister resigned, and the İttihat ve Terraki's members began to flee Istanbul.

It had only been four months since the opening of Parliament, and the regime was already in jeopardy. In order to put down the rebellion the Hareket Ordusu (Action Army), comprising the army units positioned in Thessaloniki, marched on Istanbul and captured the city, arresting the leaders of the rebellion. Later, however, some of them were released. Some historians think that foreign powers played a role in this incident.[149] Once the rebellion was subdued Parliament convened and decided to dethrone Abdülhamit. The era of a sultan who had come to the throne as a supporter of democracy, approved the first Constitution, summoned the first Parliament but later shelved them all and ruled the country under an oppressive regime for 30 years had come to an end.

In 1909 amendments were made to the Constitution, freedoms were extended and the foundations of a true democracy were laid down. From then on the only authority of the sultan was to appoint the prime minister and the Sheik ül Islam (religious leader). Parliament could only be abolished if the government failed to obtain a vote of confidence. In such an event the elections had to be held within three months.

In the meantime the government embarked upon new reforms. The size of the army and the bureaucracy was decreased and a better organization was formed. Mahmud Şevket Pasha, who had put down the counter-revolutionaries, was appointed chief of staff. He declared that the role of the army was the protection of the Constitution and tried to keep the army away from internal political struggles.

From 1909-1911 various political parties having different ideologies were established. One of these was the Ottoman Socialist Party, founded in 1910. The Hizbi Cedid (New Party), headed by Colonel Sadık, was among those formed to

---

[149] Ibid., p. 102, Kongar, op. cit., p. 68.

oppose the İttihat ve Terraki. They published a 10-point declaration on the development of the Ottoman Empire, recommending that it benefit from the experiences of Western civilization.[150] The newly established parties formed an alliance against the İttihat ve Terraki and later united under a new party called the Hürriyet and İtilaf (Freedom and Alliance Party). In 1912 elections were held in which the İttihat ve Terakki won the majority of seats. The opposition was able to put only a small number of representatives in Parliament. There were allegations that the elections had been unfair.[151] Political activities against the İttihat ve Terraki continued after the elections were over. In May-June 1912, a group that called itself the Halaskar Zabitan called for new elections to be held and respect for constitutional freedoms. They were effective; the government resigned, and a new government was formed.

It would not be wrong to say that behind all these clashes was the search for identity by Ottoman intellectuals. Which civilization should the Turkish nation follow? While some were defending the strictest code of Islam, some demanded reforms while preserving time-honoured traditions, saying that Islam was not an obstacle barring the way to modernization. There were disagreements among the proponents of Westernization as well. Celal Nuri (İleri), who was one of their leaders, stated that "technical civilization" should be imported from the West but that the core Islamic civilization should be preserved. In contradiction to this, Ahmet Muhtar in 1912 said that they would either "Westernize or perish." Abdullah Cevdet, another proponent of Westernization, said, "There is no second civilization; civilization means Western civilization; we must adopt this civilization with its roses and its nails." He thought that Turkey should embrace and become one with Western civilization.[152] While these things were being discussed, no one was thinking whether or not the West

---

[150] Lewis, The Emergence of Modern Turkey, op. cit., p. 216.
[151] Zürcher, op. cit., p. 108.
[152] Lewis, The Emergence of Modern Turkey, op. cit., p. 231.

wanted to have Turkey as part of its civilization. The answer to this question would be opened up to debate in the Western media and in political circles years afterwards, towards the end of the century.

While these first steps towards democracy were being taken, the authorities in various regions were trying to put rebellions down. There were big riots in Kosovo and Montenegro in 1910, 1911 and 1912. During the same years there was another uprising in Yemen. In 1911 the Italians, with the support of the British, the French and the Russians, landed in Libya. Their excuse was to protect the Italians living there from the "fanatic Muslims." A year later, Serbia, Montenegro, Greece and Bulgaria gave an ultimatum to the Ottoman Empire, demanding significant reforms under the supervision of foreign countries. On October 8 they declared war on the Ottoman Empire.

Under these circumstances the Ottoman Empire could not emerge victorious in the Balkan wars. When it heard that the government would give Edirne to Bulgaria, the İttihat ve Terraki party overthrew the government. The prime minister was changed once again. Later, helped by the disagreements among the Balkan states, Edirne, which had been lost during the first Balkan War, was recovered. The Ottomans had lost almost all of their land in Europe in the Balkan wars. The size of the lost territories totaled almost 153,000 sq km. Four million people used to live there. Macedonia, Albania and a part of Thrace, Ottoman lands for more than 500 years, were all abandoned.

This is the period when the İttihat ve Terraki was in direct control of the administration. From among the leaders of the party, Talat Pasha was interior minister, Enver Pasha was minister of war and Cemal Pasha was governor of Istanbul. New elections were held in 1913. The Hürriyet ve İtilaf Partisi, which was in opposition, did not participate in the elections. Parliament was under the complete control of the Ittihat ve Terraki. Enver Pasha, who became their most prominent leader, proposed a military pact between the

Ottoman Empire and Germany to German Ambassador Wangheim. Emperor Wilhelm II accepted this offer, and the conditions to ally the Ottoman Empire with Germany in World War I were thus put in place. On August 2, 1914 a secret agreement was signed with Germany. Immediately after this Parliament recessed.[153]

History books explain the internal and external developments of this era, the wars, the international agreements as well as the conspiracies against the Ottomans in great detail. Here our goal is not to give a summary of the political history of the period. We just want to bring to mind the circumstances and difficulties that the Constitution, the parliamentary regime and democracy in the Ottoman Empire had to grapple with.

In order to better understand and evaluate the political developments, the struggle for democracy and modernization, the difficulties faced, the successes and failures between the Constitution of 1876 and World War I, it would be useful to consider the evolution experienced in Western countries during this period.

---

[153] Zürcher, op. cit., p. 118.

The Ottoman Empire and the West in the 20th Century

While explaining the situation in the mid-19th century, Bernard Lewis says that the leaders and intellectuals of Islamic countries were becoming conscious of the poverty of their societies and the weaknesses of their countries, whereas the wealth, power and self-confidence of the West that at times led them to be aggressive was just the antithesis of this situation.[154]

If a holistic approach to the period that begins with the start of the 19th century up until World War I is taken, the following picture can be seen: The Ottoman Empire had entered into a period of decline from the end of the 18th century. As the years passed, the decline accelerated. At the beginning of the 19th century sultans like Selim III and Mahmud II tried to embark on reforms in order to halt the decline and preserve the power and existence of the state. Similar moves for reforms could be seen in the West as well. However, there the demand for reform came from the people, whereas with the Ottomans it was mostly the authorities of the state who felt the need for change. In the beginning the movements for reform did not have a democratic nature. The goal was to modernize the military and the government by looking at the more advanced examples of the West. To this end, friendship and cooperation was established with the West.

The Ottomans encountered the French Revolution in such an environment. At first, there was sympathy towards it. But

---

[154] Lewis, Why Turkey is the Only Muslim Democracy, op. cit., p. 41.

after a while it was realized that this revolution acted as an encouragement to the nationalist and independence movements in the Ottoman Empire. The Western countries that the Ottomans were trying build good relations with started to carve out territories from the Ottoman Empire. Sometimes the Ottomans benefited from the disagreements among the European nations, but most of the time the Ottomans were the ones on the loosing end. This is the period of decline of an empire. Just like any other empire in the world, the Ottoman Empire entered such a process for various reasons. The state tried to prevent the decline by trying to modernize itself. Before reaching the middle of the century, in 1839, the Tanzimat Fermanı, a decree by the sultan restricting his own authority, was declared. In later years the ideologies of liberty and democracy in the West started to be echoed in the Ottoman Empire. Intellectuals, thinkers and some government officials expended great effort and made great personal sacrifices to bring constitutional order and a parliamentary political system to the country. Some of them risked their lives to this end. Some spent the rest of their lives in exile. Despite all this they keep the idea of democracy alive.

There were also Christians among the Young Turks who fought for democracy. The state barely discriminated among different ethnic or religious groups, either. There were numerous Christian citizens who became high-ranking officials and ambassadors. For centuries Turks, Greeks, Armenians and Jews lived together as citizens of the same country. However, some of the minorities, influenced by the French Revolution and encouraged by foreign countries, started seeking a separate identity during that century. First came demands for autonomy, then full independence. Hence, the state entered into a process of disintegration.

It was only natural that these currents would end up stirring the nationalistic feelings of the main element of the empire, the Turks. Especially towards the end of the 19th century Turkish nationalism, even pan-Turkism, started to develop.

These currents were effective in the İttihat ve Terraki Partisi as well. Among the supporters of this ideology was Enver Pasha, who was one of the leaders of the İttihat ve Terraki Partisi during the period leading up to World War I and who was also the minister of war. But most of those struggling for freedom and the Constitution during the 19th century were proponents of an Ottoman Empire that had more freedom for all and was more modern, where people belonging to different religions and ethnic groups could live together in peace.

In 1876 there was a brief experience with the first Constitution and Parliament. After 30 years of an oppressive regime, exile and hardship the Constitution and Parliament were reinstated, while the rebellion of the fundamentalists was crushed with the help of the army. During these troubled times the empire shed its blood. Territories were lost one by one. Foreign countries applied pressure to secure more favours for minorities, pretending to be their protectors while at the same time oppressing their own people. Their treatment of people in their colonies bore no relation whatsoever to the ideas of equality, freedom and brotherhood of the French Revolution.

During that period being powerful was sufficient; there was no need to be right. The great powers did not have concerns such as securing the approval of the people for their policies, because democracy and the press were still not adequately developed. The fact that the Ottoman Empire was legally within her rights in most of her international relations did not matter much, since she did not have the power to protect her rights. She did not have a modern army with which to defend herself, nor did she have the financial capability to build such an army. She was left behind in the industrial and technological revolution. She also had to grapple with the feelings of religious and cultural hostility and enmity stemming from history. Most of the time European countries did not find it difficult to form alliances against the Ottomans.

The Ottomans also found it hard to maintain unity within the empire. They thought that granting equal treatment for all, irrespective of their religious or cultural backgrounds, would ease the pressures on the empire. However, the real goal was to use the problems of minorities to further weaken the empire so as to hasten its disintegration. Some Ottoman intellectuals were bewildered to see that foreign countries would not ease their pressure and demands on the Ottomans despite all the reforms undertaken. Actually there was nothing to be bewildered about. These pressures and demands were a part of their game. In the 19th century such were the rules the game of international relations. Those without enough power would always lose.

However, the Ottomans were not the only losers. Western countries used to engage in fierce struggles among themselves as well. Taking a long-term view it can be seen that everybody actually lost. Every country lost hundreds of thousands of its people to these political games. The territories captured from the Ottomans at the cost of thousands of lives were later lost by the captors. New states and new nations were established in those lands.

The 19th century was not the period when the Turkish nation achieved democracy, as is understood today. But it was not a time when those countries viewed as the backbone of democracy started to fully implement democracy either. Moreover, some of these countries spent a good part of the 19th century trying to abolish slavery. In some of them brief episodes as republics were followed by oppressive empires. Until the 20th century there was no country in the West that could be called democratic and that gave equality and voting rights to all, men and women alike, without discrimination. In these countries too there were major struggles for liberty and democracy.

The shift to democracy during the 20th century was not easy either. Turkey is not a new country arriving in the contemporary world, just learning the meaning of justice and equality among human beings. She was not a country that had to take lessons on tolerance from others. Turkey reached today's world with a lot of experiences throughout her long history. She got to know her friends and foes very well. She knows who suggested what Turkey do and why they did it. The Turkey of the 20th century has learned a lot from the 19th century as well as the earlier periods of her history. Therefore, those who today are trying to teach Turkey lessons in democracy, humanity, freedom and understanding should first closely study Turkey's past experiences.

Turkey after World War I

Last Years of the Empire

The common denominator of all the struggles for freedom in the 19th century was that the Ottoman Empire longed for a Constitution that would restrict the authority of the sultan and establish a parliament whose members would be elected by the people and which would have extensive powers. During that period replacing the sultanate with a republic was still not a widely discussed issue. Moreover, the sultan carried the title of "caliph," which meant he was the leader of all Muslims.

During the war years Parliament was working, and elections were held. There was more than one party. The İttihat ve Terraki gained and lost strength at different times. But towards the end of the war it was almost the single power in the country and had total control of the government. During this period reforms were enacted in education, government and especially in the military. Secular ideas and their applications gradually surfaced. In 1916 the Sheik ül Islam's seat in the Council of Ministers was abolished, and the government made an effort to set religion apart from the state.

In 1917 the religious courts were tied to the Ministry of Justice and divinity schools to the Ministry of Education. Learning a Western language became obligatory even in secondary schools. Women were encouraged to be more active in social life and were given the right to divorce their husbands. Elementary schooling became obligatory for girls as well in 1913, and in later periods secondary and high schools were opened for female students. In 1914 girls were allowed into universities. During the second Meşrutiyet period that began in 1908 an environment existed whereby all social and political problems could openly be discussed. Serious arguments took place between pro-Westerners and conservatives. Intellectuals like Namık Kemal claimed that a synthesis could be achieved between the positive aspects of Western culture and Ottoman traditions. During the war the capitulations were unilaterally abolished. There were efforts to boost the economy, and between 1914 and 1918 more than 100 private companies were established in various sectors. In the meantime, the war caused great devastation; almost 3 million Turks lost their lives during World War I.[155]

The war ended with a great defeat for Turkey and her allies. On October 31, 1918 a cease-fire agreement was signed in Mondros. The senior officials of the İttihat ve Terraki assumed all responsibility for the defeat and left the country. But this party still continued to be influential in the army and the police. That same year Sultan Mehmet V died, and Sultan Vahdeddin ascended the throne. The Hürriyet ve İtilaf Partisi, which had taken a back seat when the İttihat ve Terraki was the dominant power, started to move to front stage. One of its leaders, Ferit Pasha, who was also the son-in-law of the sultan, was appointed grand vizier. The sultan engaged in close cooperation with the British to secure the best possible peace agreement for the Ottomans. But all these efforts would be to no avail, and the Sevres Treaty would be nothing short of a total surrender. Meanwhile, together with the encouragement of the British, Greek troops landed in Izmir in May 1919. The goal was to break the local resistance and completely break the back of the Ottomans.

Following the disintegration of the İttihat ve Terakki the Teceddüd party was established in its place. Those who opposed this party formed one of their own called the Osmanlı Hürriyetperver Avam Partisi (Ottoman People's Freedom Party). More than 100 supporters of the İttihat ve Terakki were arrested.

---

[155] Mantran, op. cit., p. 624.

Under such circumstances Mustafa Kemal Pasha landed in Samsun as inspector of the Third Army on May 19, 1919. From then on a resistance and independence movement was under way in Anatolia.

The strength of the resistance in Anatolia could be felt in Istanbul. Despite the reluctance of the Ottoman government, elections were held in the autumn of 1919 due to pressure coming from Anatolia. Parliament convened in January 1920. Most of the elected representatives were also members of the resistance movement in Anatolia and established the Felahı Vatan group in Parliament. The first task of Parliament was to accept the new national borders of the country in the Misakı Milli, as decided upon by the resistance groups in Anatolia. This text had earlier been approved by the Erzurum and Sivas congresses organized by Mustafa Kemal.

In summary, the Misakı Milli stated that the areas with Ottomans in the majority were an indivisible whole; that the fate of areas where Arabs were in the majority would be decided through referendums; that plebiscites would be held in Batum, Kars and Ardahan; that the security of Istanbul and the Sea of Marmara would be secured; that talks would be held with the relevant countries regarding the passage of commerce through the Bosporus; that the rights of minorities would be protected in accordance with international agreements; that judicial, economic and financial independence would be protected; and that the reinstatement of the capitulations would be opposed.

These political decisions were made in Istanbul, the capital of the Ottoman Empire, about a year-and-a-half after the end of the war. This atmosphere of political debate continued until March 16, 1919, the day when British landed troops to occupy the city. One of the primary goals of the British was to cut any ties that existed between the resistance in Anatolia and Parliament as well as all other governmental institutions in Istanbul. The nationalists were aware of this fact. Still, they refused to go underground and chose to continue their work in Parliament. The British soldiers entered Parliament and arrested some members of parliament. The legislative body protested this act and on April 1, 1920 disbanded itself. This date marked the end of the Ottoman parliamentary system, which had been inaugurated in 1876 and reinstated in 1908 after a long hiatus, ended with a British raid on the Ottoman Parliament. The Ottomans had lost the war; however, there weren't many examples of soldiers raiding a parliament and arresting MPs. During those days 14 of the 150 Ottomans arrested by the British were members of Parliament. Those who were arrested were sent to Malta, which was under British sovereignty.

Turkish Democracy During the War of Liberation

It would not be incorrect to view the landing of Mustafa Kemal Pasha in Samsun as the birth date of Turkish democracy. Democratic attempts in the past had relied on the balance of power between the sultan and representatives elected by the people. But the idea that the people were the sole source of sovereignty had developed with Atatürk's arriving in Anatolia and his starting to organize a national resistance. It did not happen all of a sudden, either. A struggle had to be waged to install the will of the people as the official basic structure of the state.

Right after the end of World War I and the official beginning of the disintegration of the empire, resistance movements in various parts of the country began to develop. The Trakya Müdafaai Hukuk Cemiyeti (Thrace Association for the Defence of Law) was established in 1918. Soon after that a similar association was formed in Izmir, and in the same month another one was established in Kars. Müdafaai Hukuk associations were formed in Trabzon and Erzurum in February 1919. The association's center in the south of the country was Urfa. Between December 1918 and October 1920 these associations held 20 congresses, considered to be signs that

democratic methods were at the forefront in determining
people's fate in Turkey from then on.

It is interesting that even after obtaining the support of
General Kazım Karabekir and General Ali Fuat Cebesoy, both
of whom were very influential in their regions, Mustafa Kemal
Pasha drew on the congresses, which reflected the will of the
people, as the base of the national struggle. Mustafa Kemal's
choice can be seen in a circular he had sent to all civilian and
military officials in Anatolia on June 21, 1919. His message
was clear: The country was under threat, and the government
in Istanbul was in no position to protect it. The country can
only be saved by the will of the people.

The Erzurum Congress of July 23, 1919 accepted a 10-
point declaration forming the basic structure of the Misaki
Milli, which aimed at preserving the unity of the country. This
congress was held with the participation of representatives
from six eastern regions, but its decisions had implications far
beyond the borders of these regions, giving a hint as to the
future of the country. The essence of these decisions was that
Turkey was an indivisible whole within its national borders;
that even if the Ottoman Empire disintegrated the people
would continue their resistance; that if the government in
Istanbul could not protect the independence of the country,
then a transitory government would be formed; that no
privileges that would destabilize society would be granted to
the Christians; that the national armed forces would be
mobilized to reinstate national sovereignty; and that a national
parliament would be convened. Alternative proposals were
discussed during this congress. Some argued that the only way
out was to become a mandated territory of the United States.
Mustafa Kemal opposed these proposals outright. His goal was
to establish "a Western-style society," not " a society controlled
by the West."[156] Protecting national sovereignty and getting
out from under these difficult circumstances by relying on the

---

[156] Kongar, op. cit., pp. 72, 86.

power and the will of the people became the prevailing view at these congresses. One of the most important articles adopted during the Erzurum Congress and approved at the Sivas Congress was the decision not to accept the mandate or protection of any foreign country. Before the congress ended a Delegation of Representatives was elected, and Mustafa Kemal was appointed its head.

Representatives from 31 regions participated in a national congress that met in Sivas September 4-11 and was called Anadolu ve Rumeli Müdafaai Hukuku Milliye Cemiyeti (Association for the Defence of Law in Anatolia and Thrace). This congress approved the decisions of the Erzurum Congress and elected another Delegation of Representatives, with Mustafa Kemal again appointed as head of the delegation. In December the Delegation of Representatives moved to Ankara and continued its work from there. In the meantime elections were held for the Ottoman Parliament in Istanbul. Most of those elected were people who agreed with the decisions of the Erzurum and Sivas congresses. Before departing for Istanbul they came to Ankara and had a meeting with Mustafa Kemal.

These developments are the cornerstones of recent Turkish history. Every history textbook in Turkey explains in great detail the landing of Atatürk in Samsun, his work after that, the Erzurum and Sivas congress and the decisions made there. These events were, at the same time, turning points for Turkish democracy. When the news reached Ankara that the British had raided the Parliament in Istanbul on March 18, 1920 and that the parliament had dissolved itself, Atatürk invited those members of parliament who had not been arrested to Ankara, the place that was to be the center of the Turkish Parliament and Turkish democracy. In a few weeks' time 92 MPs had arrived in Ankara.

On April 23, 1920, together with 232 representatives elected from different regions of the country, they participated in the first session of the Grand National Parliament of Turkey. It had only been 21 days since the Ottoman

Parliament in Istanbul had disbanded itself. Turkey was no longer willing to live without a parliament. More importantly, Turks had attained the consciousness of a nation. Even as early as those days, Atatürk grasped the importance of having this notion as a prerequisite for establishing a contemporary state. It took years for Western democracies to develop this national consciousness. Turkish intellectuals and thinkers had been seeking an identity since the Tanzimat Fermanı. What the Young Turks were after was a national spirit.[157] Turkey completed this process much more rapidly, and the new Turkish state and Turkish democracy were established upon this national consciousness. The Turkish nation found its national identity with Atatürk.

What is important is that the Parliament was established right at the start of the national War of Liberation that would be waged against the Greek army, which had occupied part of the country. Atatürk did not want to enter a war solely by relying on the support of commanders with whatever troops remained from the Ottoman Army. He conducted the war by relying on the will, consent and political support of the people. So much so that the First Grand National Assembly of Turkey assumed the executive as well as the legislative role and actually governed the country during the war.

The will power of Mustafa Kemal and the members of the Grand National Assembly was not to be broken, even when the government in Istanbul, controlled by the British, sentenced Mustafa Kemal to death and sent troops for his capture. Nor was it destroyed when the Sheik ül Islam declared all members of the resistance enemies of Islam and issued a decree saying it was the duty of all Muslims to kill the resistance fighters. Mustafa Kemal and his friends were confident, because they derived their power from the people and not from the sultan. Actually most of the clergy had confidence in Mustafa Kemal and not in the Sheik ül Islam in

---

[157] Güvenç, op. cit., p. 11.

Istanbul. On May 5, 1920 the mufti of Ankara issued a fatwa (religious decree) opposing the fatwa of the Sheik ül Islam, saying his fatwa had been issued under the duress of foreigners. A total of 152 muftis from all around the country supported him. Two weeks later, on May 19, 1920, the Grand National Assembly declared the Grand Vizier Damat Ferit Pasha a "traitor."[158]

In later years April 23, the founding day of the Grand National Assembly, was declared the National Day of Sovereignty and Children's Day. Establishing a Grand National Assembly actually meant that from then on sovereignty belonged to the people. The fact that the sultanate had not yet been abolished could not change this fact. The assembly prepared a new Constitution. Adopted on January 20, 1921 this Constitution was evidence that the assembly had taken over the administration of the country. Article 3 of the document said that the Grand National Assembly would administer the "State of Turkey" and that the government would be called the "Government of the Grand National Assembly." Elections would be held every two years, a period that could be extended for a maximum of one year. The assembly appointed the government, and the head of the assembly was also the head of the government.

During this period there were several political factions in Turkey. Together with anti-Western Islamists there was a group representing anti-imperialism and socialism, calling themselves the Green Army. This group, formed in May 1920, was actually a political movement and not an army. But when some armed groups joined, it lost its political character and was abolished in July. During the same month the radicals in the assembly formed a group called the Halk Zümresi (People's Group). The Türkiye Komünist Fırkası (Communist Party of Turkey) was formed in opposition to it. This party was not accepted by the Third International since during the

---

[158] Lewis, The Emergence of Modern Turkey, p. 247.

same period there was another Communist Party of Turkey, established in Baku in the spring of 1920. Its leader was Mustafa Suphi, and his friends too established a pro-Communist party called the Halk İştirak Fırkası (People's Participation Party) in Ankara.

During that period of time extreme-left organizations did not pose a threat to the regime. The veterans of the İttihat ve Terraki were much more experienced and organized. Enver Pasha was in the Soviet Union. He went to Batum to find a way back into Anatolia, but his compromising attitude towards the Soviets caused concern among the MPs in Ankara. In March 1921 the Muhafazai Mukaddesat Cemiyeti (Association for the Protection of Sacred Things) was established. This group consisted of MPs who were loyal to the sultan and the caliphate and included representatives of various ideologies. Among these the Tesanüd Grubu (Solidarity Group), the İstiklal Grubu (Independence Group), the Halk Zümresi (People's Group) and the Islahat Grubu (Reform Group) were the most active. There was also another called the Müdafaai Hukuk Zümresi (Defence of Law Group).[159]

The fact that such groups existed clearly shows that even from those early stages the idea of a multi-party system was finding ground and that different thoughts could be expressed in the assembly. Although a single party system was adopted for a while, in the end a multi-party system would be accepted as the norm in Turkey's political life. The existence of so many groups at this early stage in the Grand National Assembly while the War of Independence was still going on caused various problems. Therefore, on May 10, 1921 Mustafa Kemal had his friends establish the Anadolu ve Rumeli Müdafaai Hukuk Grubu (Anatolia and Thrace Group for the Defence of Law), which enabled the assembly to work in a more organized fashion. Meanwhile some of the former members of

---

[159] Kongar, op. cit., pp. 93-94.

parliament from the İttihat ve Terakki Partisi returned from exile in Malta, joined the assembly and early in 1922 established the İkinci Grup (Second Group), representing opposition. The Müdafaai Hukuk group had the majority with 200 MPs, whereas the Second Group had only 120. The Müdafaai Hukuk Group took the name of the Halk Fırkası (People's Party) on December 6, 1922. Mustafa Kemal prepared a nine-point manifesto, the most important article of which was one that would later become the primary motto of Turkish democracy: "Sovereignty belongs to the people without any reservation or condition." On April 16 the Assembly dissolved itself, and new elections were held in June and July in two stages. The Halk Fırkası won a great majority of the votes. There were only a few elected from the İkinci Grup. The Assembly met on August 9.

While these developments were taking place in the political arena, the country was waging a life-or-death war against Greece. The Greek army had reached Central Anatolia. Three months after the assembly had adopted the Constitution, on April 7, 1921, the advance of the Greek forces was halted at a place called İnönü. However, the Greek attacks continued during the summer.

The Greek soldiers had reached Eskişehir, and there was talk about moving the assembly to a safer place than Ankara. The president requested authority from the assembly and assumed all its powers for three months.

Even in this most difficult of times nothing was done without the consent of the Assembly. All the remaining strength of the people was called upon. A crucial battle was waged in Sakarya and won through the military genius of Mustafa Kemal and the selfless sacrifice of the Turkish soldiers. The Greek army started to retreat on September 13. It would take almost a year for a full withdrawal, but the power of the government in Ankara was by now well understood. On March 16, 1921, even before the Battle of Sakarya, the Soviet Union signed the first agreement with new Turkish government. Right after the battle at Sakarya the

French government sent a representative to Ankara to sign an agreement ending their occupation of the Adana region. The British also understood that the Greek withdrawal from Anatolia was inevitable; yet, it would take much longer for the British to sign an agreement. By then everyone had realized that the government in Ankara would never accept the Treaty of Sevres and that that a new treaty would be have to be negotiated. It was out of the question for the Istanbul government to represent Turkey any longer.

On November 1, 1922 the Grand National Assembly abolished the sultanate. The Ottoman Empire, established in 1299, had come to an end. The empire that Western countries and Russia had tried so hard to destroy for centuries had been done away with by the Turks themselves in order to establish a modern and contemporary state. The Istanbul government resigned, and its last prime minister, Tevfik Pasha, handed over his seal to Refet Pasha, the representative of the government in Ankara. A few days later, on November 17, the last Ottoman sultan left for Malta on a British battleship, without leaving behind a new sultan. His cousin, Abdülmecit Efendi, remained behind as caliph, but only for a short while.

Lausanne Conference and the Foundation of the Turkish Republic

The Peace Conference met in Lausanne on November 20, 1922, three days after the sultan had left the country. Apart from Turkey, England, France, Italy and Greece attended. The Soviet Union, the Ukraine, Georgia, Romania and Bulgaria would attend the relevant parts of the conference. The Lausanne Conference was different from other conferences held after the end of World War I. The Ottoman Empire had lost the war; however, it was not the Ottoman Empire but rather a new Turkish state at the negotiating table. This state was the heir to the empire, but it was also the victor of a War of Independence. Therefore, the winners of World War I were in no position to dictate their terms to the Turks. Minister of Foreign Affairs İsmet İnönü headed the Turkish delegation and put up a tough struggle in Lausanne. From the start he realized that diplomacy was the art of struggle, saying: "Before going to Lausanne I used to view diplomats as people who did nothing more than wander around in elegant clothes and who valued pompousness more than anything else. I saw in Lausanne for the first time that the clothes were the least important part of the task. I saw that diplomacy was a constant struggle. Just as in war, one had to be prepared for a new test every day."[160]

İnönü carried out his task with great success. He defended Turkey's interests with vigor. He did not bow to pressure. The Turkish delegation had to expend great effort to stand up to pressure on issues such as defining borders and abolishing the capitulations and privileges of minorities. Turkey had granted the maximum amount of rights conceivable in a democracy to non-Muslim minorities; however, there had long been some circles that wanted to have different groups recognized as minorities. In the meantime, there were those who frequently mentioned the Kurds. İsmet Pasha had this to say on the issue in Lausanne: "Kurds have always benefited from being citizens of Turkey. They never viewed the Turkish government, with which they always have shown political and social cooperation, as a foreign government. They have members in the Grand National Assembly, and they actively participate in the governmental as well as administrative affairs of the country."[161]

Following tough negotiations an agreement was reached on July 24, 1923. Henceforth, there was a Turkish state whose independence and territorial integrity were recognized, and the capitulations were abolished, resulting in equal rights and status with the rest of the European states. All citizens were

---

[160] Erdal İnönü, op. cit., vol. I, . 22.
[161] Kongar, op. cit., p. 300.

subject to Turkish laws, irrespective of their faith. The Grand National Assembly of Turkey approved the Treaty of Lausanne, and the occupation forces began to leave Istanbul, with the last British soldiers departing on October 1, 1923.

In his telegram to İnönü, congratulating him on the success of the Lausanne Treaty, Mustafa Kemal said: "This time, you have crowned this life of yours that so far has been a series of valuable services to your country, with historic success."

What did Turkey gain with the Treaty of Lausanne? İnönü explained this briefly in a speech he gave when presenting the treaty for parliament's approval. "A united and integrated homeland that has gotten rid of both extraordinary restrictions vis-à-vis the outside world as well as privileges, some of which had meant a government within a government; a land liberated from extraordinary financial obligations; a country which we have the absolute right to defend, that has abundant resources and freedom. The name of this homeland is Turkey."

The value of Lausanne was better recognized in later years. In 1968, at the anniversary of Lausanne, İnönü said: "Other nations would be hard pressed to produce another example of a political agreement signed after World War I that continues to be a valuable document 45 years after its signing. Future generations should never loose sight of this fact. Thanks to Lausanne a 45-year-long period of peace was able to be enjoyed by the secular republic that was also the product of the conference.

Seventy-five years after the Lausanne Treaty, this victory and the words of İsmet İnönü are now better understood.

Representatives of other nations negotiating the Lausanne Treaty with İsmet Pasha viewed each of Turkey's gains as their loss. British Prime Minister Lloyd George, who resigned following a crisis between Turkey and Britain in 1922, said immediately after the end of the Turkish War of Independence, "Lausanne is the worst agreement signed by England so far." However, independent historians have done more justice to Turkey in their analyses. One of them was

Stephan Ronart, who in his 1937 book, "Contemporary Turkey," had this to say on Lausanne: "The Lausanne Treaty was the first peace after the Great War that had been negotiated and not dictated. This peace was the victory of both guns and politics. It was won in the midst of conflicts of interest of twelve nations, at the heart of confusion following the occupation of the Ruhr region and when world domination policies of the global financial powers playing with millions were going on. This victory was almost torn off from the rest of the world. There was nothing left from the Sevres Treaty. All the shameful memories of the Ottoman era were erased. Capitulations, controls, areas of influence, financial auditors. These were the nightmares of a bad dream, and they were all gone now. Henceforth, a new Turkish state that recognized no boundaries or conditions in its policies or economy was a reality that could be seen and touched."[162]

Now that the Lausanne Treaty had been signed, it was time to name the new state. Upon the suggestion of Mustafa Kemal the Grand National Assembly proclaimed the Republic of Turkey on October 29, 1923. Following a period of constant war that lasted for almost 10 years, a large part of the population of the country had been lost, resources depleted, its infant industry already destroyed. Anatolia had lost 20% of its population. Turkey's international trade was down to one-third its level of the previous decade. Turkey was unable to return to its pre-war GDP levels until 1930.

Political Life and Reforms in the First Years of the Republic

During the early stages of establishing a new state, Mustafa Kemal, commander in chief of the War of Liberation, had described the national goal as ensuring the security of the national borders and developing within these borders, and not having any ambitions on other territories following pan-

---

[162] Hamza Eroğlu, 70. Yıldönümünde Lozan, Ankara, 1993, p. 94.

Turkist or pan-Islamist policies. He knew very well that winning the war was not sufficient to reach that target. At a speech he gave in 1923 Mustafa Kemal said: "The success of our army so far does not come to mean that the real salvation of our country has been achieved. These victories have only established the foundations of our future victories. Let's prepare for new victories in economy and science."

Soon after the declaration of the Republic, the caliphate was abolished on March 1, 1924. All members of the Ottoman dynasty were exiled. That same day legislation entitled "Tevhidi Tedrisat Kanunu," dealing with the integration of various institutes of education, was also passed.

Mustafa Kemal explained his views on abolishing the caliphate in a speech he gave at the Grand National Assembly in November 1924 as follows: "The Turkish nation feels great happiness in the removal of obstacles in its path to join the civilized countries moving on the road to development." In another one of his speeches Atatürk stressed that those people who remain uncivilized would remain under the pressure of the civilized countries; that by civilization he meant Western civilization and the modern world; and that Turkey had to join this civilization in order to survive, He added, "Finally, our nation has adopted in shape and essence, absolutely and as a whole, the lifestyle and potential offered by contemporary civilization to all nations."[163]

These words of Atatürk put forward the ideological basis of Turkey's 75-year-long struggle to integrate with Western civilization and of the revolutionary reforms she has made. It is a pity that 75 years after these words were uttered there are those in the West who identify Western civilization with Christianity and claim that Turkey cannot become a part of this civilization due to religious differences. The declaration made to that effect after a Brussels meetings of the leaders of

---

[163] Lewis, The Emergence of Modern Turkey, op. cit., pp. 250, 262.

Christian Democrat parties in March 1997 are deplorable for Western civilization.

Atatürk, however, saw Western civilization as a world of values wherein there were no walls of religion or culture built around nations, which countries that had adopted a modern, contemporary and positivist world outlook would join of their own accord, without being subject to the permission or will of others. He labored constantly to prepare Turkey for this world of contemporary civilization. The reforms of Atatürk were, actually, a project of civilization. In its broadest sense Atatürk's revolution was a cultural revolution. "The foundations of the Turkish Republic will be culture," are his very words. The target was "A culture suitable to our national identity and history, removed from influences coming from the East and the West."

This, however, did not mean distancing Turkey from Western or contemporary civilization -- to the contrary. Ataturk said, "The goal of the reforms we are conducting is to ensure that the Turkish people become contemporary and civilized in all ways."[164] Cultural differences would not keep Turkey out of Western civilization; they could even enrich Western civilization. This was the dominant thought in Turkey at the time. Turkey would take her place in the civilized system formed by contemporary, democratic, Western countries, and she would do this by relying on her own cultural resources, preserving her historic riches. During that period, with such contemporary thoughts, they visualized integrating states and peoples; however, even today there are those who unfortunately view cultural differences as a factor distancing nations from each other.

During visits to İnebolu and Kastamonu to explain his thoughts on reform of the dress code, Atatürk said the following: "The Turkish nation that established the Turkish Republic is a civilized nation. However, as a brother, friend and father I would like to tell you that those who claim to be

---

[164] Güvenç, op. cit., p. 34.

civilized must prove this with their way of thinking, family life and lifestyle. The truly civilized people of Turkey must prove this civilization through their outer appearance."[165] Atatürk's contemporary views resulted in a constitution that adopted the most advanced state structure and system of freedoms of its time. The republican assembly accepted this document in 1924, and Turkey now had a contemporary Constitution.

Article 3 of the new Constitution defined the basic structure of the state: "Sovereignty rests with the people without any conditions or reservations." Some of the most important articles of the Constitution involved the following: The Parliament would elect the president, the president would elect the government. The Parliament would have full authority to inspect the government. The principle of division of power was accepted, and the judiciary would be independent. Elections would be held every four years. The government or the members of Parliament could propose legislation. The MPs would have immunity regarding their speeches in Parliament. They could be tried in court, subject to a decision of the Parliament's general assembly. The Parliament and the Council of Ministers could not interfere with the decisions of the courts and could not change them.

These articles defined the characteristics of the state. Article 68, which addressed freedoms, said: "Every Turk is born free and lives as a free person. Freedom means retaining every right that will not inflict damage on anyone else. The boundary of everyone's freedom is the boundary of someone else's freedom. This boundary can only be determined and designated by law." Having defined basic freedoms, the Constitution went on to say that every Turk was equal before the law, that Turks had a natural right to their conscience, to express and publish their thoughts, to travel, own property, assemble, establish associations and establish companies. Article 72 said that no one could be arrested except for

---

[165] Lewis, The Emergence of Modern Turkey, op. cit., p. 263.

conditions specified by law. Article 73 outlawed torture, cruelty, confiscation and forced labor. Article 75 clearly indicated the basic philosophy of the Constitution: "No one may be called to account due to his beliefs, religion or sect." Every religious ceremony could be held as long as it conformed to the law. Article 77 prohibited censorship and established the principles of freedom of the press.

Article 88 was another important article, defining Turkish identity. Who is a Turk? Anyone who has Turkish citizenship is considered a Turk, irrespective his/her religion or race. Anyone who was born in Turkey of a foreign parent but who chooses Turkish citizenship at his or her coming of age is also considered a Turk.

This approach to citizenship, which rejects racism, is considered a modern approach even today, let alone in 1924, the year it was drafted. Considering the strong opposition to giving citizenship to foreigners or the efforts to impose restrictions on it in some European countries, the approach of the 1924 Turkish Constitution sets an example to all, even today.

So the Turkish Republic assumed a modern character soon after its establishment and took its position among the few democratic countries in the world.

The world began to realize the democratic character of the Turkish revolution from its early periods. Edouard Herriot, who was the prime minister of France at the time of the birth of the Republic, wrote these words in the prologue of the book, "Le Kemalisme," written by Tekin Alp: "Atatürk thought that an effective result could be achieved only through the contribution of the people. He became a champion of democracy. He worked with the people for the people. The Turkish nation immediately adopted the principles and methods of Western civilization. Just like passing from the Anatolian to the European side of Istanbul, the Turkish nation rapidly became a Western society. Some may call this a miracle. In fact, this was a result desired, pre-planned and based on logic that received its inspiration from dedication to the people. A democratic, secular republic, a system and a regime for development was established upon the ashes of the Ottoman Empire, the Caliphate and the Sultanate."[166]

The democratic character of the modern Turkish state established by Atatürk was understood and appreciated by the Western statesmen in such a manner.

The basic characteristic of Turkish democracy was in its application of the principle of sovereignty resting with people at every level of public life. Atatürk said: "Sovereignty belongs to the people. In drafting laws, in forming governments, in all details of public administration, in national education, in economy, the faith of the people is determined by the Grand National Assembly. In all these areas decisions should be taken in accordance with the principle of national sovereignty."

This was the main trait distinguishing the Turkish Republic from the Ottoman Empire. In Atatürk's words, leaving aside its experience with a constitutional regime in its last 15 years, the Ottoman state had been based on the sovereignty of a single individual, the sultan. The will of the people and their interests were simply not taken into consideration. In a sense the Turkish Republic was established as a reaction and antithesis to this fact. The founders of the Turkish Republic were so set on the concept of national sovereignty and superiority of the will of the people that they even shied away from some restrictions on people's sovereignty seen in Western democracies. In some Western countries sovereignty was shared between the parliament, the senate, the president and the government, whereas in Turkey the will of the Grand National Assembly was above all else. The assembly not only prepared legislation, it also elected the officials of the government from among its own members. In a sense the government was an organ that worked with the authority granted by the Assembly. That is why they called ministers "vekil" (representative); the ministers were working in a

---

[166] Tekin Alp, Le Kemalisme, Paris, 1937, pp. 6-8.

representative capacity for the Grand National Assembly. The constitutions of other democratic countries of the time did not usually grant such extensive powers to their parliaments, and thus they did not have the same kind of authority granted by the Turkish Constitution to the Grand National Assembly of Turkey.

The Parliament was not the only place where they had this understanding. Even in villages, which were the smallest units of settlement, the local administration was in the hands of a "muhtar," and the assembly of elders was elected by the locals. Atatürk saw it as a must to abolish the privileged classes if the concept of national sovereignty was to be established. All titles of royalty that are still seen in some Western countries, titles implying a kind of superiority such as "efendi" or "pasha," were abolished. It would not be correct to view the abolishment of the "tekke" and "zaviye" (Dervish Convents) merely as efforts to give the state a modern and contemporary look. It would be more accurate to interpret it as Atatürk's desire to establish a true democracy, which in some respects did not possess the shortfalls of Western democracies. According to him, the people should have the ability to govern the state without any discrimination. The secret of Atatürk's success lay in the fact that he had relied on the will of the people and had received their support in all of his reforms. He was a leader. General Sherill, the US ambassador in Ankara during the early days of the Republic, had this to say about Atatürk: "Turkey rarely raised a great man like Mustafa Kemal. There is no statesman today who can be considered more remarkable than Mustafa Kemal. The President of Turkey is a savior, a reformer, a national hero and a contemporary statesman." Sherill's view on the Turkish statesmen of the period as well as the Turkish government is also a source of pride for Turks: "Regarding the ability of the Ministers to administer their own Ministries I would like to express my personal opinion: There is no government in the world which is more outstanding than the Turkish government."[167]

When judging today's Turkish democracy, these basic thoughts and attitudes from its early stages must be taken into consideration. As in all other democratic countries, democracy in Turkey developed step by step. There were some difficult times that necessitated taking a step back; yet, in time Turkish democracy continued its stride along the contemporary, civilized, rational path drawn by Atatürk in the early 1920s that relied on the national will of the people.

As is the nature of democracy, opposition groups began to form from the early years of the Republic, and in 1924 it started to grow strong. Prime Minister İsmet İnönü asked for a vote of confidence from Parliament. Once the government took the confidence vote, Hüseyin Rauf and 32 of his supporters left the People's Party (Halk Partisi) and established the Terakkiperver Cumhuriyet Partisi (Progressive Republican Party). During the same period the Halk Partisi became the Cumhuriyet Halk Partisi (Republican People's Party). The Terrakiperver Cumhuriyet Partisi adopted a program similar to those of liberal parties in the West. They were proponents of giving more weight to local administrations, of following an evolutionary, not revolutionary path and of a more liberal economic system. In the meantime İnönü resigned and was replaced by Ali Fethi Okyar. In February 1925 the Sheik Said Rebellion erupted. Although some of the rebels were intent on Kurdish nationalism, a great majority of them wanted to re-establish religious law and bring back the caliphate.[168]

Parliament passed legislation placing the use of religion for political purposes among the definitions of treason. On March 2, 1925 the government lost a vote of confidence and İnönü once again became prime minister. The government then

---

[167] Ibid., pp. 178, 181-183, 187-188.
[168] Zürcher, op. cit., p. 178.

crushed the rebellion with tough measures. Its leaders were caught and punished.

In the meantime the government put forward a comprehensive reform package, the goal of which was to secularize and modernize society.

The Sheik ül Islam and the Ministry for Religious Affairs and Funds were abolished in 1924, and the Religious Affairs Administration and the General Administration of Funds were established in their place. The religious lodges were shut down in 1925. The wearing of the fez was prohibited in November. At the start of 1926 the Gregorian calendar and the system of time used by the West were adopted. In the same year the Swiss civil code and the Italian criminal code were adopted, and a great reform in the judiciary was carried out. The alphabet was changed in 1928, with Latin characters replacing Arabic. Banking legislation was passed. Rewriting the civil law, which had significant connotations for family life, in accordance with secular principles, was in itself a revolution.

Westerns units of weight and other measurements were adopted in 1931. A law on the use of family names was passed in 1934, and Mustafa Kemal Pasha was given the surname Atatürk (Father of all Turks). That same year the Constitution was amended, and women were given the right to vote. Granting suffrage to women was one of the turning points in the history of Turkish democracy, and at that time many Western countries still had not bestowed this right on women.

The following table gives the dates that the right to vote was granted to women in some Western countries.

Dates that Women Gained Suffrage
Rights in Some Western Countries

Country	Date
New Zealand	1893
Australia	1902
Finland	1906
Norway	1913
Denmark	1915
Netherlands	1917
Germany	1919
Sweden	1919
Turkey	1934
France	1944
Italy	1946
Japan	1946
Belgium	1948
Switzerland	1971

Source: Encyclopaedia Encarta

This table shows that Turkey granted this democratic right to women far earlier than many Western countries.

In 1935 the government decided to move the weekend holiday from Friday to Sunday, a decision that had special significance within the framework of efforts to secularize and westernize.

In 1937 the Constitution was amended once again to make the principle of secularism one of its articles. Article 2 of would read as follows: "The Turkish state is republican, nationalistic, populist, pro-state, secular and revolutionary." This change was also in itself a revolution. Turkey was the first among all Islamic countries to declare itself secular. This was not limited to Islamic countries, either. The constitutions of some Western countries also have articles stating that the official religion of the state was Christianity. Even today there are countries with such articles in their constitutions.

The reforms of the Atatürk period were revolutionary both in content and implication. They were far more advanced than all the reforms the Ottoman Empire had tried to achieve since the early 19th century. When compared to other nations, it is difficult to find a similar example in recent history that was so comprehensive and profoundly influential on the government as well as on the lifestyle of the people. All of Atatürk's reforms are very important, but perhaps the most important of all was the reform in democracy. The right to sovereignty that had been in the hands of a dynasty for more than 600 years now belonged to the people. The people identified with democracy; they owned it and turned it into an irreversible lifestyle. In fact, had it not been for the support of the people, a reform of this magnitude could not have been achieved.

It is also difficult to find another revolution which tried so hard to remain legitimate. Even under the most difficult conditions Atatürk remained loyal to the principle of supremacy of law and legitimacy of the regime. The Turkish nation did not leave him alone in this fight for democracy; they adopted his reforms and took ownership of the democracy. Most books published in the West on Turkey in the early years of the Republic express admiration for this great masterpiece. In his book "Mustafa Kemal, or Walking East," Paul Gentizon says: "What has happened in Turkey between 1922 and 1928 has no match in the world. It was as if a whole nation was changing around."[169]

Other nations' experiences with democracy demonstrate the significance of the success achieved in this area by the Turks. The first republic established after the French Revolution, considered to be the greatest revolution for democracy in the world, was able to exist for only 14 years. The Turkish Republic, which is the foundation of Turkish democracy, has been alive and strong for 76 years.

---

[169] Tekin Alp, op. cit., p. 9.

Single-Party Period

The development of democracy was not without its problems in Turkey. Starting from the early periods of the Republic, opposition groups began to form in Parliament. This was seen as a natural event at that time, as opposition was a part of the nature of democracy. Since the time of the Ottoman Parliament there had been opposition groups and parties. But what was not natural was for the opposition to resort to violence. Even when the Republic was in its first years, there were those who chose to take up arms against the state, the regime and the leaders. Apart from the Sheik Said rebellion, various rebellions erupted in different regions of Anatolia. Intelligence was obtained that an assassination attempt would be made on the life of Ataürk during his visit to Izmir on June 15, 1926. The members of the opposition who were behind this attempt were found out, put on trial and convicted. Various laws were passed giving the government extraordinary powers to put down rebellions. The government established internal security. Rebels, or those who wanted to change the regime through violence, were caught, tried and punished. The Independence Courts established specifically for this purpose passed harsh sentences, some of which became issues of debate in later times. But the young Republic was kept alive, and internal stability was achieved. These laws that enhanced the authority of the state remained in force until 1929. During that period the Cumhuriyet Halk Partisi (Republican People's Party or CHP) became the sole political power in the Parliament. The efforts of small opposition groups of royalists, Islamists, liberals and socialists remained futile. Within the CHP itself, the leader of which was President Atatürk, party discipline was strictly imposed. During this period the state and the party were almost one.

However, the single-party system started to cause public discontent, highlighting the need for an opposition party.

Fethi Okyar, who had returned from Paris where he had served as ambassador, established the Serbest Cumhuriyet Fırkası (Free Republic Party or SCF). Atatürk declared that he would remain unallied with both of the parties. Some of Atatürk's close friends, and even his sister Makbule Hanım, became members of this new party. Fifteen members of Parliament also joined the SCF. Okyar's party published an 11-point program that defended liberal economic policies and encouraged foreign investment. The party also supported freedom of thought and single-level elections. Once again Turkey had a multi-party system. Local elections were held in October 1930. The SCF won 30 out 512 municipalities, but following this election the struggle between the two parties reached critical levels. Okyar realized he would not be able to keep the party alive under the prevailing conditions of the time, and he closed it on November 16, 1930.

Turkey had returned to a single-party regime. But Atatürk was aware of the drawbacks of such a situation for Turkish political life. Because of this, 30 seats in the 1931 elections and 16 seats in the 1935 elections were reserved for independent candidates.

There were various groups of different social and political views outside of Parliament as well. Foremost among these was the Türk Ocakları (Turkish Hearths), which defended nationalist ideas. By 1931 this organization had 267 branches and 30,000 members; however, it was closed that year. In its place the Halkevleri (People's Homes) were established. These were mobilized to educate and culturally develop people in all corners of the country. By the end of World War II they had 500 branches.

Atatürk's ideology relied on the one hand on the will of the people and on the other, positivism. It put the guidance of science in the forefront.

İsmet İnönü, who was prime minister between 1925 and 1937, was an ardent defender of Atatürk's ideology. In 1937, upon the request of Atatürk, he handed over his position as prime minister to Celal Bayar. However, following the death of Atatürk in 1938, he became president and remained in that position until 1950. İnönü worked hard to keep the country secure and stable. Movements that had caused major social unrest in Western Europe were unable to gain ground in Turkey. The regime tried the multi-party system in two short episodes, but ultimately preserved its single-party character until the end of World War II. Parliament remained continuously open during this period. The Constitution was in force, and elections were held regularly. The regime had imperfections primarily in the fields of multi-party democracy as well as in freedom of the press and freedom of thought, but it maintained the supremacy of the will of the people and prepared the groundwork for later political developments. These main characteristics of the Republic were preserved until the end of World War II. Thanks to the masterful diplomacy pursued by İnönü, Turkey remained non-aligned until the war was over. Hence, Turkey was not directly affected by the catastrophe that devastated the whole of Europe and parts of Asia, costing the lives of millions. The warring countries did not dare attack Turkey. Turkey declared war on Germany towards the end of World War II and attended the San Francisco Conference to become a founding member of the United Nations, taking her position among the civilized nations of the world.

Difficulties and Collapses in Western Democracies after World War I

World War I was the most extensive and destructive war the world had ever seen. Thirteen million people lost their lives. On average, for every minute of the war, there were four dead and nine wounded soldiers.[170]

Millions of people were left starving and homeless. The social and economic costs of the war were too great to be calculated. In France alone 300,000 homes were totally destroyed, and 450,000 were damaged beyond repair. By the end of the war the German, Austro-Hungarian, Russian and Ottoman empires had all collapsed.[171]

The effects that the dire conditions of the war and the agreements signed following its conclusion had on Western European countries were reflected in their political lives in later periods. In many countries it proved impossible either to keep democracy alive or fully abide by its rules. While the Turkish Republic preserved its regime based on the will of the people in peace and stability, dictatorships developed and clashes evolved in most of Europe, all of which drew Europe into World War II. After taking a closer look at the political events in Europe after World War I, the value of Turkey's success in preserving her Republic and continuing her stride along the path to democracy can be better appreciated.

---

[170] Johnson, op. cit., p. 162.
[171] Peacock op.cit., p. 131.

France: Fight for Survival of the Third Republic and the Vichy Government

France was one of the countries that had suffered the most during World War I. A total of 1.4 million people lost their lives in the war. This was 17.6% of the army and 10.5% of the active male population of the country. Despite this France recovered with relative ease from the effects of the war, entering into a period of rapid development in agriculture and industry and becoming one of the most advanced nations in Europe. In 1917 Georges Clemenceau obtained the support of the right-wingers and the moderates to become prime minister.

The Treaty of Versailles stipulated that Germany pay reparations for war damages far exceeding her ability to comply. When Germany failed to pay, France, together with Belgium, occupied Germany's Ruhr region. In Alsace-Lorraine, which was recaptured during the war, the German language was replaced with French at schools. In reaction to these policies the local German population formed an underground organization. Their leaders were captured and punished in 1927. The Communist Party grew stronger in France, and in 1924 it managed to put 29 members of parliament in the Assembly, resulting in the organizing of the extreme right. Organizations known as the Corps of the King, the Young Nationalists and the Flaming Cross started to work and resorted to violence to re-establish the nobility. The Action Française paper published by Leon Daudet, son of well-known author Alphonse Daudet, criticized the republican democracy for being too weak and defended the view that France should be run with an autocratic regime.

Fascist movements were also seen in France in the 1930s. The French People's Party led by Jacques Doriot was sympathetic towards Hitler. The Catholic Church, although not openly supportive of fascism, was influenced by Italy and started to suggest the establishment of a "state of institutions" in France. These developments resulted in violent demonstrations in Paris in May 1934. First the extreme right-wingers, then, acting against them, the socialists and communists organized large demonstrations. Twenty-five people were killed and many injured during these demonstrations. Prime Minister Daladier had to resign.

The threat of fascism united the radicals, socialists and communists, who formed the People's Front against fascism. This front won a landslide victory in the elections of May 1936, securing 378 seats to the 200 won by the right.[172] Socialist Leon Blum became prime minister; however, the social policies of his government, especially its decision to lower wages, caused great social unrest. Large strikes were staged, and factories were occupied. It was the communists who benefited the most from the People's Front, managing to put 72 members of parliament into the Assembly and building their membership to 380,000. The French Communist Party, led by Maurice Thorez, was vehemently opposed to fascism and Nazism but was pushing for closer ties with the Soviet Union. Under such circumstances the People's Front coalition was only able to last for one year, and Blum was forced to resign. During the term in office of Daladier, who became prime minister in 1937, France shifted to the right. There was an inclination to reach a compromise with Hitler and Mussolini. The idea of using the Nazi Germany against Russia started to gain credence. Daladier was one of the negotiators of the Munich Accord, which paved the way for reaching a compromise with Hitler.

In between the two wars the Catholic Church had increased its influence in France. This was clearly evident in the education system. From 1920 to 1936 secondary schools of the secular government became fewer in number, while schools tied to the Church went up from 632 to 1,420. There were various ethnic and religious groups in France. The number of Jews had increased from around 35,000 at the end of the 19th century to more than 100,000 by 1920. France's

---

[172] Ibid., p. 165

tolerance for foreigners made this country an attractive center for them in between the wars. Between 1889 and 1940 2.3 million foreigners had gained French citizenship. Yet, this was not easy for everyone, and Africans in particular, had great trouble becoming French citizens. In addition to them there were 2,613,000 people living in France in 1931 without French citizenship.

Having said this, French attitude towards the subjects in her colonies was quite different. They were denied basic rights and freedoms. Efforts on the part of some French intellectuals to remedy the situation were not effective. The atmosphere of freedom developing in France had not reached the colonies. But there was no racially motivated violence against foreigners living in France, either. France had been a multicultural society since the 19th century. Therefore, one should not view Daladier's efforts to soften Hitler or the publications of a group of people connected to the French daily Action Française against Jews, Protestants and foreigners as evidence that the French people nurtured racist trends. Fascist propaganda was unable to find a following in the masses, and the pro-fascist coup planed in 1934 could not be carried out.

During the period between the two wars, France tried to increase its influence over her colonies. Investment in the colonies quadrupled between 1914 and 1940. In the meantime, people living in the colonies started to ask for the same rights as the French people. Ho Chi Minh, who had participated in preparatory talks for the 1919 Paris Peace Conference ending World War I, presented a program with eight items reflecting the demands of the people of Indochina; however, these were rejected. At that time an oppressive regime ruled Indochina, where 700 executions were carried out in 1930 alone.

The position of the colonies in Africa was not much different, either. The French who had settled there had representatives in the French Parliament in Paris who subverted any attempt to grant more rights to the indigenous inhabitants of these colonies. The income of Europeans living in the African colonies was on average eight times higher than that of the local people.

Rene Maran's book "Batouala," reflecting the views of the African people on their colonial masters, had won the Goncourt Prize in Paris, but the sale of the book was prohibited in the French colonies in Africa. In 1926 10,000 Africans lost their lives in the construction of the Congo-Ocean railroad due to appalling working conditions. By 1936 only 2,000 Africans had been granted French citizenship.

Some French intellectuals leveled harsh criticism against the inhumane treatment in the colonies and demanded radical reforms. During his term as prime minister Leon Blum made a failed attempt to grant French citizenship to 25,000 Algerians. Especially in the years approaching World War II France viewed her colonies and the people living in them as a source of strength in the power struggle in Europe. There were quite a few politicians who, considering the people in the colonies as well, talked about a "100-million strong France." The French colonial minister, Georges Mandel, had said in 1939 that he had 2 million Arab and black soldiers available on demand.[173]

Such was the situation in France when the country entered World War II. When the French Army was defeated in the early stages of the war and the Germans entered Paris on June 14, 1940, the French government asked for a cease-fire. The government fell, and Petain, one of France's heroes in World War I, became prime minister. According to the terms of the cease-fire Alsace-Lorraine, northern France and the Atlantic shores would be left to Germany. Central and southern France would be left to the administration of the French government led by Petain, whose capital was the city of Vichy. The French government would continue to rule its colonies. Petain later became president, and in his place Laval became prime minister. During this period anti-occupation underground

---

[173] Johnson, op.cit., pp 145,146,149,151.

forces started to form. These were directed from London by General Charles de Gaulle, who worked in close cooperation with the Allies and played a crucial role in the victory against Germany. The Vichy government that had felt obliged to establish good relations with Nazi Germany remained in power until the liberation of France.

These were the experiences of France from the start of World War I to the end of World War II. Although a few reforms were enacted, one could not say that it had been a stable and uninterrupted period for democracy. During the war effort, rights and freedoms were pushed aside, perhaps out of necessity, and a fight for survival was waged. At the top of the agenda was ridding the country of the German occupation. The oppressive regime in the colonies continued, and there weren't any signs of a movement towards a democratic regime based on human rights.

Britain: Clouds of War and Democratic Survival

The price of war was heavy for Britain as well. They had lost 702,410 people during World War I, and the country's economy was almost destroyed. The war had important repercussions in internal politics as well. The defeat of Great Britain at the Dardanelles forced Churchill to resign. While that turmoil was going on, pro-independence supporters in Ireland organized a rebellion. Following a major uprising in Dublin, the Republic of Ireland was declared on April 24, 1916. There was a four-day bloody battle between the Republicans and the British Army. In the end the British suppressed the rebellion and executed its leaders.

The economic difficulties faced at the end of the war in 1918 forced the country to ration basic consumption materials. Surcharges were imposed on the wealthy. Britain made an important democratic reform in the last year of the war; it gave women the right to vote. But still, only women who were over the age of 32 and had paid municipal taxes could exercise this right.

Prime Minister Lloyd George won the elections of 1918, which were a great success for the Conservative Party. Seventy-three members of parliament elected from Ireland refused to enter Parliament and established their own legislative body in Dublin. There was social unrest following the war, with strikes following one after another. The number of unemployed went up to 1 million in 1920 and 2 million in 1921.

During this period the government passed several pieces of legislation that extended the social rights of the people. Thanks to an amendment enacted in 1920, the number of those who could benefit from health and unemployment insurance went up from 3 to 12 million.

Meanwhile, those working for the independence of Ireland organized themselves under the umbrella of the Irish Republican Army and initiated assassinations of British soldiers and police. To combat them the British formed a special force called the Black and Tans, who started a campaign against the Irish. The extra-tough methods used by this force evoked a strong reaction in Britain, and the government was strongly criticized. In 1922 England recognized the independence of Ireland; however, three regions in northern Ireland remained within the United Kingdom. The Conservatives maintained their majority for a while but faced defeat in the next elections. The Labour Party, which was the largest group in the House of Commons, became the ruling party at the end of 1924. Yet the government's decision to recognize the Soviet Union and sign a commercial agreement with that country caused a strong reaction, and the government was forced to resign.

Working conditions worsened once again in 1925, resulting in a general strike. In 1927 legislation was passed prohibiting all strikes that threatened to destabilize the government. Hence, general strikes became outlawed. During this period a few social reforms were implemented, most important among which was legislation passed in 1928 that granted unconditional, equal voting rights to men and women. Turkey granted this right only six years after Britain.

Following the 1929 elections Labour once again came to power and formed a government with the support of the Liberals. During that time, the British government rejected Gandhi's demand for India's independence. While this government was still in power a great economic crisis that had started in the United States hit the whole world. In 1931 the number of unemployed in Britain went up to 2.7 million. The government's stability measures and decision to lower wages caused a major crisis, and a new government was formed in 1931. Due to harsh economic conditions "hunger walks" were held in parts of the country. But the economic policies of the government proved to be effective, and the British economy entered a period of growth until World War II.

In those years extreme elements in both the right and the left of the political spectrum began to have an influence on the political life of Britain. The British Fascist Party led by Mosley staged demonstrations. On the left were efforts to form a people's front. In May 1937 Chamberlain became prime minister.

The war gave rise to significant developments in Britain's internal politics. The Extraordinary Powers Act gave the government extensive powers, the likes of which could not be easily found in any other democratic country. One of these was the right to apprehend people without a court decision in cases where the security of the state was under threat.[174]

On May 1940 Churchill took over as prime minister as well as minister of defence and assumed all responsibility for the war effort.

The situation in the British colonies was not in line with the democratic measures in Britain. The rights of the locals were extremely restricted. In 1931 there were 1.8 million

---

[174] Peacock, op. cit., pp. 184, 188, 239.

Europeans in South Africa. While they held 1,126,000 sq km. of land, 6 million Africans only held 87,000 sq km. The situation in Rhodesia was not much different. Perhaps the policies that were initially planned were different from what worked out in practice. In fact, the colonial secretary, the duke of Devonshire, issued a declaration in 1923 that said: "Kenya is first an African country. The interests of the native Africans are above all else." Yet, in 1930 Africans owned 135,000 sq km. of land, the Europeans 42,700 sq km. and Britain 253,000 sq km. of land in Kenya.[175]

Germany: Farewell to the Weimar Democracy

Defeat in World War I and the economic and social crisis caused by the heavy war reparations affected German political life. Immediately after the war the socialists in the Parliament demanded the resignation of Kaiser Wilhelm II, who bowed to their demands. Socialist Friedrich Ebert became president. Extreme leftists tried to structure Germany based on the Soviet model, and a Council of Commissioners was formed. The extreme leftists led by Karl Liebknecht and Rosa Luxembourg tried to establish a proletariat dictatorship as Lenin did in Russia. On January 6, 1919, all major buildings in Berlin were occupied during a demonstration in which a 100,000 people participated. The interior minister asked for the help of extremely conservative ex-soldiers to suppress the uprising. The communists were pushed back with this counter-attack, and Berlin was brought under control. During the fighting many were killed, including Liebknecht and Luxembourg. The struggle between the socialists and the newly formed German Communist Party went on for 12 years. This struggle is viewed as one of the factors that brought Hitler to power.[176]

---

[175] Johnson, op. cit. p.279.
[176] Peacock, op. cit., p. 173.

The socialists won the general elections, but the conservative nationalists managed to put 12 members of parliament in office. Compared to the pre-war period, the regime was much more liberal. The prime minister and the ministers were accountable to the Parliament; however, the president continued to be politically strong, and he had the right to abolish the legislative body. This new state is referred to as the Weimar Republic. Even as early as 1920, influential writers such Carl Schmitt started to write of the need for Germany to have a more authoritarian constitution and government.[177]

The communists organized riots in the Ruhr region and in Munich, which they controlled for about a month. The president ordered the army to suppress these uprisings. In the meantime, members of an extreme right-wing organization called the Free Corps took control of Berlin and reinstated the kaiser.

While these clashes were taking place, France and Belgium occupied the Ruhr region in 1923. The social and political consequences of this occupation were devastating for Germany. The German Mark became a worthless piece of paper, and there were general strikes everywhere. Thanks to the efforts of Minister of Foreign Affairs Gustav Stresemann, who assumed that position during the same year and continued there until 1929, things took a slightly positive turn and the economy started to stabilize. The French and Belgian soldiers began to withdraw from Germany in 1925. Yet this was also the period in which the Nazi movement started to develop. Hitler had tried in 1923 to overthrow the government in Munich and had declared himself president of Germany. His attempt failed. He was arrested and given a five-year prison term but was released nine months later. During his incarceration he started to write "Mein Kampf," which later

---

[177] Johnson, op.cit., p.279.

became the handbook of the Nazi movement. It preached the "superiority" of the Arian race and planted the seeds of anti-Semitism.[178]

On the other hand, a republic was declared the very same year in Turkey, replacing the Ottoman Empire with a modern state.

The Nazis had 24 members of parliament in 1924, but this number fell to 12 in 1929. Hitler later started a campaign calling for an end to war reparation payments, which helped increase the number of Nazi members of parliament to 107 in the 1930 elections. Next to the social democrats his party had the most seats in Parliament. The communists won 77 seats in the same elections. Paramilitary troops organized by Hitler numbered almost 400,000. There were frequent clashes between them and the socialists and communists all around the country. During the presidential elections of 1932 Hindenburg received 18 million votes and Hitler 11 million. After a year of continual clashes, Hindenburg appointed Hitler as prime minister in January 1933. A month later an arson attack was made on the Reichstag, the German Parliament. The communists were immediately blamed for the arson, and their leaders were swiftly arrested. Attacks on Jews began. The Nazis won 341 seats out of 647 in the general election of 1933, which was held under oppressive circumstances. The rest is history. By 1945 12 million Germans had lost their lives.

Italy and Spain: Years of Authoritarianism

Italy and Spain could not maintain their democracies after World War I and were ruled by dictators, which led to great suffering. The war had caused tremendous losses and destruction in Italy, where almost 600,000 people had lost

---

[178] Peacock, op. cit., p. 176.

their lives. In this environment, extremist groups got organized and gained strength. Mussolini was the leader of the fascists, and he held his first major political demonstration in Milan in 1919. The Fascist Party was officially established in 1921. In the beginning, just as with the Nazis, they were not that strong and in the elections of 1921 were able to win only 22 seats. On October 28, 1922 they organized a large march on Rome. Instead of dispersing the fascists with force, King Victor Emmanuel III appointed Mussolini prime minister. Gradually the fascists organized armed militias and used force to eliminate those who opposed them. Many people were killed during the elections of 1924, among them the Socialist leader Matteotti. The opposition left the Parliament. What followed was a period of coercion that included crackdowns on the opposition press, coercing university professors to take an oath of loyalty to fascism and using force against anyone opposed. Italy entered the war under these conditions. The result is common knowledge.

The history of the same period is filled with agony for Spain as well. Following the overthrow of the monarchy by the Republicans in 1931, there were intense clashes among conservatives, communists, socialists, liberals and anarchists. Within the Catholic Church, the army and businessman were many who opposed the Republicans. During the elections of 1936 a People's Front formed by the left-wing parties won a great victory. Under these circumstances a backlash led by General Francisco Franco started against the Republicans. Franco, who landed his troops in Spain through Morocco, came to the outskirts of Madrid, and as a result, the civil war spread all over the country. Germany and Italy helped Franco, and Russia helped the Republicans. With the outside aid he received, Franco managed to take control of all Spain in 1939 and established a dictatorship.[179] Until his death in 1975 Spain was ruled by Franco's authoritarian regime.

---

[179] Ibid., pp. 168, 211.

Such is the general picture of political developments in Europe from the start of World War I to the end of World War II. One hundred-fifty years after the French Revolution many European countries had distanced themselves from democracy and were ruled by dictators. In those countries that had maintained their democracies there was major economic, social and political turbulence. While granting new political and social rights to their own citizens, they followed a different policy in their colonies. The French Revolution's ideas of freedom had never reached those places. Ideologies developed that defended violence and totalitarian states. Jews suffered tremendously, but they were not the only ones. Anyone opposed the totalitarian regimes was subjected to oppression and coercion. Turkey was one of the places to which people running from this oppression escaped.

Flight to Turkey for Freedom

Since the time of the Ottoman Empire, Turkey had been a place of refuge for those fleeing oppression. Protecting refugees is a time-honored tradition of the Turkish people. During the 15th and 16th centuries thousands of Jews escaping the oppression of Christians in Western Europe had taken refuge in the Ottoman Empire. Many Jews who were forced by the Spanish Inquisition to convert to Christianity also fled to Turkey in the 16th and 17th centuries. In the 17th century thousands of Jews came to the Ottoman Empire as a result of Habsburg attacks on neighbouring countries. The place of refuge for Jews who had escaped from the massacres in the Ukraine carried out by Boghdan Chmielnicki was again Turkey. In the 19th century, more than 1.5 million Muslims and Jews fled to Turkey from southeastern Europe.

Following the capture of North Africa by the French, Egypt and Cyprus by the British and the occupation of Bosnia by Austria, thousands of people sought refuge in the Ottoman Empire. The refugees were not limited to Muslims and Jews.

Hundreds of Christians who were oppressed following the 1815 Vienna Congress and the 1848 rebellion during the time of Metternich also took refuge with the Ottomans. Turkey was one of the main destinations of Jews who fled the 1881 massacres in Russia. The numbers of those seeking shelter in Turkey increased even more after a great fire in the Turkish and Jewish parts of Thessaloniki.

In the 1930s, thousands of intellectuals fleeing the oppression of the Nazis came to Turkey. Among them were world-famous professors, scholars, doctors, lawyers and actors. Most of them secured prestigious positions in Turkey, especially at universities in Istanbul and Ankara, six months after the Nazis had fired them from their jobs. Their arrival in Turkey was organized by the Zurich-based Organization for Emergency Aid To German Scientists. The representatives of this organization visited Ankara in July 1933 and met with Minister of Education Reşid Galip, who secured Atatürk's approval and reached an agreement with them. Among those who came to Turkey under this agreement were well-known scholars such as economist Alfred Isaac, economist and sociologist Alexander Rustow, professor of Roman law Professor Andreas Schwarz, professor of criminal law Richard Honig, professor of international commercial law Ernst Hirsch, famous city planner and the ex- mayor of Magdeburg and Berlin Ernst Reuter and professor of economics Fritz Neumark.[180]

Turkey was among the leading countries that helped the Jews during World War II. During the early days of the war some Turkish citizens of Jewish origin were living in Western European countries, with 10,000 in France alone. Most of these people had regularly renewed their nationality papers, but some had failed to do so for various reasons, and their citizenship was questionable at the very least. The war caught

---

[180] Stanford Shaw, Turkey and the Holocaust, New York, 1993, pp. 3, 7.

them under these circumstances. When Paris was occupied by the Germans, there were 3,381 Jews living there who were also Turkish nationals. On September 27, 1940 the commander of the German occupation forces issued a series of restrictive measures against the Jews living in France. Later these were made even stricter.

On June 2, 1941 a census of Jews living in Europe was taken, and their houses, factories and shops were confiscated. The schooling of Jewish children was also restricted. There were constraints in the regions controlled by the Vichy government as well. The forced emigration of Jews from both the German-occupied as well as the Vichy government-controlled regions to concentration camps started in 1942. There were severe restrictions imposed on those who were allowed to stay in their homes, and Jews were prohibited from owning radios, telephones or bicycles.

Even under such difficult conditions, Turkish diplomats in France and other European countries made an extraordinary effort to rescue Turkish Jews. These diplomats' efforts were not confined to official attempts. They also engaged in behind-the-scene activities, even at the risk of their own lives, and managed to save the lives of thousands of Jews. Namık Yolga, who was at the time serving as deputy consul in the Turkish Consulate in Paris, wrote to Stanford Shaw: "Anti-semitism that has shown itself in numerous countries to varying degrees never existed in Turkey. Therefore, it was only natural for our consulate to protect our citizens of Jewish origin just like any other Turkish national." Ambassador Necdet Kent, who was then deputy consul at the Turkish Consulate in Marseilles and who had expended great efforts to save Jewish lives, has written about how they tried to rescue even those Jews who had lost their Turkish citizenship.[181]

At first they attempted to save Jews one by one; however when the pressure began to mount and people started to be

---

[181] Ibid., pp. 55, 60, 65.

sent to concentration camps, Ankara gave the order for Jews to be brought to Turkey in groups.

In addition to Paris and Marseilles the Turkish consulates in Lyon, Athens and Thessaloniki as well as Turkey's representative offices around Europe made great attempts in the same direction. Turkish representatives in Thessaloniki gave Turkish citizenship papers even to Jews of Greek nationality in order to be able to save them from the Nazis. The Jewish community in Turkey established a special organization to sneak those who were being oppressed out of Greece. Some of them were taken to Izmir and some to Alexandria. Among thcm was George Papandreou, who later became prime minister of Greece. A total of 859 people were saved in this in way.

One of the most meaningful examples of the humanitarian efforts made despite all danger was the struggle of Selahattin Ülkümen, Turkey's consul general on the island of Rhodes, against the commander of the German occupation forces.

When the Germans decided that the Jews on Rhodes should be "temporarily transferred to another island," they met with strong opposition from Ülkümen, who prevented the transfer not only of Turkish Jews but also of their relatives having Greek and Italian citizenship. At that time there were 1,673 Jews living in Rhodes, and those who could not be saved by Ülkümen were sent to Greece. Only 151 of them survived the war. In the final months of the war, soon after Turkey declared war on Germany, German planes bombed the Turkish Consulate in Rhodes, killing Selahattin Ülkümen's pregnant wife and two consulate officials. Ülkümen was sent to Piraeus and put under house arrest until the end of the war. Despite this 44 Jews protected by Ülkümen had not been deported from Rhodes. When the German commander learned that the Red Cross would come to the island in January 1945, he allowed the Jews to be sent to Izmir.

The Yad Vashem Foundation in Israel, which bestows the "Righteous Gentile" award to those who risked their lives for

Jews although they are not Jews themselves, presented this award to Ülkümen and planted a tree in his honor in front of the Genocide Museum in Jerusalem. In 1998 the state of Israel put his picture on one of the stamps issued in memory of those who had contributed to the rescue of Jews from genocide.

Turkey played an important "bridge" role in the escape of Jews from Western Europe to Palestine, organized by the Eretz Association in Istanbul. On January 30, 1941 Turkey issued the Transfer Passages Decree and organized this transit. The Turkish Parliament approved this decree, which gave the Jewish Refugee Agency in Istanbul full authority over the matter. In 1941 alone, 4,400 Jews arrived in Turkey under this decree. By the end of the war around 100,000 Jews had transited Turkey on their way to Palestine.[182]

Turkey continued her efforts to rescue the Jews until the very end of the war. Minister of Foreign Affairs Numan Menemencioğlu ordered a ship named the Tarı to transport Jews out of the Balkans. However, because the countries involved could not guarantee the ship safe passage, the operation was carried out in secret with smaller boats. The Turkish government ordered representative offices in Burgas, Constanta and Budapest to issue visas to Jews quickly so as to facilitate their speedy arrival in Turkey.

At a speech he gave in 1947, Prime Minister Recep Peker said, "Anti-Semitism will remain a source of shame of the 20th century." Since that time Turks of Jewish origin have continued to live in peace, harmony and security in Turkey as they have done for centuries.

So this is the Turkey that is accused by some of being uncompassionate and which was kept out of the EU with the excuse of not having enough respect for human rights. After all the bitter experiences witnessed by history, it would not be incorrect to say that Turkey tops the list of countries that does not need a lesson in compassion and tolerance.

---

[182] Ibid., pp. 149, 252-254, 266.

Turkish Democracy after World War II

Before the war came to an end there were signs that Turkey would soon have a more contemporary and advanced democracy. In his opening speech at Parliament on November 1, 1944 President İnönü had strongly emphasized the democratic, parliamentary nature of the Turkish political system. He had declared on May 19, 1945 that the government would take important steps in that direction. The same year, while legislation for land reform was being discussed in Parliament, a group of parliamentarians led by Celal Bayar came forward as the opposition group. On June 7 Celal Bayar, Adnan Menderes, Refik Koraltan and Fuat Köprülü submitted a motion to Parliament asking for the full implementation of the Constitution and a strengthening of democracy. Meanwhile, in 1945 a businessman from Istanbul, Nuri Demirağ, established the Milli Kalkınma Partisi (National Development Party). On January 7, 1946, Adnan Menderes and his three colleagues, together with some friends, established the Demokrat Parti (Democrat Party or DP), and hence Turkey returned to a multi-party system. A great effort to have a more liberal regime had begun. Restrictions on the press were relaxed, and universities were granted a certain degree of autonomy.

The elections held that year were considered to be the first and most important step towards multi-party democracy after the war. The Demokrat Parti won 62 out of the 465 seats in Parliament, but there were allegations that the elections were not carried out in full compliance with the law. Quarrels erupted between the government and the opposition during this period. The Demokrat Parti was asking for a more democratic political system and a more liberal economy. In the meantime, the Sosyalist Parti (Socialist Party) and the Türkiye Sosyalist İşçi Köylü Partisi (Socialist Party of Workers and Villagers of Turkey) were established in 1946.

When the political disputes between the Cumhuriyet Halk Partisi (Republican People's Party or CHP) and the Demokrat Parti started to have adverse effects on the country's political life, President İnönü consulted with the leaders of both parties and issued a memorandum on July 12, 1947 asking all government organs to remain unbiased towards all of these parties. This intervention by the president is viewed as an important turning point towards fully establishing a multi-party system in Turkey.[183] During this period important reforms were implemented. The September 7, 1947 decisions that would facilitate Turkey's membership in the IMF were accepted. Together with the devaluation of the Turkish lira, a few measures geared to make the economy more liberal were also agreed upon. In 1947 new legislation on trade unions was implemented.

This was a period in which democratic ideology began to be fully established in Turkey. Şemsettin Günaltay, who was then prime minister, had said at a speech on January 23, 1948: "We must take as an example the rules of Western democracies. For us, freedom of conscience is a sacred concept." The following day he gave a speech in Parliament on the same issue: "I will work earnestly to establish democracy. That is the only way for our country. I would like to tell you as a historian that demagogy will bring disintegration and dictatorship."[184]

General elections were held on May 14, 1950 in which 80% of the electorate participated. The Demokrat Parti won 53.4% and the Cumhuriyet Halk Partisi 39.8% of the vote, resulting in the DP coming to power. Celal Bayar became president and Adnan Menderes prime minister. After 14 years as prime minister and 12 as president, İnönü made a democratic hand-over and became the opposition leader. This

---

[183] Zürcher, op. cit., p. 224.
[184] Lewis, The Emergence of Modern Turkey, op. cit., p. 303.

was the first election in which the government had changed hands through democratic means in Turkey. Following the first Constitution and parliamentary elections in 1876 Turkey had tried a multi-party system in 1908 and 1913. Between 1923 and 1925 and later in 1930 she again had experiences with multi-party democracy. In the meantime she went through a period of a single party system and returned to multi-party democracy after 1946. In 1950 she reached a stage whereby the government could change hands by means of free elections.

During this new period Turkey took important steps towards liberalizing her economy. A Turkish brigade under the UN flag was also sent to Korea, where some 25,000 Turkish soldiers fought for peace. Turkey lost 730 soldiers in the Korean War. On February 18, 1952 she became a member of NATO.

In that same year Türk-İş (Confederation of Turkish Labor Unions), which would make important contributions to the Turkish labor union movement, was established. Despite internal political struggles, the democratic parliamentary regime was kept alive. Elections were held on May 2, 1954. The Demokrat Parti increased its returns from 53.6% to 58.4% of the vote, while the Cumhuriyet Halk Partisi fell from 39.9% to 35.1%. The DP won 503 and the CHP 31 seats. The Millet Partisi (Nation Party), which had won a single seat in Parliament in the elections of 1950, was shut down in 1953 for mixing religion with politics. It was later re-established as the Cumhuriyetçi Millet Partisi (Republican Nation Party) and received 4.8% of the vote in the 1954 elections, giving it five seats in Parliament.

Worsening economic conditions with increasing inflation on the one hand and internal political struggles on the other forced the government to move forward by a year the elections that were scheduled for 1958. In the October 27, 1957 elections the DP lost support but still won 47.3% of the vote and remained in government. The opposition CHP increased its share to 40.6%. In the new Parliament the DP had 424 representatives and the CHP 178. Although the gap was still significant, the imbalance was not as large as it once had been. The Hürriyet Partisi (Freedom Party), established by people who had left the DP, received 3.8% of the vote and managed to win four seats in Parliament. This party later integrated with the CHP. Although the Cumhuriyetçi Millet Partisi received only 7%, it still won four seats. According to the majority system in place since 1946 the party that received the majority of votes in a region received all the seats allocated for that area.

During those years important developments took place in the region. The Balkan Pact was established with the participation of Turkey, Greece and Yugoslavia in 1953. The Baghdad Pact was formed with Turkey, Iraq, Iran, Pakistan and Britain in 1955. In 1956 Egypt's President Gamal Abdel Nasser nationalized the Suez Canal, and Israel, Britain and France landed troops in Suez. The British sent troops to Jordan to suppress a coup against King Hussein in 1957. In 1958 Egypt and Syria joined forces to form the United Arab Republic; however, it turned out to be short-lived. In 1958 the monarchy in Iraq was overthrown after a coup, and the king and prime minister were both killed. The Baghdad Pact lost its significance when Iraq left the organization in 1960. In its place another organization called CENTO was established with the participation of Turkey, Iran, Pakistan, Britain and the United States.

1959 and 1960 witnessed a hardening of internal political struggles in Turkey. On April 18, 1960 the government introduced a motion to set up an investigative committee on the activities of the opposition. Freedom of press was restricted. Large-scale student protests started, and universities were closed. The army was called upon to subdue the student demonstrations.

The army took over the government on May 27, 1960. A National Unity Committee was formed under the leadership of General Cemal Gürsel. However, unlike most military regimes in other countries, the goal of the army was not to establish a dictatorship that would take over the administration of the country. To the contrary, its goal was to hand over the administration to civilians once a constitution that would strengthen democracy was put in place. For this reason, Istanbul University President Sıddık Sami Onar and four other law professors were invited to Ankara the very same day of the coup to write a new and contemporary constitution. Constitutional law professor Bülent Tanör said, "The coup of May 27 was undemocratic in its means of execution but democratic in its philosophy and in the nature of the residual elements upon which the intervention was based."[185]

When analyzing the military interventions in Turkey, Bernard Lewis says that more than the interventions themselves, the return of the soldiers to their barracks and their efforts to return to democracy were the interesting aspects of these operations.[186]

A temporary constitution prepared by the law professors was put in force on June 12, 1960 and would remain effective until a new one was drafted and elections held. A government of technocrats was appointed that would be accountable to the National Unity Committee. During this period some extreme measures met with adverse reaction from the people. A total of 147 university professors were dismissed, and a large number of generals and officers were sent into retirement. After a while it was realized that an injustice had been done to the academicians, and all 147 were reinstated. But some of the decisions proved impossible to reverse. Former Prime Minister Menderes, Minister of Foreign Affairs Fatin Rüştü Zorlu and Minister of Finance Hasan Polatkan were sentenced to death by the court, and following approval of their sentences by the National Unity Committee were executed. Bayar's death sentence was commuted to life in prison due to his advanced

---

[185] Bülent Tanör, İki Anayasa, Istanbul, 1994, p. 15.
[186] Lewis, Why Turkey is the Only Muslim Democracy, p. 45.

age. In addition a number of Demokrat Parti members of parliament and officials were sent to prison.

The statesmen who had been executed were later exonerated; memorial burial sites were built in their honour and their names were given to roads, schools and airports. Those imprisoned were released after a few years, and some of them returned to political life. However, whatever the reason, the treatment meted out to former statesmen and politicians during that period is one of the sad pages in the history of Turkish democracy.

On January 6, 1961 a constituent assembly was established to prepare a new constitution. Taking into consideration the proposal put forward by the law professors from Istanbul and Ankara universities, it drafted the new Turkish Constitution and approved it on July 9, 1961.

The opening passage of this Constitution explains its aims and outlines its basic goal as "establishing a democratic state of law with all its legal and social foundations that will enable the development of human rights and freedoms, national solidarity, social justice, individual and societal peace and welfare." Article 2 of the Constitution defines the character of the Republic as follows: "The Turkish Republic is a national, democratic, secular and social state of law based on human rights."

The Constitution reorganized the balance of power and contained clauses preventing the government from becoming overly powerful. Accordingly, the Parliament, which used to have only a single house, now had two with the introduction of the senate. An independent Constitutional Court was established that would verify the constitutionality of new legislation; freedom of press was accepted in its most extensive form; and the electoral system was changed into a representative one enabling parties to be represented in Parliament in proportion to the votes they had received. The principle accepted with the 1924 Constitution had been the "supremacy of the Parliament." The Constitution of 1961, however, brought with it the principle of "supremacy of the

Constitution." The Constitutional Court had the right to inspect the constitutionality of legislation drafted by Parliament. Moreover, the independence of the courts was safeguarded, and a Supreme Committee of Judges was established to decide on the promotions of judges. The Council of State could now inspect all activities of the administration. These were the requirements of a democratic state of law.

The Constitution of 1961 was very progressive in democratic rights and freedoms as well. Rights and freedoms could only be restricted for reasons specified in the Constitution; restrictions had to conform to the word and spirit of the Constitution, had to be accomplished by law and could in no way infringe upon the essence of rights and freedoms.

The new Constitution aimed at achieving economic development, social justice and democracy all together. It was well known that in earlier days in the West, however, economic development had been achieved either by postponing or limiting democratic rights and expectations of social equality.[187]

This liberal and democratic Constitution was put to a referendum on July 9 and was adopted with 61.7% of the vote. Earlier, on January 13, all bans on political activities had been removed. In a short period of time 11 new parties, including the Cumhuriyetçi Köylü Millet Partisi (Republican Villagers' Party or CKMP), were established. The largest of these was the Adalet Partisi (Justice Party or AP), which was seen as the continuation of the Demokrat Parti.

Elections were held on October 15, 1961. That is to say, Turkey returned to a parliamentary democracy 17 months after the intervention by the army with a new, contemporary and more liberal Constitution. The CHP won the highest number of votes in the elections, with 36.7%. The AP, which

---

[187] Tanör, op. cit., pp. 19-24, 82.

received 34.7%, followed. The CHP put 173 and the AP 158 members into Parliament. The Yeni Türkiye Partisi (New Turkey Party or YTP) received 13.9% and the CKMP 13.4% of the vote. The Türkiye İşçi Partisi (Turkey Labor Party), established in February 1961, garnered around 3%. One of the most important issues on the agenda of the CHP-AP coalition government led by İnönü was reducing the sentences of imprisoned politicians. Disagreement over this issue ended with the collapse of the coalition.

İnönü formed a new government with the two smaller parties in Parliament, the YTP and the CKMP. The local elections held in November 1963 ended with a victory for the AP, which had been in opposition. İnönü resigned upon the withdrawal of the YTP and the CKMP from the coalition. When the first leader of the AP, Ragıp Gümüşpala, could not form a government, İnönü was once again given the task of doing so. On December 25, 1963, together with the independents, he formed a minority government. Following her first experience with a coalition government, Turkey now encountered a minority government. That government stayed in power for about a year, but when its budget was not approved by Parliament, it had to resign, on February 13, 1965.

The government formed by Suat Hayri Ürgüplü, an independent member of parliament, ran the government until the elections scheduled for October of the same year. After the death of Gümüşpala, Süleyman Demirel took over the leadership of the AP. In the elections of October 1965 the AP won a landslide victory by garnering 52.9% of the vote. The CHP's votes fell to 28.7%. All others received less than 7%. Demirel became prime minister, and the first single-party government since the 1960 intervention was thus formed. Turkey entered a period of internal stability. In the elections of 1969 the AP received 46.5% of the vote and again managed to form the government by itself. The CHP's share of the vote fell further to 27.4%. In 1970 Demirel resigned due to a conflict within the party; however, he was later again appointed prime minister and established a new government. At the end of the same year 41 members of parliament resigned from the AP and founded the Demokratik Parti (Democratic Party or DP) led by Ferruh Bozbeyli.

In the elections of 1965 the CHP shifted to the center left and entered into a process of new political structuring. This time there was a division in the CHP. Forty-seven members of parliament who did not accept its left-of-center policy deserted the CHP and formed the Güven Partisi (Reliance Party) led by Turhan Feyzioğlu. Although the CHP achieved good results in the elections of 1968, especially from large cities, they were unable to meet their expectations in the general elections of 1969. In the meantime the extreme right and extreme left started to organize as well, and armed clashes began to take place between these extremist groups. Pro-violence youth movements that had begun in France in 1968 and later surfaced in various other European countries spread to Turkey. Some people were killed during these clashes.

On March 12, 1971 the army gave a memorandum to the government asking it to form a strong, new government that would be able deal with the anarchy going on in the country. Demirel resigned, and a new government was formed under the leadership of Nihat Erim, a member of parliament from the CHP. İnönü declared his support for the new government. During this period the Parliament continued to meet. The right-wing Milli Nizam Partisi (National Order Party), led by Necmettin Erbakan, and the Türkiye İşçi Partisi were both shut down by the Constitutional Court. Erbakan established a new party called the Milli Selamet Partisi (National Salvation Party or MSP) in October 1972. Forty-four articles of the Constitution were changed by Parliament. In this case the goal was to strengthen the government and prevent the abuse of rights and freedoms. The independence of state radio, television and universities was also curbed. State Security Courts were established to try those involved in politically motivated violence.

In the meantime, Erim asked Parliament to increase the authority of the government and be given the right to pass decrees instead of laws on certain issues. When Parliament refused this request, Erim resigned. Ferit Melen, one of the leaders of the Güven Partisi, formed the new government. Bülent Ecevit, who opposed the CHP lending support to these governments, first resigned from his post as secretary-general of the party; then, in May 1972 he was elected to replace İnönü as leader of the CHP. At that time, elections were also held in Parliament to replace President Cevdet Sunay, since his term had ended. Faruk Gürler, who was then Chief of General Staff, was unable to attract sufficient votes, and instead Fahri Korutürk, a retired admiral, was elected. Korutürk appointed economist Naim Talu as prime minister until the elections of October 1973.

Under Ecevit's leadership the CHP received 33.5% of the vote and became the most successful party in the general elections of 1973. The AP received 29.5%. The CHP formed a coalition government with Erbakan's MSP, and Ecevit became prime minister. Hence the period of the March 12 memorandum was over in two-and-a-half years. During this period the army did not suspend the operations of Parliament. It even respected Parliament's decision as to who should be the next president, although it was not in line with the military's wishes.

Following a coup in Cyprus staged by the Greek junta, Turkey militarily intervened on the island on July 20, 1974 based on her rights and obligations as a guarantor power that stemmed from the 1960 London and Zurich agreements, saving the lives of the Turkish Cypriots. Following the intervention, the foundations of a democratic state were laid down in the Turkish north of the island. Soon after the intervention, on September 16, 1974, Ecevit resigned. After a brief period with a caretaker government led by Sadi Irmak, Demirel formed a coalition government with the participation of the AP, the MSP and a few other smaller parties. This government stayed in power until the elections of 1977.

The CHP led by Ecevit won 41.4% of the vote in the 1977 elections, becoming the largest party. The AP won 36.9%. Ecevit failed in his attempt to form a government with the participation of the independent members of Parliament. Demirel put together a new government with the MSP and the Milliyetçi Hareket Partisi (Nationalist Movement Party or MHP), which did not last long and was forced to step down when some of the members of parliament from the AP resigned.

In January 1978 Ecevit became prime minister once again and formed a government with the independents that was in power until October 1979. However, clashes between the right- and left wing extremists could not be prevented during this period. The partial elections that were held in 1979 to fill the vacant seats in the Senate were a disappointment for the CHP. Ecevit, who lost his majority in Parliament, resigned. Demirel became prime minister again, forming the government with the support of the independents. When Korutürk's term ended in 1980 the political parties failed to agree on a replacement, and despite 100 rounds of voting they were unable to elect a president.

In the meantime the extremist clashes took a turn for the worse. In 1977, 230 people were killed as a result of political violence. Two years later this number went up to 1,500. The Ecevit government had declared martial law in 13 regions. That did not prove to be sufficient, and the number of regions under martial law was increased to 20. The clashes between the extremist factions later turned into political assassinations. In May 1980 one of the former deputy leaders of the MHP, Gün Sazak, and in July former Prime Minister Nihat Erim were assassinated. In the same month Confederation of Revolutionary Workers' Unions leader Kemal Türkler was also murdered. In 1980 the number of those killed in anarchistic attacks had gone up to 2,206.

The Turkish Armed Forces intervened and took over the government on September 12, 1980. Just as in previous interventions, the goal of the army was not to establish a military dictatorship but rather to put democracy back on firm ground and hand it over to politicians once security and order in the country were achieved. The violence ended with the intervention of the army, and guns and ammunition worth around $500 million were confiscated from the extremist groups.[188] The sheer magnitude of the arms seized indicated the extent of the games being played on Turkey by other countries.

The political violence in Turkey could not be seen as the work of small terrorist groups within the country. It was no longer possible to conceal the fact that outside forces were involved in this game as well. Not everyone wished to see Turkey to develop in peace, democracy and stability. However, as Professor Emre Kongar points out, it was not possible to put the entire burden on the work of outside forces. Activities of some organizations were prohibited. Some of the old politicians were put under short-term arrest. Freedoms were restricted for a period that continued until the elections of November 6, 1983. In the meantime a constituent assembly met on October 23, 1981 and started to work on a new constitution. Once drafted, it was put to a referendum and received the support of 91.4% of the electorate. The Anavatan Partisi (Motherland Party or ANAP) led by Turgut Özal received 45% of the vote in the 1983 elections and became the sole ruling party. Among other parties that had participated in the elections the Halkçı Parti (People's Party) won 30%, and the Milliyetçi Demokrasi Partisi (Nationalist Democratic Party) received 23% of the vote. Once again, Turkey had returned to a multi-party democracy, which has continued uninterrupted since that time.

During this period democracy developed even further. Some of the old prohibitions were removed, and various political parties that had been closed down were allowed to participate in the local elections of 1984.

Prohibitions on some of the old politicians imposed during the "September 12 period" were eliminated with a public vote held on September 6, 1987. The Anavatan Partisi received 36.3% of the vote in the general elections of November 29, 1987 and maintained its majority in Parliament. The Social Democrat Party, which had merged with the Halkçı Parti and assumed the name of the Sosyal Demokrat Halkçı Parti (Social Democrat People's Party or SHP) received 24.8% of the vote.

---

[188] Kongar, op. cit., 200, 209.

The Doğru Yol Partisi (True Path Party or DYP) established by Süleyman Demirel, whose political restrictions imposed after the 1980 military intervention were lifted, won 19.5%. The Demokratik Sol Parti (Democratic Left Party or DSP) formed under Ecevit's leadership garnered 8.5% of the vote.

During this period parties like the Radikal Parti (Radical Party) and the Yeşiller Partisi (Green Party) were established. In the local elections of March 1989 the SHP received 28.2% of the vote and became the leading party. The DYP with 25.6% and ANAP with 21.9% followed. Turgut Özal was elected president to replace Kenan Evren, whose term expired in November 1989. Yıldırım Akbulut replaced Turgut Özal as prime minister. On June 17, 1991 Mesut Yılmaz became prime minister in place of Akbulut.

Subsequent governments continued the social and economic liberalization movement that had started during Özal's term as prime minister. New steps were taken in the human rights area. Articles 141, 142 and 163 of the penal code, which had been criticized for restricting freedom of thought, were abolished. There were also decisions taken regarding trade unions. Elections were again held on October 20, 1991. The DYP, led by Süleyman Demirel, came out on top with 27%. Yılmaz's ANAP received 24% and came in second. The SHP was third, with 20%. A DYP-SHP coalition was formed under Demirel's lead. Upon the death of Özal, Parliament appointed Demirel as the new president. Tansu Çiller, who was elected DYP leader to replace Demirel, became the first-ever female Turkish prime minister. She too continued with the same coalition.

In the elections of December 1995 the Refah Partisi (Welfare Party or RP) received 21.6% of the vote and came out ahead of all the others. ANAP and the DYP were next, each with around 20% of the vote. The DSP came in fourth. The CHP led by Deniz Baykal received a little over 10%, barely passing the threshold to enter Parliament. After the elections an ANAP-DYP coalition led by Yılmaz, then an RP-DYP coalition led by Erbakan and after that an ANAP-DSP-DTP (Demokrat Türkiye Partisi or Democratic Turkey Party) coalition again led by Yılmaz were formed. After a brief period of a transitional minority government led by Bülent Ecevit, general elections were held on 18 April 1999 in which the DSP received the greatest number of votes. The MHP led by Devlet Bahçeli came in second, followed by the Fazilet Partisi (FP), the ANAP and the DYP. The other parties were unable to pass the 10 % treshold and remained outside Parliament. A coalition comprising the DSP, the MHP and the ANAP was formed under the leadership of Bülent Ecevit.

During all these periods Turkey engaged in significant political and economic reform. The Constitution was revised. Except for 1995, the economy showed rapid growth every year. The effect and frequency of terrorist attacks that had been going on for 14 years diminished. The democratic system was kept alive despite fundamentalist moves and various other internal problems. Elections were conducted under the supervision of the judiciary and were held in a fair and just manner. Freedom of the press was improved. Independent Turkish journalists made it known that at least some of the internal and external criticism directed at Turkey on this issue was unjust or exaggerated. Despite numerous problems on a variety of issues Turkey managed to preserve her democracy, and the Turkish people adopted democracy as a way of life. Participation in elections has been higher than in most European countries. Since the elections of 1950, when 89.3% of all voters went to the polls, the turnout rate has been above 70% and in some elections more than 80%.

When studying the steps taken by Turkey to solidify her democracy as well as her experiences after World War II, the experiences of European countries during the same period should be looked at. What was happening there while all the aforementioned developments were taking place in Turkey?

Post-War Democracy in Western Nations

The U.S.A.: Effects of the Cold War on American Democracy

Upon the death of President Franklin Roosevelt in April 1945, Vice President Harry S. Truman took office. Truman believed in the social policies of Roosevelt; however he had a difficult time convincing Congress. When major strikes that shook the economy were staged after the war, Congress passed the Taft-Hartley Act in 1947, restricting the rights of labor unions to strike, despite Truman's veto. Truman won the election of 1948, and the Democrats won the majority of seats in Congress. The Korean War was fought during his term in office.

The Republican Dwight D. Eisenhower, who won the election of 1952, worked to give African-Americans rights equal to those of whites. In 1954 a struggle was waged against the racial discrimination that was still prevalent in the southern states. In that same year Supreme Court Chief Justice Earl Warren ruled that racial discrimination among blacks and whites was a violation of the US Constitution. The Supreme Court also ruled against the local practice of racially segregated schools and decided in favour of the integration of such schools. In 1957 the city of Little Rock, Arkansas, declared its rejection of this ruling, upon which Eisenhower sent in the National Guard to enforce the decision.

Legislation adopted in 1957 and 1960 gave the federal government authority to safeguard the voting rights of African-Americans. That is to say, 15 years after the end of

World War II and 180 years after the establishment of the United States and the adoption of the Bill of Rights, there were still regions in that country with problems in recognizing the equal rights of people of different races. Eisenhower was re-elected in 1956. In the 1960 election John F. Kennedy defeated Richard Nixon, who was Eisenhower's vice president. During the Eisenhower period the US economy had shown rapid growth; however, distribution of wealth continued to be a major problem. In 1959 the annual income of half of American families was less than $2,000, and in 1960 there were 4.5 million unemployed in the United States.

One of the most significant developments having a great impact on the domestic politics of the United States during the Truman-Eisenhower period was the anti-communist campaign led by Senator Joseph McCarthy. Accusations reached drastic proportions. There were claims that 57 Communist Party members were working in the US State Department, yet this and similar claims were never substantiated. But this campaign proved effective. A law passed in 1951 allowed for the dismissal of civil servants if there was reasonable doubt regarding their loyalty to the country. In 1953 McCarthy was appointed chairman of the Senate Igovernment Operations Committee as well as its subcommittee on investigations. During this period, the books of some American authors were found to be "destructive" and burned. In 1954 McCarthy started to malign army generals. The extremely anti-communist John Birch Society went so far as to accuse Eisenhower of being a supporter of the communists.

Kennedy's agenda contained numerous social projects, such as giving equal rights to Blacks, improved social benefits and more financial aid to students. However, some of these projects were either forestalled or delayed by Congress. This was also the period of the Cuban missile crisis as well as the Vietnam War. President Kennedy was assassinated in 1963. Lyndon B. Johnson replaced him and managed to finalize some of Kennedy's initiatives. In the meantime, the Civil Rights Act was also passed; however this new legislation did not satisfy those struggling to better the rights of African-Americans. In the mid-1960s there were black riots in many cities. There were also groups that resorted to violence, such as the Black Panthers. In 1968 Martin Luther King, a black clergyman and a peace activist, was murdered. Richard M. Nixon won the elections of 1968 and 1972. He pulled out of Vietnam; however, his interventions in Laos and Cambodia in the final stages of the war and in particular the bombing of North Vietnam that killed thousands of civilians were heavily criticized.[189]

The Watergate scandal that surfaced in 1973 forced Nixon to resign from office. The public had been particularly outraged at the cover-up that emerged after the Democratic Party's headquarters were broken into and some documents stolen. Upon Nixon's resignation Vice President Gerald Ford became president in August 1974, but he lost to Jimmy Carter in 1976. Carter's term in office was a time when human rights were put at the forefront of government policy. While opposing apartheid in South Africa, Carter also imposed sanctions on governments that violated human rights.

The Republican candidate, Ronald Reagan, won the election of November 1980. Reagan became known for his tough attitude against the Soviet Union and communist movements in Latin America. However, high-level meetings were held during his presidency between the United States and the Soviet Union, and agreements were signed to decrease the amount of nuclear arms maintained by the two countries. George Bush and then Bill Clinton followed Reagan as president. The Gulf War was one of the major challenges faced by the United States during the Bush administration. The disintegration of both the Soviet Union and the Warsaw Pact caused dramatic changes in East-West relations. President Clinton's term has been a period of developing relations with Russia and the former Soviet republics as well as the former

---

[189] Peacock, op. cit., pp. 268, 270, 272.

members of the Warsaw Pact. Human rights once again came to the fore and began to occupy an important place in the foreign relations of the United States.

France: Fifth Republic and Powerful President

The Vichy government led by Petain in wartime France came to a conclusion with the end of the German occupation. The Vichy period was one in which France, under outside influence, took a total departure from her traditional democratic line. When the Vichy regime collapsed, the French National Committee established in London under Charles de Gaulle's leadership was recognized as the legitimate government of France. The results of the elections of 1945 were very close among the communists, socialists and the Catholic left, the Popular Republican Movement. De Gaulle resigned in January 1946. The French Parliament prepared a new Constitution initiating the period of the Fourth Republic. With this Constitution, French women, for the first time in the history of France, were granted suffrage. By then, women in Turkey had possessed this right for 11 years.

Critical of the new Constitution and annoyed by the growing support for the communists, de Gaulle formed the Union for the New Republic Party. This group won 40% of the vote in the 1947 elections and put 120 members into the Parliament after the elections of 1951. During this period France still had problems with her colonies. Independence movements were growing stronger both in Indochina and in Africa, particularly in Algeria. The Indochina problem was resolved in 1954 with the Geneva Agreement. Tunisia won its independence in 1956. French soldiers in Morocco used force against the rebels, but Morocco also managed to win its independence.

The major problem was with Algeria. More than a million French nationals were living there at the time. A large number of French troops were sent to Algeria to protect both the lives

of these people as well as French sovereignty. The number of
these troops reached 500,000 in 1954.[190] The struggle of the
pro-independence movements in Algeria intensified after
1954. The Algerian Liberation Front (FLN) was fighting for
independence as well as for the abolition of privileges granted
to French nationals living in Algeria. The FLN had bases in
Tunisia and Morocco. From these bases they launched attacks
on French military targets, resulting in extremely bloody
battles. After four years of fighting the Algerians had lost
200,000 men and the French 13,000. Allegations regarding
methods used to question suspects caused a great uproar in
France, thus strengthening anti-war sentiments in the country.
There were difficulties controlling the units in Algeria from
France, and local commanders started to oppose the policies of
the French government. When Pflimlin, who supported a
peaceful settlement to the Algerian problem, was appointed
prime minister, two of the commanders in Algeria, General
Salan and General Massu, staged a coup. There were rumors
that the French units in Algeria would carry out a military
operation in France, where total chaos reigned.

On June 1, the French Parliament voted, 329 for and 224
against, to appoint de Gaulle president with full authority. De
Gaulle was also asked to draft a new constitution. The Fifth
Republic of France began with this new Constitution, which
was quite different from the previous one. Executive power
was considerably increased at the expense of the Parliament.
Article 16 states, "In the event that the institutions of the
Republic, the independence of the country, its territorial
integrity or capacity to fulfil its international obligations is
under serious and immediate threat and the constitutional
public administration's regular functions are disrupted, the
president will take the necessary precautions in consultation
with the prime minister and the heads of the Parliament and
the Constitutional Court." Article 36 of the same Constitution

---

[190] Ibid., p. 282.

gave the Council of Ministers the right to declare martial law. If the duration of martial law exceeded 12 days, then the government had to secure the approval of the Parliament.[191]

If this legislative body delayed its approval of the budget for more than 70 days, then the government had the right to collect taxes by decree. The government also had extensive powers to determine the agenda of the Parliament, and in times of internal strife the president could dismiss it. The new Constitution also changed the electoral system in France. Ministers, although responsible to Parliament, lost their parliamentary seats. It became more difficult to overthrow a government with a vote of no confidence. Hence, with the Constitution of 1958, France moved to a semi-presidential system. The authority of the president was expanded to levels unmatched in other European democracies.

In the mid-1990s France started to debate whether or not these articles were in line with democratic principles. New constitutional proposals were drafted that aimed to remove Article 16 and make various other modifications. These are still under discussion. However, the problems with internal security summarized above, in particular the war in Algeria, forced France, one of the oldest and strongest democracies in Europe, to undertake such restrictive measures. This draft was approved in a September 1958 referendum by 79 percent of the electorate.

The elections that followed were a great success for de Gaulle's Union for the New Republic Party, winning 188 seats. The socialists won 40 and the communists only 10 seats. De Gaulle's party formed the government together with the conservatives. On January 8, 1959 de Gaulle assumed his presidential functions and stayed in office for 11 years. During this period, upon initiatives to grant independence to Algeria, there were again uprisings in the French Army, and in 1961 General Salan revolted against the French government. But de

---

[191] Maurice Duverger, Constitutions et Documents Politiques, Paris, 1996, pp. 288, 297.

Gaulle preserved his government and his power. Some of the rebels were caught and imprisoned. Those who escaped formed the Secret Army Organization and engaged in terrorist attacks against the government. They even made a failed attempt on the life of de Gaulle.

Algeria won its independence in July 1962. Starting in 1958, de Gaulle changed France's policy regarding her colonies in Africa. He gave these countries a choice between immediate independence or remaining territories within the French community. Those who opted for the latter would benefit from financial aid from France, but France would control their foreign policy. With the exception of Guinea, all chose to remain with France. A few years later, however, they all opted to become fully independent.

At the time of the May 27, 1960 military intervention in Turkey France also was facing domestic problems of security and stability. It was the early years of the then Common Market, and France's policy was to direct the market together with Germany. De Gaulle vetoed Britain's application to join, claiming British membership would bring the influence of the United States to Europe. He later repeated his veto, this time saying the condition of the British economy was not favourable enough.

Trade unions reacted angrily against wage freezes in 1968. Keeping information services under the control of the government also sparked strongly adverse reactions. When coupled with various other social protests, these issues brought about large student demonstrations and violent clashes in Paris. The government resorted to the use of force to disperse these demonstrations. De Gaulle talked with commanders to call upon the armed forces if necessary. He once again won the elections held at that time and gained public support. Yet the economy had suffered from the upheaval. Representatives of international financial organizations met in Bonn and decided to extend financial aid to France. De Gaulle refused to devalue the franc. Instead, he resorted to some tough economic measures, which resulted in violent demonstrations. He resigned when his project on the reorganization of local governments was rejected and was replaced by Georges Pompidou. During the elections of 1972 the socialists and the communists formed a common front. During Pompidou's term France reversed her policy and accepted Britain's membership into the European Economic Community. Following Pompidou's death in 1974 Giscard d'Estaing won the elections by a slight margin, receiving 50.8% of the vote, against his rival François Mitterrand. Taking into consideration strong public demands, d'Estaing abolished controls on the press and cinema, and he put an end to the tapping of phones by security authorities.[192]

Hence, in France such contemporary, liberal, democratic requirements were put into effect only 20 years after the end of World War II. The economic problems and unemployment seen in other European countries between 1970 and 1980 were experienced in France as well but to a lesser degree. During this period the French economy exhibited rapid growth; however, things began to change in 1980. Annual inflation went up to 13.1%. The number of unemployed reached 1.5 million. The 1981 elections were held under these economic conditions, and this time it was the Socialist Party led by Mitterrand that won the elections, after whose death Jacques Chirac became president of France. During this period France made major headway in economic and democratic development. However, the rise of the extreme right has become a source of concern, leading politicians to find legal means to deal with threats of this type.

---

[192] Peacock, op. cit., pp. 282, 291.

British Decolonialism

The post war era was full of economic difficulties for Britain. The rationing system was maintained in place for a long time after the end of the war. People had to make great sacrifices to heal the wounds of war. The Labour Party won the first elections after the war, securing 393 seats in the Parliament, whereas the Conservative Party managed to win only 213 seats. This was a period when basic industrial concerns as well as banks were nationalized. The number of unemployed went up to 2 million in 1947. Bread was rationed. The Conservative Party led by Winston Churchill won the elections of 1951. Once again the government gave the private sector the lead in the economy. Anthony Eden replaced Churchill, who left politics in 1955. Conservatives won the elections of 1955 as well. The most important problem during Eden's term in office was the nationalization of the Suez Canal by Egypt's President Nasser. Britain's decision to militarily intervene together with France and Israel met with strong reaction both at home and abroad. Nasser's prestige in the developing world was enhanced, and independence movements all around the globe found additional strength. Eden resigned in January 1957. He was replaced by Harold Macmillan, whose term saw major economic problems and high inflation rates. The balance of payments went into deficit. De Gaulle's veto of the British application to join the EEC created a problematic situation. The Labour Party led by Harold Macmillan won the elections of 1964. During his term Britain started to pull out of some of her old colonies. British troops left Yemen in 1967. Britain decided to end the British presence in the Persian Gulf and parts of the Far East in 1968. Rhodesia declared independence in 1965 but was not recognized for a long time. After 1968, the violent incidents in Northern Ireland grew worse. There were claims that the local government was discriminating against the Catholics. The British Army was given the responsibility to end the fighting between Catholics and the Protestants. The IRA, which wanted to unite Northern Ireland with the Irish Republic, intensified its attacks in 1971. That was followed by the activities of Protestant extremists. Faced with these developments, the British government abolished the local assembly and assumed the functions of the local government. A state secretary was temporarily tasked with the administration of Northern Ireland.

In 1970 the Conservative Party led by Edward Heath won a clear victory in the general elections. The new government took measures to liberalize the economy, and on January 1, 1973 Britain joined the EEC. In 1974 it experienced major social unrest. The country was shaken by strikes staged by miners. None of the parties could win a clear majority in the elections of February 28, and Harold Wilson formed a minority government. The Labour Party won enough seats to form the government by itself in the elections held in October of the same year. Wilson resigned in March 1976 and was replaced by James Callaghan. In 1975, for the first time ever, a female politician, Margaret Thatcher, became leader of the Conservative Party. After becoming prime minister in 1979, Thatcher completely overhauled British economic policy, resulting in significant improvement in the economy during her term in office. However, violence continued in Northern Ireland. In 1980 and 1981 some imprisoned IRA militants died after staging hunger strikes. Yet despite all the pressure, the British government refused to accept these people as political prisoners. In 1981 major riots took place in London, Liverpool and Manchester. The harsh actions of the police during these riots, especially in mainly black areas, became a subject of investigation. The conduct of the police force in London's Brixton and Liverpool's Toxeth districts was heavily criticized.

The major problem faced during Thatcher's term as prime minister was the Falkland Islands crisis. Argentina landed troops and occupied these islands, which it had long claimed as its own. Britain took back the islands in a large-scale military operation. Hence, Britain made it clear that she did not intend to withdraw from all of her overseas territories. Thatcher remained in office for 10 years and was followed by John Major, who replaced her as leader of the Conservative Party. The Labour Party, led by Tony Blair, won the elections of 1997 by a large margin.

Germany: Establishment of Democracy and New Problems

Compared to the rest of Europe, the events in Germany after World War II took a different course. Following the Yalta and Potsdam agreements after the war, Germany and its former capital, Berlin, were under the control of the United States, Britain, France and the Soviet Union. East Germany became a Soviet satellite, while in West Germany a democratic, federal and liberal state was established. The integration of the two Germanys became possible only 45 years after the end of the war. Throughout that period the Germans had to live in two countries with different regimes, separated from each other by barbed wire fences and walls.

Germany came out of the war as a burned out, devastated country. Millions of Germans had lost their lives. There were 1.1 million prisoners of war in the Soviet Union, most of whom were unable to return home.[193] Industry was totally destroyed, and some German towns were completely wiped off the map. When the Americans entered Cologne, there were only 32,000 people left in the city which had formerly boasted a population of 750,000. It was their first chancellor after the war, Konrad Adenauer, who established the foundations of a modern and contemporary country upon the ruins of the war. He drafted Germany's post-war Constitution, taking all the legal precautions necessary to prevent a repetition of the bitter experiences of the past. Together with Ludwig Erhard, Adenauer won the elections of August 14, 1949. He repeated this success in later elections as well and remained chancellor for 14 years. In this period, also thanks to liberal policies designed by Erhard giving priority to the private sector as well as incentives for exports, the German economic miracle was created. During Adenauer's term the German GDP tripled. A strong organization of trade unions was formed with whom the government cooperated regarding political and economic issues. Politically motivated strikes became impossible. The right to strike in general was put under strict restrictions. German democracy was strengthened. Meanwhile a labor

---

[193] Johnson, op. cit., p. 585.

uprising in East Germany in 1953 was violently suppressed by the Red Army. Adenauer encouraged defections from East to West. In order to prevent this flow of people out of the country, Walter Ulbricht, the leader of East Germany, ordered the construction of a wall between East and West Berlin on August 13, 1961.

During this period Germany held on to the ideals of the European Union. The close friendship established after de Gaulle and Adenauer's first meeting on September 14, 1958 paved the way for strengthening the Common Market. The two leaders met 40 times until 1962, when Adenauer left politics. They made decisions concerning not only Germany and France but also the future of all of Europe. The conditions prevailing at that time did not allow for the reunification of Germany. The Federal Republic of Germany became oriented towards the West and followed a policy of close cooperation with Western European countries. Together with Adenauer, the Italian Prime Minister De Gasperi as well as French Prime Minister Robert Schumann promoted the idea of a united Europe with foresighted policies. In 1969 the Social Democrats took over the West German government from the Christian Democrats. Germany soon felt the effects of the 1968 student riots in Paris. There were demonstrations in most German cities, and street clashes occurred between the police and youths. The terrorist attacks during the 1972 Munich Olympics deeply affected both the German people and the public administration. The terrorist organization Beider-Meinhof continued its assaults until the mid-1990s. Germany formed a special anti-terrorist squad known as the GSG-9. After German unification extreme right-wing activists and neo-Nazis stepped up their activities. Anti-foreigner demonstrations became more frequent. Turkish nationals were burned to death in arson attacks in Mölln and Solingen. There were further similar incidents. The German authorities determined the average number of racist attacks to be around 1,000 a year. The government took some precautionary measures and closed down several of these organizations but could not manage to completely wipe them out.

Despite all these difficulties Germany managed to preserve its democratic system uninterrupted. Economic development continued. The German state system and the German Constitution were maintained. The private sector continued to take the lead in the economy. Germany continued to have coalition governments. In fact, Christian Democrats and their natural allies in Bavaria, the Christian Social Union, have had a long history of close cooperation. After a brief attempt at a coalition with the Christian Democrats, the Social Democrats entered into a long-term coalition with the Liberal Party led by Hans Dietrich Genscher. The Christian Democrats and the Liberals formed a coalition government in 1982 and were consistently successful in the general elections until 1998, when the Social Democrats won the elections and formed a coalition government with the Greens Party. Gerhard Schroeder became chancellor.

Troubles in Other Western Democracies

Some European countries managed to establish and develop democratic governments soon after the end of the war. Among these are the Scandinavian countries, Finland, Austria, Belgium and the Netherlands. However, some other European countries continued to have authoritarian governments until the mid-1970s, either continually or at different periods of time.

Antonio Oliveira Salazar, who became prime minister of Portugal in 1932, established an authoritarian regime that lasted until 1974. In Spain, Francisco Franco preserved his grip on the power he had established during the civil war until his death in 1975. Following these periods, Western European-style democratic systems gradually developed in both of these countries.

Greece has had military dictatorships since the end of World War I. Gen. Metaxas, who made his first attempt to seize power in 1923, achieved his goal in 1936. A civil war led by the communists in the north after World War II continued for 10 years. Between 1945 and 1949 160,000 Greeks lost their lives to the civil war. Approximately 20,000 people were arrested, and around 5,000 were either executed or imprisoned for life. A total of 700,000 Greeks became refugees. The civil war was brought to an end by Metaxas's former chief of staff, Gen. Papagos. Between 1946 and 1952 Greece had 16 governments. The elections of 1952 were won by the Nationalist Party led by Papagos, who stayed in power for 11 years. Upon his death Konstantin Karamanlis became leader of the party and won the elections of 1958 and 1961. Left-wing PASOK, led by George Papandreou, won the next elections, and Karamanlis left the country. The domestic struggles during Papandreou's term shook Greece's political stability. In 1967 Col. George Papadopoulos took power with a coup and remained in government until 1974. Following Turkey's Cyprus operation on July 20, 1974 the junta was forced to resign, and once again Karamanlis came to power. Later, the PASOK party, led by Andreas Papandreou, the son of George Papandreou, won the elections. During his term Greece became a full member of the EU. After a brief period of the conservative New Democracy Party government led by Mitsotakis, PASOK once again came to power. Kostas Simitis, who succeeded Papandreou as party leader after his death, became prime minister.

An Overview of European Democracies

The developments summarized above provide an outline of the developments experienced by some Western democracies after World War II. When taken as a whole, the following can be seen: After the war even some of the most advanced democratic nations had problems with their systems of government. Except for perhaps a few small European countries, democratic regimes all around Europe were jeopardized from time to time. Some of the current EU countries lived under military dictatorships years after the end of the war. It took 20 years for democracy as we know it today to establish itself in Western Europe following World War II. During this period the larger countries of Europe started the decolonization process, which did not prove to be an easy task.

Hundreds of thousands of people lost their lives during wars or armed clashes waged in overseas places. Even today as the new millennium approaches, some Western countries continue to possess overseas territories. It took them many years to apply the democratic principles adopted at home in their colonies. As can be seen, even countries considered to have well-advanced democracies do not see their systems as perfect and continue to reform their laws regulating democracy and elections.

The state structures of the Western European countries are different from each other. Today, almost half the EU members are constitutional monarchies, and the other half are republics. There are differences among constitutions as well. Countries such as Germany and Austria have federal systems, whereas countries like France and Greece are unitary states. France has a semi-presidential system, whereas the rest have constitutional systems that give more weight to the parliament.

Some constitutions give extraordinary powers to the president if the security of the country is at risk. Up until the early 1980s some European countries had restrictions or controls imposed on the press. Secularism does not mean the same thing in each and every one of these countries. Among EU members there are those who still accept Christianity as the official religion of the state. The constitutions of some do not contain the concept of minorities. For example, the French Constitution does not even refer to minorities.

When the democratic evolution of Turkey is analyzed, these factors should all be taken into consideration. Since the early 1920s Turkey has had a system of government whereby sovereignty unconditionally belongs to the people. Her Parliament was operational during the War of Liberation, which lasted until 1922. In 1923 the structure of the state was accepted as being a republic, and no changes have been made to this structure since then. The value of this is better appreciated considering the short lifespans of some of the first republics in Europe.

The Turkish Parliament operated continuously for 40 years between 1920 and 1960. The purpose of the interruption in 1960 was not to disrupt the democratic regime and establish a military dictatorship; to the contrary its goal was to overcome the bottlenecks experienced by the democracy and establish a more democratic and contemporary structure. It would certainly have been better if this could have been done without a military intervention, but this did not prove to be possible under the conditions prevailing at the time. It is true that regrettable events took place during that period, but it is not true that the government was taken over by those who had ambitions of establishing a dictatorship. This is evidenced by the fact that free democratic elections were held only a year later in 1961. The intervention of 1971 did not close down the Parliament; rather, a transitory government was formed by the members of parliament and with its support. If problems could have been solved within the normal framework of democracy, of course, that would have been preferable. It was not possible, however, to do so.

An analysis of the causes of the 1960 and later interventions is not the subject of this study. The point here is that even when Turkish democracy was interrupted, there were no ambitions for dictatorships such as those that were found in Europe during those periods. The reason behind this is the close attachment of the Turkish Armed Forces to the principles of Atatürk and the awareness that his most valuable creation was the democratic system of government based on the will of the people. Foreigners who criticize Turkish democracy from time to time should bear this fact in mind. Military dictatorships in European countries such as Spain, Portugal and Greece, however, continued for many years after World War II.

Turkey returned to democracy after the elections held in 1973. The goal of the 1980 intervention was again not to establish a dictatorship. Terrorism had paralyzed the government. Parliament was unable to elect a president, even after 100 rounds of voting. In a sense, the regime was blocked. The problems of that period are well known. Soon after the intervention a constituent assembly was formed.

A new Constitution aimed at preventing a reoccurrence of similar conditions was drafted, and after a brief period democracy was put back on track and became operational. The Constitution was amended in 1995 to improve its democratic character. Old restrictions were removed. Political parties could now operate freely. No official body other than the Constitutional Court had the right close down political parties. All general and local elections were subject to the control of the judiciary. Freedom of the press was achieved. Private radio stations and television channels were allowed. There was no censorship. The broadcasts were not inspected prior to being aired, although their compliance with general public moral values is inspected after the broadcast by an independent agency and by the government. Trade and labor unions have complete freedom over their activities; however, discussions are still under way on how to grant government employees' unions the right to strike. Yet, there are discussions in Turkey about the shortcomings of the 1982 Constitution and the necessity to design a new one. Both the Constitution and legislation protect the territorial integrity of Turkey. What is prohibited is acting against the unity and territorial integrity of the country, that is to say, against its very existence. No independent observer could fail to understand the fact that in general the amount and tone of criticism leveled on various subjects against the government by the media in Turkey is much higher than the number and intensity of criticism in the media of other European countries against their own governments.

According to the Turkish Constitution, international agreements signed by Turkey have the power of legislation and are directly binding on the courts. Some European countries do not have such a law. Since 1949 Turkey has been a member of the Council of Europe, which only accepts democratic countries as members. By signing and approving the European Convention on Human Rights at its inception, she showed herself to be one of the most democratic countries in Europe and the world. In those days no one could even imagine that some of the countries which are now EU members would ever gain membership in the Council of Europe.

By the time Central and Eastern European countries were taking their first steps towards democracy, Turkey's democracy had been well established and institutionalized. Moreover, as Bernard Lewis rightly points out: "Turkey had never been colonized, Turks have always been sovereign in their lands. Democracy in Turkey was not established by foreign powers, as was the case for some European countries after World War II. It was not established by a country that ruled and then pulled out after a certain period, as was the case with the former French and British colonies. It became established with the free will of the Turkish people. This fact gives the democratic institutions in Turkey a far better chance to survive."[194]

Today, there are those who claim that Turkish democracy is behind those in all of Eastern Europe. Is this a fair assessment to make considering the facts presented above? There can be no reasonable explanation for the decision to leave Turkey out of the EU accession process by citing lack of democracy as an excuse, while this country started to reform itself 200 years ago, had its first Constitution and elections 112 years ago, has been ruled by a parliamentary system for 78 years, has been a republic for 75 years and has had a multi-party democracy for 52 years. As the examples summarized above show, there has been no country that has managed to develop democracy without any interruptions or problems.

Samuel Huntington claims that there are periods when democracy around the world develops in waves, then counter-waves push it back, and another wave pushes it forward again. The first wave of democracy took place between 1828 and 1926, followed by a counter-wave between 1922 and 1942. The second wave of democracy came in 1943 and lasted until 1962, and its counter-wave was between 1958 and 1975. Finally, the third wave of democracy arrived in 1974. According to Huntington, there were 29 democracies in 1922; in 1942 this number went down to 12. In 1962 it rose to 36 but declined to 30 in 1973. In 1990 it was back up to 58. Yet he says not even half of the countries around the world have democratic systems.

Huntington also establishes a link between democratic and economic development. Laureano Lopez Rodo, who was the minister of planning in Spain during the Franco regime, said that Spain would switch to democracy when her GDP per capita exceeded $2,000. Yet Spain switched to democracy soon after the death of Franco, before a major economic development had taken place. In 1974, only 18 of all the

---

[194] Lewis, Why Turkey is the Only Muslim Democracy, op. cit., p. 45.

democratic countries around the world had a per capita GDP of more than $3,000. There were four democratic nations whose per capita income was less than $1,000.

When Turkey switched to a multi-party democracy in 1946, her per capita income was much less than $1,000. Huntington explains democratic development in conjunction with a religious dimension. He claims a strong relationship between Christianity and democracy, stating that in 1988, 46 of the 39 democratic countries were dominated by the Catholic and Protestant faiths. Only seven countries with other religions were considered to be democratic. He further adds that among these seven, there are some like South Korea, where Christianity is on the rise. It seems that by 1980, 25% of the South Korean population were Christians, whereas this proportion was less than 1% at the end of World War I. Apparently, the Christian clergy led the struggle against military regimes and helped develop democracy.[195]

If this theory is correct, shouldn't the democratic achievements of Turkey, 99% of whose population is Muslim, carry a special significance and be encouraged? Yet as indicated above the practice is just the reverse. As stated previously while evaluating the applications of Greece, Spain and Portugal, the EU Commission saw EU membership as a significant element that would strengthen democracy in these countries. It warned of the danger that anti-European trends could become more powerful in those countries unless they were accepted into the EU. However, there is no reference to that effect in the opinion of the commission on the Turkish application. If this is because of the adequate strength of Turkish democracy and not a result of double standard, then why has Turkey been prevented from joining the accession process, showing a lack of democracy as a justification?

---

[195] Samuel Huntington, 3. Dalga, translated by Ergun Özbudun, Ankara, 1993, pp. 60-67, 71.

Huntington too touches upon the relationship between EU membership and democratic development. He says: "For Greece, Portugal and Spain democratization and EU membership went hand in hand. Membership into the Union will strengthen democratic ties." As the EU cannot be expected to discriminate against nations due to their religion or culture, then how can the fact be explained that a similar view was not presented for Turkey?

Most of the criticism leveled against Turkey on lack of democracy is related to problems of implementation rather than the structure of the democracy itself. These criticisms are concentrated on the human rights issue. Therefore, a closer look at human rights must be taken. How did it develop in Turkey and in Western Europe, and what is the current situation?

Human Rights

One of the most frequently discussed issues around the world today is human rights. In fact, it is not possible to separate democracy and human rights from each other altogether. Countries that are truly democratic are those that respect human rights at the same time. If democratic institutions in a country are working as they should, then it must be assumed that human rights are also protected, since democratic countries around the world are also signatories to human rights conventions and have adopted their legislation in accordance with their obligations. One of the main principles of democracy is the division of power. Therefore, courts should be able to pass sentences, independent of the government, on those who violate human rights.

This subject should be considered independently of the sensitivity shown by governments for human rights issues. If those governments that make it their policy to violate human rights have also taken control of the independent judiciary, then those countries cannot be considered democratic. That is to say, the human rights issue is closely linked with the independence of the judiciary. The laws of the country, of course, are binding on the judiciary. There might be discrepancies in the legislation of countries regarding the limits on freedoms; however, the common denominator among all of them are texts that safeguard basic freedoms, such as the European Convention on Human Rights, which Turkey has been a party to since 1954.

Therefore, in a country like Turkey that made its international obligations part of its own legislation, claims of lack of democracy can not be based on "lack of regulations," since international agreements on human rights have already become a part of the laws of the country. This does not imply that national legislation on human rights should not be improved. On the contrary, every country including Turkey should constantly review its laws so as to further human rights. Yet if international agreements signed are binding on the judiciary of a country with independent courts, then one must be very careful when talking about lack of democracy or gaps in legislation regarding human rights in that country. Moreover, although there might be differences between pieces of legislation, no democratic country can have a legal code that exempts those who violate human rights from punishment.

Human Rights and Turkish Constitutions

One of the oldest and most basic texts on human rights is the French Declaration on Human and Citizen Rights, dated August 26, 1789. This text, which would later become the introductory section of the French Revolution's Constitution in 1791, lists the inalienable rights that humans have from birth. The first article of the declaration says people are born free and are equal before the law. This principle is mentioned in Article 68 of the 1924 Turkish Constitution. Article 68 is a total reflection of articles 1 and 4 of the Constitution of the French Revolution. Articles 68 and 83 of the 1924 Turkish Constitution comprise rules, most of which are taken from French constitutions, that safeguard human rights. For example, Article 70 says: "Individual freedoms, freedoms of conscience, thought, speech, press, travel, assembly are natural rights of Turks." Article 72 asserts that "Except in those instances that are specified by law, no one can be put in police custody or arrested." Article 73 is as follows: "Torture, cruelty, seizure and forced labor are prohibited." Article 75 summarizes freedom of thought and religion as follows: "No one can be held accountable for his thoughts, religion or sect."

As these examples clearly indicate, Turkey had put articles addressing human rights that can be considered advanced even according to today's standards, in her Constitution as far back as 75 years ago and since then developed the structure of the state in accordance with those articles.

The Constitution of 1961 follows the same philosophy and takes it even further. Article 10 of this Constitution talks about every individual's inalienable rights and freedoms that cannot be separated, touched, transferred or relinquished. Article 14 of the Constitution reads: "No one can be subjected to cruelty or torture." The same article says that no punishment can be given that violates human dignity. In 1971 an amendment was made to the Constitution regarding the boundaries of basic rights and freedom. It says that basic rights and freedoms can only be restricted for protection of the integrity of the country with its people and territory, the republic, national security, public order, public benefit, public morality and general health in line with the word and spirit of the Constitution and only by law. While imposing such restrictions, it stresses that laws cannot infringe upon the essence of basic rights.

Constitutions of other countries have similar articles, and even the European Convention on Human Rights says that under such conditions some restrictions can be imposed provided that basic rights and freedoms are not violated. In the above sections examples were given of the kinds of restrictions imposed by Western European countries on democratic rights and freedoms, even after World War II, when their national security was threatened. Some countries go even further and preserve articles in their constitutions that are still debated with respect to their compliance with the basic principles of a democratic state that accepts the supremacy of law. It seems that those who had drafted these constitutions gave equal weight to the protection of rights of the individual and preservation of the security of their country.

The Turkish Constitution does not have an article similar to that of Article 16 of the 1958 French Constitution that gives extraordinary powers to the president in the event national security is at risk. Moreover, as mentioned above, Article 15 of the European Convention on Human Rights clearly indicates that rights and freedoms can be restricted when national security is threatened.

Just as in the constitutions of other countries, the Turkish Constitution also underwent some changes through time. The current 1982 Constitution contains the same basic rights and freedoms. Article 12 of the 1982 Constitution deals with general rules regarding human rights. Even Article 15, which mentions the restriction on basic rights and freedoms that may be imposed during times of war or mobilization, says that such restrictions may be imposed "provided that they do not violate international obligations." Considering that Turkey has signed numerous agreements on human rights other than the European Convention on Human Rights, we see that the Constitution specifies that those obligations will be respected even under conditions of war. Article 25 concerning freedom of thought says: "Everyone is free to have their own thoughts and opinions. No one can be forced to express his thoughts and opinions under any circumstances, or blamed or accused due to their thoughts and opinions."

Some articles of the 1982 Constitution were amended by the Turkish Parliament in 1995 to make them more liberal. Apart from the introductory section, improvements were made in Article 33 on the freedom of founding associations, Article 52 on the activities of trade unions, Article 53 on collective bargaining, Article 67 on the right to elect or be elected, Article 68 on establishing and becoming a member of a political party and Article 69 on rules regarding the conduct of political parties. Changes were recently made in the penal code, and work is under way on new legislative proposals.

The predominant view prevailing when the first Constitution of the Republic was accepted in 1924, namely that Turkey should accept the most advanced norms of Western Europe regarding human rights, is still shared by the vast majority of Turkish society. There is consensus among political parties that the citizens of Turkey should enjoy the most extensive rights and freedoms possible. However, this does not include such things as the freedom to resort to violence or to destroy the territorial integrity of the nation. The constitutions and laws of Western European countries do not have such freedoms either. There is no country in the world that sees the destruction of democracy or the use of violence as freedoms. Still, there are some differences between the laws of Turkey and some Western European countries. In those countries, for an act to be considered an assault on the integrity of the nation it must involve an element of violence. Yet none of these differences are significant enough to change the fact that Turkey is a democratic country based on laws and respect for human rights.

No one can claim that the laws of Western European countries are mirror images of one another; indeed, they are significantly different from one another. For example, some European countries grant the right to vote to foreigners living there, whereas others don't extend that privilege. Some of them accept dual citizenship, while others refuse to do so. There are striking discrepancies, especially on the protection of the rights of foreigners. Yet no one claims that one European country is more democratic than another merely by looking at such differences. This is because the basic rules of democracy are well known. Every democratic country including Turkey abides by these rules.

Legal Supervision of Human Rights

Most of the accusations and criticism related to human rights stems from problems with the implementation of rules and regulations rather than the lack of legislation or constitutional rights. These criticisms come not only from human rights organizations but also from Turkish statesmen and the Turkish press. Therefore, it would be wrong to dismiss claims against Turkey without due diligence. Human rights organizations claim that civil servants in many countries violate laws and regulations and subject prisoners to ill treatment. They organize campaigns and work to prove their accusations, which become more acute against countries grappling with terrorist activities.

The existence and work of nongovernmental organizations (NGOs) have become indispensable to contemporary democracies. Therefore, it would be unfair to criticize these organizations for making such allegations. Criticism from the media and NGOs is helpful and even necessary to have healthier democracies that can develop themselves and help correct mistakes in social order. But on one condition: These allegations cannot be deemed as realities unless confirmed by independent courts. No public official can be considered guilty unless condemned by independent courts. This is one of the basic rules of international law. Article 9 of the 1791 Constitution of the French Revolution deals with this issue. Article 11 of the Universal Declaration of Human Rights adopted by the United Nations in 1958 says that anyone accused of a crime is presumed innocent until proven guilty by an official court.

Therefore, accusations of human rights violations against governments or individuals cannot constitute evidence in and of themselves or be reason enough to deem that countries or individuals are guilty of such crimes. Today, the judicial organs of international organizations such as the Council of Europe, which accepts as members only countries with well-established democracies, have the right to investigate allegations of human rights violations against governments and render verdicts based on their investigations.

Individuals as well as governments have the right to apply to these organs. Countries such as Turkey that accept the decisions of these courts cannot argue that human rights violations are their domestic affairs. In this respect, too, allegations of human rights violations do not constitute reason enough to accuse governments of being guilty of such crimes. The European Commission of Human Rights or the European Court of Human Rights, which have since been joined together, must find that country guilty of human rights violations.

Since 1987, Turkey has been among those countries that grant its citizens the individual right to apply to the European Commission of Human Rights. It also accepts the obligatory jurisdiction of European Court of Human Rights regarding these applications. However, accepting its obligatory jurisdiction does not mean that the decisions of the court are always seen as correct and just. There are well-known cases in which the court's decision has been strongly criticized by individual nations. Having said this, is it really possible for countries to accept such international inspection mechanisms if they commit human rights violations as a matter of government policy? Turkey has also signed various other international agreements in the human rights field that also involve mechanisms of inspection. One of these is the Convention on the Prevention of Torture.

Up until the present time there have been applications to the European Commission of Human Rights filed against almost all members of the Council of Europe regarding alleged violations of the European Convention on Human Rights. Yet there are rules that claimants must abide by. For example, internal judicial mechanisms must first be exhausted before making any applications. The applications of those who do not fulfil these requirements are rejected. There may be exceptions to this rule, but when it grants these exceptions, the council comes under heavy criticism. If the commission thinks that the right of application is being abused, then it again rejects the application.

According to Article 28 of the convention, once it accepts an application alleging violation of certain rights, the commission seeks the opinion of the relevant country and if necessary undertakes an investigation. It then tries to reach an amicable settlement between the individual making the accusation and the country involved. If that proves impossible, the commission looks at whether or not that country has fulfilled its obligations under the European Convention on Human Rights. Later, the commission's view is presented to the Committee of Ministers of the Council of Europe. The commission may also put forward its view regarding violations of the terms of the convention directly to the European Court of Human Rights, where a two-thirds majority is required. That is to say, there are numerous rules and regulations that one must abide by before giving a verdict on human rights violations.

These rules were put in place while the convention was being drawn up in order to prevent anyone from making groundless allegations or accusations against the signatory countries. Yet now we see that some NGOs and government officials have accused even those governments that have accepted the jurisdiction of international human rights courts of violations of these rights in various incidents, as if no such rules were in place or as if certain procedures did not exist. There is no international agreement that gives a country or an organization the right to decide unilaterally whether or not human rights violations exist in other countries. According to international law no one can be both claimant and judge at the same time.

If these rules are not adhered to, if decisions are going to be made without even hearing the other party or conducting a judicial investigation, what use is there for commissions or conventions on human rights? International rules of conduct between states require everyone to wait for the court verdict, at the very least; otherwise, the claimants become both the prosecutor and the judge. Therefore, such allegations not only fail to conform to the code of conduct in international relations but also offend the dignity of nations.

In particular, if allegations of human rights violations are used as a vehicle to achieve various political goals, to humiliate a country in front of the international community or to obstruct some rights or expectations of a country, then this jeopardizes international relations as well as the substance of human rights. The same goes for human rights organizations. Unless national or international courts confirm their allegations, they cannot portray anyone, let alone any country, as being guilty of human rights violations. At the very best, these allegations can be considered claims well worth investigating. The increased influence of these organizations in recent years on world public opinion as well on the media does not change this fact. This is all the more so, considering that their power stems from their credibility. If the claims of these organizations are discovered to be unfounded or designed to attain some political ends, then their credibility and trustworthiness gradually become eroded. Therefore, the measure in such issues is the decisions of international human rights courts.

What does the record show regarding decisions of the European Court of Human Rights on valid applications regarding claims of human rights violations in various countries? The following table gives the answer.

European Court of Human Rights Decisions on Various Countries (1960-1997)

Country	Applications	Decisions on Violations	Friendly Satlement
Austria	87	44	-
Italy	260	98	1
U.K.	96	50	-
France	103	45	1
Hollanda	50	27	-
Belgium	40	24	1
Greece	33	22	3
Sweden	40	21	-
Swit•erland	39	19	-
Germany	33	15	-
Turkey	31	11	3

Source: Document d'Information du Greffier de la Cour Europeenne des Droits de l'Homme

An analysis of this table gives the following results: Until the end of 1997 Turkey was found guilty of not complying with her obligations under the European Convention on Human Rights 11 times. But similar judgements were passed against other countries as well. For example, Austria was found guilty 44 times. This number is 24 for Belgium, 40 for France, 22 for Greece, 27 for Holland, 21 for Sweden, 50 for the United Kingdom and 98 for Italy.

In total, signatory countries were found guilty 412 times. Only 11 of these involve Turkey. Both states and the European Commission of Human Rights have the right to apply to the European Court of Human Rights. The numbers above refer to such applications. Applications are also made to the European Human Rights Commission. Individuals have the right to apply to this organization as well. In recent years various international organizations have been working in a systematic manner to bring the complaints of Turkish citizens to the commission. For this reason there has been an increase in the number of applications by Turkish citizens. As an example, a comparative look will be taken at decisions passed in 1997 on appeals made in that year or earlier. According to a press statement issued by the secretary of the European Commission of Human Rights, the commission studied 3,619 applications from various countries in 1997, 490 of which were found worthy of investigation. Reports were prepared for 468 of these and sent to either the European Council of Ministers or the European Court of Human Rights for a decision. Forty-five applications were settled amicably; 3,073 were rejected; and 4,750 new applications were made within that year. The following table shows the work of the commission on various countries for 1997.

Action Taken by the European Human Rights Commission on Various Countries (1997)

Country	Registered Applications	Applications Worth Investigating	Registered Applications	Applications Submited to Government	Friendly Settlement	Decisions on Substance
Austria	238	28	126	27	3	24
Belgium	58	4	53	12	-	6
Bulgaria	42	3	25	6	1	2
Denmark	34	-	36	3	1	-
France	558	102	573	150	12	71
Germany	383	7	304	7	-	2
Greece	56	2	50	13	-	7
Italy	833	351	281	507	2	276
Holland	155	12	144	12	1	6
Poland	430	11	201	37	1	4
Slovakia	81	4	38	2	1	3
Spain	153	3	144	9	-	6
Sweden	146	4	161	17	-	2
Switzerland	155	8	162	13	-	6
Turkey	365	29	34	344	1	20
UK	451	83	411	113	8	16

Source: Press release from the Secretary of the European Commission of Human Rights

This table contains actions on applications carried over from previous years as well. It is also possible for some of the 1997 applications to be processed in later years. As can be seen the number of applications against some countries is higher than against others. Turkey is one of these. The number of applications found worthy of investigation differs from one country to the next. This is because in some countries exhausting all internal mechanisms is very difficult and time-consuming. In general there are more cases against larger countries. However, the number of cases against some Eastern European countries, which only recently became members of the Council of Europe, is not small either. The large number of applications against Turkey is an indication of the human rights problem in Turkey. However, there are only 20 rulings against Turkey. It must also be remembered that terrorist activities against Turkey cannot even be compared with those in other countries and that most of the applications against Turkey concern allegations of misconduct by the security forces against detainees found guilty of terrorist activities.

Having said this, there can be no excuse for human rights violations in any country. Such is the importance of the European Commission of Human Rights and the European Court of Human Rights. Turkey showed how serious she was about protecting human rights by accepting the jurisdiction of the commission and the court; she also took a step further by granting her citizens the right of individual application.

Human Rights Associations' Allegations

As indicated above, most of the criticism reflected in the world media on human rights violations in Turkey is not based on the decisions of international courts but on the allegations of some NGOs. These organizations started to come into being in the early 1960s. In those years criticism against Turkey was almost next to none. Their reports for 1964-1965 do refer to Turkey, but only in a few sentences. Interest grew after 1966, when communist propaganda was prohibited in Turkey. During that period the military junta in Greece, the Soviet Union and Eastern European countries were the focus of their attention. From 1969-1970 the sentencing of an author in Turkey attracted a great deal of attention. By the mid-1970s Turkey's name began to be mentioned more frequently. Allegations of mistreatment of prisoners came onto the agenda as well as the prohibitions on communist propaganda based on articles 141-142 of the Turkish Penal Code. Following the intervention in Cyprus in 1974, Turkey became the focus of attention for the European media as well as for human rights organizations. In order to obtain their support, circles unfriendly to Turkey systematically fed allegations to these organizations.

Accusations intensified after the military intervention in 1980. There were numerous allegations of mistreatment of prisoners. While human rights reports used to have only about one paragraph on Turkey, after 1980 entire sections began to be devoted to various allegations. Though categorically denying the allegations, Turkey opened investigations into each and every one of them. Politicians who accused Turkey for the benefit of their public based their accusations on the allegations of these human rights organizations. Which brings us to a question: If the allegations of these organizations are so credible, are they considered to be as important and valid when made against other countries? These human rights organizations publish reports not only on Turkey but also on various countries around the world on serious human rights violations. Claims against Turkey mainly concern mistreatment or even torture of prisoners convicted of terrorist activities, but there are serious claims against other countries as well. The fact that there are allegations against other countries does not, of course, minimize the importance of allegations against Turkey. This does prove, however, that a holistic view should be taken regarding the claims of these organizations.

In order not to repeat the mistakes of others, Western countries accused by international organisations or NGOs of violation of human rights will not be named here. Those who want to learn can look them up in the publications of Amnesty International or the Helsinki Human Rights Federation or visit their Web sites. What they will see is this: There are serious allegations of human rights violations in countries accepted as candidates for EU membership. Allegations against current EU members are even more serious. Reports on EU countries, which frequently criticize Turkey, give concrete examples on mistreatment of prisoners, torture that resulted in death and police brutality. They also stress that the majority of these crimes are racially motivated against minorities or foreigners in those countries. They give examples of months-long imprisonment without trial of those seeking asylum. There are serious accusations against countries that have filed lawsuits against other countries on claims of human rights violations. There are allegations that they forcefully uprooted the local people living in their territory, with the excuse of establishing military bases, and did not pay compensation for decades.

The same reports also contain allegations that most security force members accused of cruelty to prisoners never get tried, with the trials of those who do lasting for many years. Most are released without being charged due to lack of evidence; otherwise they receive minimal sentences.

What has been the authorities' reaction in those countries? One official said that these allegations were "totally unfounded, and that this human rights organization had cast a shadow over its credibility in its allegations against other countries." A minister claimed that the human rights organization making the allegations had collected its information with a "one-sided approach." That is to say, the organizations whose reports are used as grounds for accusing Turkey are deemed as biased and not credible when they accuse other countries of similar allegations.

The Turkish media and public are becoming increasingly convinced that those who wish to keep Turkey away from Europe or the EU are using the human rights issue as an excuse to achieve their goal. Although this may be an unfounded suspicion, it is becoming a widely held view in the face of Turkey being targeted with allegations that are not based on any proof or court decisions.

Apart from human rights organizations, we must give serious consideration to the work of the U.N. Human Rights Commission. This commission analyzes the human rights issue in its entirety. In a report prepared by Maurice Glele d'Ahanhanzo, the special rapporteur appointed by the commission, for the 1995-1996 period and published as a U.N. document, practices in various Western countries are studied in detail. The report contains worrisome observations and criticism regarding these countries.

Naturally, the existence of human rights violations, police brutality and even torture in other countries cannot justify the existence of similar crimes in Turkey. A bad example cannot be used as an example at all. Yet for countries that are faced with similar accusations to come forward and act as if they were without fault, that they can set an example to the rest of the world and even have the right to check and verify countries on human rights is surprising, to say the least.

In reality, we see that acts of policy brutality that sometimes result in death do take place, even in countries that are considered to be centers of democracy and leaders in human rights. All countries must work and cooperate with each other to prevent such incidents and to secure the human rights of their citizens, not only in theory but also in practice. The way to achieve this is not by publicly accusing each other of incidents that are not based on concrete evidence or the decisions of international courts. As a prominent Western European statesman said in his reply to a fellow member of parliament who hurled baseless accusations at Turkey in his parliament: "Today everybody around the world lives in glass houses; those who wish to break the windows of others may end up breaking their own."

What is important is to take an independent view on the human rights issue and be able to see one's own faults, not make excuses for the acts of some public officials who violate human rights; to incriminate those who commit such crimes; and to work at eliminating problems in this field. Turkey is working towards these goals. She is adopting new legislation, training her security forces and cooperating with other countries regarding this issue. The cooperation between Turkey and Sweden is a good example of efforts in this direction.

Regarding human rights, the most serious mistake that can be made at an international level is to use this issue for other political intentions and purposes. Such approaches jeopardize human rights as well as international relations. They also diminish the effectiveness and credibility of organizations that work very hard and very sincerely to improve human rights around the world. Making false allegations against a country may backfire on the party making the allegations. Therefore, those who do make such allegations against countries like Turkey, which has accepted the jurisdiction of international courts on this matter, should take more care in basing their claims and analysis on the decisions of such courts.

As the above examples clearly indicate, allegations of human rights violations have lately concentrated on the mistreatment of prisoners. This is certainly an important matter, and every nation that has accepted the U.N. Universal Declaration of Human Rights is obliged to protect prisoners in its country from inhumane and degrading treatment. Article 5 of the declaration addresses this matter. Yet there is much more to the human rights issues than this. The declaration consists of 30 articles, each referring to obligations that must be diligently complied with. It would be a mistake to confine the human rights issue just to the treatment of prisoners. For example Article 2 of the declaration says: "Everyone is entitled to all the rights and freedoms set forth in this Declaration, without distinction of any kind, such as race, color, sex, language, religion, political or other opinion, national or social origin, property, birth or other status. Furthermore, no distinction shall be made on the basis of the political, jurisdictional or international status of the country or territory to which a person belongs, whether it be independent, trust, non-self-governing or under any other limitation of sovereignty." Do all countries, and in particular members of the EU, comply with this article?

Article 19 of the law on Greek nationality adopted in 1955 reads as follows:

"If a person of non-Greek ethnic origin departs from Greece with the intention of not returning, then a decision may be taken to annul their citizenship." This article refers only citizens who are not ethnically Greek. Does this fall in line with the second article of the Declaration of Human Rights or with the first article of the European Convention on Human Rights? This article of the Greek Nationality Law was removed in mid-1998. Yet up until that time many people who were not ethnically Greek lost their nationality because of this law.

Articles 9 and 10 of the Universal Declaration of Human Rights are as follows:

"Article 9

No one shall be subjected to arbitrary arrest, detention or exile."

"Article 10.

Everyone is entitled in full equality to a fair and public hearing by an independent and impartial tribunal, in the determination of his rights and obligations and of any criminal charge against him."

Does the months-long detention of asylum seekers in the prisons of some EU countries, without being charged with any crime, comply with these articles?

"Article 11

(1)Everyone charged with a penal offense has the right to be presumed innocent until proven guilty according to law in a public trial at which he has had all the guarantees necessary for his defence.

(2)No one shall be held guilty of any penal offence on account of any act or omission, which did not constitute a penal offense, under national or international law, at the time when it was committed. Nor shall a heavier penalty be imposed than the one that was applicable at the time the penal offense was committed."

As mentioned above this is one of the oldest principles of law. Isn't portraying government officials as criminals prior to a fair trial and sentencing a violation of this article?

"Article 16

(1)Men and women of full age, without any limitation due to race, nationality or religion, have the right to marry and to establish a family. They are entitled to equal rights as to marriage, during marriage and at its dissolution.

(2) Marriage shall be entered into only with the free and full consent of the intending spouses.

(3) The family is the natural and fundamental group unit of society and is entitled to protection by society and the State."

Do immigration laws that prohibit workers from bringing, sometimes for years, their wives or husbands from their country of birth, comply with this article?

"Article 18

Everyone has the right to freedom of thought, conscience and religion; this right includes freedom to change his religion or belief, and freedom, either alone or in community with others and in public or private, to manifest his religion or belief in teaching, practice, worship and observance."

When an EU member country obstructs the work of the mufti elected by the Turkish minority and sentences him for trying to do his job, is this not a violation of this article?

We can enlarge this list. Yet the examples above clearly illustrate that the Universal Declaration of Human Rights, which is an integral part of the U.N. Charter, was not solely prepared to protect the rights of prisoners. Neither were the European Convention on Human Rights, its additional protocols or the numerous agreements and conventions of organizations such as the United Nations or the International Labour Organization. As mentioned above, protection of the rights of prisoners is an important human rights obligation. But those who limit their struggle for improved human rights only to that issue are unwittingly pushing the inspection of the human rights of millions of people backstage. Today, 3 million Turks live in Western Europe. They went there as workers in the early 1960s. However, is it possible to still view second, third and even fourth generation Turks as migrant workers from the day they were born? Do these people, who are part of the society they live in, have rights in the political and social arenas, in professional life, in education and in other areas equal to the rest of the population of that country? Isn't it true that even people who arrive from other EU member states have more political and social rights, let alone the local population? Does this discrimination comply with the word and spirit of the U.N. Universal Declaration of Human Rights?

Do those who regularly criticize Turkey's human rights record support the expansion of the human rights agenda to include these issues as well?

General Assesment of Human Rights and Democracy

The facts presented above show that Turkey has a lot to say on democracy and human rights. Lacking solid grounds, no one has the right to accuse a country that has waged a 120-year-long struggle to assure supremacy of the will of the people, has kept alive a republican regime based on that will for 75 years, has proved that a Muslim nation can successfully sustain democracy, has had free elections overseen by the judiciary for many years and has continuously defended freedom of the press of being a failure in democracy. Moreover, the appreciation of other cultures and religions is an integral part of Turkish tradition. Even when such concepts were undeveloped in other countries, Turks were known as a people who came to the help of the oppressed. Bernard Lewis says, "If we define tolerance as the nonexistence of oppression, then the Ottomans had a perfect record until the end of 19th century."[196]

As mentioned in earlier sections, just as in European countries, democracy and human rights have passed through various stages in Turkey as well. Democratic rights were curbed when internal or external security was in danger. Prior to World War II, the British government had been given the right to have suspects arrested without a court decision. In France, when the war in Algeria was threatening the internal security of the country, the Constitution gave the president extraordinary powers, the likes of which could not be found in

---

[196] Lewis, The Emergence of Modern Turkey, op. cit., p. 349.

any other democracy. In the United States the Congress, worried about the threat of Communism, had put restrictions on public employees, which were removed only when conditions returned to normal. Some of the restrictions that remain are not implemented. Democracy grew stronger once internal and external security improved.

Development seen in human rights also followed a similar course. After the end of World War II there were problems with legislation and practices. The practices and strong measures of the police in Northern Ireland, Spain, Italy, France and Germany, when faced with the real threat of terrorism, were the subject of much criticism. They still are. Yet the existence of such criticism did not cause anyone to doubt the existence of democracy in those countries. Improving democracy and human rights has become the common goal of a majority of people in Western countries. People are trying to leave behind the bitter experiences of the past. Those groups who want to resurrect the inhumane theories and practices of the pre-war period face the reactions of the major part of their society. The existence of such groups as well as their actions, which from time to time succeed in inflicting great suffering, is deemed shameful by the leaders of those countries. People are trying to find ways to prevent such incidents. Yet no one questions whether these countries are democratic or not. This is because democratic mechanisms are operating. Elections are held regularly. Freedom of the press and freedom of thought are protected, the principle of division of power is respected, and democratic institutions are functional. Problems that may arise from time to time are resolved within the democratic system.

The same evolution is valid for Turkey as well. The country is following the path of democracy. No one is considering replacing democracy with another regime. Elections are held regularly. Democratic institutions are working. Freedom of thought and freedom of the press have advanced significantly. Issues once considered taboo are now freely and publicly discussed. In the past there have been periods when the armed forces intervened in administration; however, these were not result of dictatorial ambitions. Their primary goal was always reinstating a multi-party democracy in a short period of time. No one can claim that in the past 75 years Turkey has ever had a dictatorial regime. Yet during the same period numerous countries in Western Europe did have dictatorships for many years. Some of these were in place long after the end of World War II.

When the past 75 years are evaluated, a picture emerges that fills Turkish democracy with pride. This does not mean that there have never been any problems or that there aren't any now. Neither does it mean that there is no need to improve legislation and practices regarding democracy and human rights. Yet it obviously is a mistake to look at a few shortfalls, erroneous practices and illegal actions of a few members of the security forces and accuse all of Turkey. There is no need for Turks to develop a guilt complex under the influence of such accusations.

Turks have long been known for their tolerance of other religions and cultures, and Turkish history and literature is filled with examples of this. Turks have had the tradition of being a multicultural community for 1,000 years. They do not need to be given lessons by nations that still have not acquired the habit of living intermingled with other cultures. This why the attempts of some foreign statesmen, politicians and journalists to show Turkey the way on issues such as democracy and tolerance, although perhaps done with good intentions, are seen as awkward by the Turkish people.

Foreigners who think they understand Turkey's political situation or problems better than Turkish politicians, academics, journalists and intellectuals do not seem to be exercising common sense. Making development of economic and political relations with Turkey conditional on improvements in the human rights area, or attempting to curb her rights that stem from international agreements by saying that she must first undertake reforms on the human rights issue causes a justifiable reaction on the part of the Turkish nation. Turkey's implementing policies or making decisions that will enable her to achieve the highest standards in the well-being, freedom, welfare, democracy and human rights of her people is dictated by reason and common sense. Is there a need for foreigners to preach to or advise Turkey on this issue?

Moreover, as respects those who would like to help or who support Turkey in these issues with good intentions, is making frequent derogatory public statements against Turkey or the Turkish people really the best method for them to use? In earlier sections detailed information on the problems faced by some Western European countries in the fields of democracy and human rights was given. Are those who do not refrain from publicly criticizing Turkey being equally critical on the same issues against Western European countries?

It seems that those who for their own reasons want to keep Turkey out of the integration process of Europe or who seek some concessions from Turkey on issues like Cyprus are using the improvements needed in democracy and human rights to their own ends.

Modern approaches in the Western world do not allow those who possess wealth or power to act as they wish. Now they also have to be justified in their actions and be able to explain them to the world public. It is becoming increasingly more evident that those who want to keep Turkey away from Europe are trying to portray Turkey as the party that bears responsibility for this decision. The Turkish public is becoming increasingly convinced that the goal of the campaigns against Turkey that intensified after Turkey applied for full EU membership in 1987 and reached unprecedented levels not seen since World War II is to create an excuse to keep Turkey out of Europe.

Terrorist activities seen in recent years in Turkey cannot be tied to lack of democracy, either. Just as the recent surge in terrorist activities in the United States, the United Kingdom and Japan cannot be tied to a lack of democracy in those countries, the same is true for Turkey as well. Today everyone knows that some countries use terrorism as an indirect method of waging war. Human rights organizations or politicians who accuse Turkey of using unacceptable methods against terrorists rarely take a position or make statements against countries that support these terrorist organizations.

Of course, as was said before, none of this means that human rights violations in Turkey should be tolerated. A single human rights violation is one violation too many. It must be thoroughly investigated, and those guilty should be incriminated. What should be stressed here is that an issue as important and sensitive as human rights violations should not be used for political purposes, and that a country and a people should not be humiliated in the world's eyes under the pretext of violations of human rights.

SUMMARY AND CONCLUSION

When elements that make up the national strength of a country are considered together, it can be seen that in many respects Turkey is one of the most prominent countries not only in Europe but also in the world. Recent achievements of Turkey have put her at comparable levels in many areas with the advanced nations of the world.

With regards to population, which is one the most important elements that make up a nation's strength, Turkey ranks second in Western Europe. Scientific estimates show that in 15 years Turkey will be the largest country in Europe with respect to population. The 1997 census shows a decline in rapid population growth, which for years has been a major source of concern. In Western countries, however, aging population is a major problem. Forecasts for the next 25 to 50 years show that the social geography of Europe, even that of the world, will change tremendously. The populations of the EU countries as well as those of the candidates for EU membership are expected to decline significantly. The same is also true for Russia.

In Eurasia, the region between Turkey and the Pacific Ocean, the population is expected to rise. By 2050, the total population of Turkey and her neighbours will exceed the current population of the EU. If peace, stability and cooperation are achieved, a large and wealthy zone of economic cooperation can be established in this region. The same can be said with regards to the Turkic republics. The richest oil and natural gas reserves in the world are located in this area. When Turkey's neighbours Russia, Ukraine and Romania are added to the equation, by the mid-21st century a market twice the size of the EU's population will come into being in this region.

Compared to Western Europe Turkey's population is much younger and more dynamic. This is an advantage for Turkey and a fact that must be carefully analyzed with respect to economic development potential as well as defence capabilities of the country. Western European countries and the United States seem to fare better than Turkey with regards to standards of education. Yet since the early days of the Republic the rate of increase in Turkey's educated population has been higher than that of most Western countries. Forecasts predict that Turkey stands a good a chance of catching up with educational levels in Western European countries by the first quarter of the 21st century. Regarding elements that define the social structure of a society, which are among the factors that must be taken into account when evaluating the strength of a nation, Turkey is not behind, but rather is ahead of Western European countries in things such as solidarity among people, strong family ties, cooperation, self-sacrifice and sharing.

The fact that today there are some 3 million Turks living in Western Europe is closely linked to the Turks' heritage of living in multicultural societies. When estimations regarding Turkey's strength are made, Turks living abroad should also be taken into consideration as an important factor. Provided that the population growth rate is decreased to a more moderate level and that targets in the field of education are reached, Turkey will soon have the human resources expected of a regional power.

Turkey has the largest territory in all of Western Europe. Her strategic position at the crossroads of north and south as well as East and West gives her significant advantages. Turkey is rich in natural resources; in fact she is one of the richest in Europe in that respect. Geographically Turkey is located on the transportation and communication links between Europe, Asia and the Middle East. Some of the pipelines that will carry the oil and natural gas reserves of the region to world markets pass through Turkey, and work is also under way to build new ones. Most of the trade from countries such as Russia, Ukraine, Romania, Georgia and Bulgaria with the rest of the world passes through the Turkish Straits. When this and similar factors are taken into consideration, it is obvious that Turkey has strategic properties that cannot even be compared with those of almost any Western European country.

In NATO, the strength of the Turkish Armed Forces is second only to the United States. The Turkish Army has modern weapons, is trained extremely well and has high morale. If conditions so require, the Turkish Armed Forces are capable of quickly sending a fully equipped corps abroad for peace operations. There are only a limited number of armed forces around the world that can undertake such an operation. Together with the help of such a deterrent force, Turkey has earned the honor of being the only country that has had uninterrupted peace for 75 years in her region.

Turkey's economic performance today cannot be compared to its past levels. When adjusted by purchasing power parity, Turkey currently has the sixth largest economy in Europe. During the past 15 years Turkey has had the most rapidly developing economy in Europe. In the production of some basic materials such as iron, steel and cement Turkey is more advanced than most other European countries. It is the fifth-largest textile manufacturing country in the world. In the production of numerous industrial goods Turkey is among the top 20 to 25 nations in the world. Turkish foreign trade has been among the fastest growing in the last 15 years.

The unemployment rate in Turkey is lower than most European countries, where it continues to be a serious economic problem. Foreign currency reserves are at record levels. The Istanbul Stock Exchange has been one of the fastest growing in the world. In net tourism earnings Turkey has surpassed most well-known tourism destinations in Europe.

These basic indicators are significant in showing Turkey's position and economic strength in the world. If Turkey can maintain her current pace of economic development, she will be able to catch up with the most advanced nations of Western Europe and even overtake some of them within the first quarter of the 21st century. By and large, Turkey has achieved this progress through the efforts of her own people, with her own strength and resources. These achievements should not lead to a neglect of problems that still exist. Turkey has various problems, such as inflation, that await a solution. However, all countries that are in a process of rapid development like Turkey have similar problems. The 1998 crisis experienced by the Far Eastern countries, which until recently were held up to the world as model economies, is a case in point. Even the EU member states, which are widely thought as having solved all of their basic problems, face serious economic, social and financial problems from time to time. Therefore, when evaluating Turkey, her problems and difficulties, the benchmark used should be the performance of countries faced with similar problems and not some ideal measure. Moreover, it would not be correct to say that all of Turkey's problems originate from within the country. There are external sources for these problems as well.

Turkey possesses the capability and experience required to deal with her problems without decreasing the growth rate of her economy. In the past she managed to have high growth rates with low inflation. There are other countries in the world that have achieved the same. The way to close the gap with the advanced nations and reach their standard of living is to have a high economic growth rate. The only way to preserve the large and modern defence force necessitated by Turkey's strategic location is also by achieving a high growth rate and increasing national income.

Becoming an EU member in the near future could help Turkey to solve her aforementioned problems in the medium term. Therefore, despite all obstructions, joining the EU has been a primary goal of Turkey for the past 35 years. As indicated by the examples given in previous sections, Turkey is more advanced than every single one of the EU candidates in almost all fields of economic activity. Consequently, leaving Turkey behind all the others in the EU's enlargement process cannot be perceived as fair treatment, especially when the fact that Turkey is the only country that has signed a customs union agreement with the EU is taken into consideration. As a result of the benefits and obligations born out of the 35-year-long cooperation and agreement with the EU, the Turkish economy has to a large extent become compatible with that of the EU.

This should not be interpreted, however, to mean that Turkey must refrain from establishing cooperation with countries outside of the EU. To the contrary, Turkey must develop economic ties and cooperation with the rest of the world, in particular with the United States, Russia, Japan and China, as well as establish new economic and commercial ties with countries in the Middle East, Central Asia, the Far East, Africa and Latin America. Economic cooperation achieved with other countries will strengthen Turkey's position in her quest to integrate with the EU. Turkey's EU vocation was a conscious choice, but whether this goal becomes a reality or not, Turkey will continue to take all measures necessary to sustain her economic development.

Coming to the issue of democracy and human rights, it is true that Turkey entered this process much later than other Western countries. Yet even in countries that are considered to be the backbone of democracy, multi-party democratic regimes based on human rights were not easily established and in most could not be sustained uninterrupted. Internal and external threats to their security or the policies of their political leaders resulted in periods when they took U-turns from democracy. From time to time they had authoritarian administrations, even periods of dictatorship. During those periods, Turkey was a place of refuge for those fleeing oppression. This is because Turkey has always been a country where people of different religions and cultures have lived side by side in peace.

Today, human rights occupy an important place on the world agenda. There are allegations even against countries considered to be well advanced in this area. Fifty years after its adoption it still is hard to say that the Universal Declaration of Human Rights is being fully implemented. The development of democracy and human rights in Turkey should be studied within this general framework.

For the last century Turkey has struggled to achieve a system based on the will of the people. Constitutions that restricted the powers of the sultan were drafted, a parliament was established and elections were held. Yet a true administration based on the will of the people came only with the establishment of the Republic in 1923. The modern Turkish Republic, founded by Atatürk, established integration with Western civilization as one of its goals. The underlying ideal of this goal is the human rights issue. Starting from the 1924 Constitution, all Turkish constitutions have placed great importance on human rights. Multi-party democracy arrived after 1946, and governments started to change with free elections. The primary goal of all the constitutions adopted in later periods has always been maintaining the democratic regime. Since 1949 Turkey has been a member of the Council of Europe, which accepts only democratic countries for membership. It has been more than 40 years since Turkey signed the European Convention on Human Rights, which involves the right of international verification regarding human rights. Turkey granted her citizens the right of individual application to the European Commission of Human Rights for claims of human rights violations.

No one can doubt the position of such a country among the democratic nations of the world. The problems faced from time to time and the mistakes in implementation cannot change the fact that Turkey is a democratic country.

Just as in the economic field, the progress made in the fields of democracy and human rights should not obscure the violations that may arise from time to time. There is a total consensus in Turkey regarding the indispensability of democracy as a way of life. This constitutes one of most important factors behind Turkey's national strength.

There are only a handful of countries around the world the size of Turkey that have as large or larger a population and that have achieved the economic and democratic levels attained by Turkey.

Within what can be considered a brief span of time in a country's history, Turkey has managed to cover a great distance towards the goal set by Atatürk of reaching the standard of contemporary civilization based on the solid political, economic and social foundations he laid down. Peaceful foreign policy, again established by Atatürk, that aims to form friendships and cooperation with all countries, has helped achieve these results. Turkey is today one of the most powerful, most democratic and most advanced nations in its region. She has become one of the most important countries in the world. The refusal of certain parties to see the development and current levels attained by Turkey or their attempts to belittle Turkey's achievements by leveling baseless or exaggerated accusations cannot change this fact.

For the past 200 years Turkey has aimed at becoming integrated with Europe; therefore, Turkey's participation in the architecture of the Europe of tomorrow and her being one of the countries shaping the Europe of the next century should be no surprise to anyone. Those who wish to keep Turkey away from Europe for religious, cultural or other reasons do not stand a chance of being successful, because following all the bitter experiences in the past, people now want friendship, cooperation and coexistence instead of division. They will refuse to let religious and cultural iron curtains replace the ideological Iron Curtain that was removed only after a 45-year struggle.

The Europe of tomorrow must be a place where people with different cultures and religions but the same principles of civilization live together. The Turkish people envision and want to be a part of such a Europe. Turkey has the power to fulfil the requirements of such an integration. The growing awareness of this power will raise the self-confidence of the Turkish people and motivate them to reach even higher goals in every field.

Turkey, which is a European country with high cultural and moral values, has become a regional power that is developing in democracy. The country that entered the 20th century as the "sick man of Europe," in the words of some foreigners, has reached the end of the century as an advanced, powerful and modern country.

Atatürk was the most successful of the 20th century leaders who set out to revolutionize and change the structure and destiny of their people. Of all revolutions only his accomplished its goal, and it still maintains its dynamism and vigor. Of all the revolutionary leaders only Atatürk still continues to shine his light and show the way for his people. Only his name is respectfully remembered by his own nation as well as by nations around the world. For his was an ideology of humanity and civilization; his guide was intelligence, and the source of his power was the will of his people. The Turkish nation will continue along the path of civilization that he opened up, and in the 21st century Turkey will take her rightful place among the most advanced, powerful and civilized countries of the world.

Bibliography

Agreements to Accession, European University Press 1996.

Alp, Tekin, Le Kemalisme, Paris, 1937.

Armaoğlu, Fahir, 20. Yüzyıl Siyasi Tarihi, Ankara 1987.

ATİAD, Almanya'daki Türk girişimciliği, Görünmeyen Güç, Düsseldorf, 1997.

Avrupa Birliği Ülkelerinde Çalışan Türklerin Ekonomik Gücü, Türkiye Araştırmalar Merkezi, Essen, Mayıs 1998.

Benchmarking Europe's Competitiveness: From Analysis to Action,UNICE, Brussels, December 1997.

Bilge, Suat, Milletlerarası Politika, Ankara, 1966.

Béhar, Pierre, Une Géopolitique pour l' Europe, Paris, 1992.

Billion, Didier, Lé Role Géostrategique de la Turquie, Paris, 1995.

Brzezinski, Zbigniew, The Grand Chessboard, New York, 1997.

Defence Policy of Turkey and Turkish Armed Forces, The White Paper, Ankara, 1996.

Doing Business in Turkey, IBS Yayıncılık, İstanbul, 1997.

Duverger, Maurice, Constitutions et Documents Politiques, Paris, 1996.

Economic Developments and Reforms, Colloqium 1997, Brussels, 1997.

Economie Europeenne, Rapport Economique Annuel pour 1995. Commission Européenne, Bruxelles, 1995.

Education at a Glance, OECD Indicators, Paris 1993.

Eroğlu, Hamza, 70. Yıldönümünde Lozan, Ankara.

European Economy, European Commission, Brussels, 1997.

Eurostat Yearbook, Luxembourg, 1997.

Executive's Handbook, Intermedia, Turkey 1998, Almanac,

Feldstein, Martin, Refocusing the IMF, Foreign Affaires, Vol.77, No. 2

Grants and Loans from the European Union, Luxembourg, 1997.

Güvenç, Bozkurt, Türk Kimliği, Ankara, 1993.

Huntington, Samuel, The Clash Of Civilizations and the Remaking of World Order.,s.85.

Huntington, Samuel, Üçüncü Dalga, çev. Ergun Özbudun, Ankara, 1993.

Images Economiques du Monde 1998, Paris, 1998.

IISS Military Balance, London, 1997-1998.

İnönü, Erdal Anılar ve Düşünceler, İstanbul 1995.

İnönü, İsmet, Hatıralar, II.Kitap, Ankara, 1985.

Johnson, Paul, A History of the Modern World, London, 1983.

Kepenek Yakup, Yentürk Nurhan Türkiye Ekonomisi, İstanbul, 1996.

Kongar, Emre, 21. Yüzyılda Türkiye, İstanbul.

Köker, Eser Danyal, Education, Politics and Women in Turkey Le Courier des Pays de l'Est, Aout 1997, no.421.

Lesourne Jacques, Lecompte Bernard, de l'Atlantique a l' Oral, l'Apres-Communisme, Paris, 1990.

L'Etat du Monde 1998, Paris 1998.

Lewis, Bernard, The Emergence of Modern Turkey, London, 1961. 32. Lewis, s.109.

Lewis, Bernard, Why Turkey is the Only Muslim Democracy? Middle East Quarterly, March, 1994.

Lohrman, Astrid Marina, Der Textil-und Bekleidungsektor in der Türkei und die Auswirkungen der Zollunion mit der Europaischen Union, Zeitschrift für Türkeistudien 2/97.

Lord Kinross, The Ottoman Centuries,New York 1977.

Mantran, Robert Histoire de l'Empire Ottomane, Paris, 1989.

Mayhew, Alan, Recreating Europe, Cambridge, 1998

Nordic Democracy, Copenhagen, 1981.

OCDE, Analyse des Politiques Educatives, Paris, 1997.

OECD, Bank Profitability, Paris, 1997.

OECD, Coup d'Oeil sur les Economies de l' OCDE, Paris, 1996.

OECD, Ecoonomic Outlook, Paris, June 1997.

OECD, Employment Outlook, July, 1996.

OECD, International Direct İnvestment Statistics Yearbook, Paris, 1997.

OECD, Le Monde en 2020, Paris, 1997.

OECD, Main Economic Indicators, Paris, December, 1997.

OECD, Statistical Yearbook of Turkey, Paris, 1997.

Organisation Mondiale du Commerce, Rapport annuel 1997, vol.I et II.

Özyavuz, Tuncer, Osmanlı-Türk Anayasaları, İstanbul, 1997.

Peacock, L., Europe and Beyond, London, 1984,

Ramses, Institut français des Relations internationales, Paris, 1997.

Regards sur l' Education, Les Indicateurs de l'OECD, Paris 1997.

Selami Sezgin, Country Survey X: Defence Spending in Turkey, Defence and Peace Economics, vol.8.

Shaw, Stanford, Turkey and the Holocaust, New York 1993

Şimşir, Bilal, British Documents on Ottoman Armenians, Vol.1.,Ankara,1982.

Tanör, Bülent, İki Anayasa, İstanbul, 1994.

Tewes, Henning, German Politics, Vol. 6, No.2, (August, 1977).

The World Bank, World Development Report, The State in a Changing World, Washington, 1997.

Turkey and the European Community, Bruxelles, 1991.

La Turquie: 10 Ans Apres sa Demande d' Adhésion a l' Union Européenne, Centre des Relations Européennes,CRE, Bruxelles, 1997.

Turkish Economy, 97, Turkish Industrialists' and Businessmen's Association, İstanbul, July, 1997.

UNCTAD, Handbook of International Trade and Development Statistics, New York, 1995.

Unesco Statistical Yearbook, Paris,1996.

UN Monthly Bulletin of Statistics, New York, vol. LI No:12, December 1997.

Uzunoğlu, Sadi, The Implementation of the Customs Union in Turkey and its Macroeconomic Effects, Zeitschrift für Türkeistudien, Essen, 1997 Heft 2.

Ülger, Eriş, Atatürk und die Türkei in der Deutschen Presse, Hückelhoven, 1992.

Van den Bempt, Paul Greet Theelen, From Europe

Vaner Semih, Akagül Deniz, Kaleağası Bahadır, La Turquie en Mouvement, Bruxelles, 1995.

Vernon, Manfred C., Devlet Sistemleri, çev. Mümtaz Soysal, Ankara 1961.

World Competitiveness Yearbook.

Zürcher, Erik J., Turkey, a Modern History, London, 1994.

Index